HG
4026
.H44
1982

Helfert, Erich A.
    Techniques of financial analysis /
Erich A. Helfert. -- 5th ed. --
Homewood, Ill. : R.D. Irwin, 1982.
    x, 304 p. : ill. ; 24 cm.
    Includes bibliographies and index.

74409

    1. Corporations--Finance.   2. Cash
flow.   3. Financial statements.
4. Ratio analysis.   I. Title

20 OCT 82   7917217   OMMMxc   81-81558

Techniques of Financial Analysis

TECHNIQUES
OF FINANCIAL
ANALYSIS

Fifth Edition

ERICH A. HELFERT, D.B.A.

Assistant to the Chairman
Crown Zellerbach Corporation
San Francisco, California

1982 **RICHARD D. IRWIN, INC.** Homewood, Illinois 60430
Irwin-Dorsey Limited   Georgetown, Ontario   L7G 4B3

© RICHARD D. IRWIN, INC., 1963, 1967, 1972, 1977, and 1982

Library of Congress Catalog Card No. 81–81558

Printed in the United States of America

2 3 4 5 6 7 8 9 0 DO 9 8 7 6 5 4 3 2

PREFACE

The purpose of this book is to provide the student, business executive, analyst, or other interested person with a concise reference collection of the more important tools and techniques of financial analysis without delving into their broad theoretical and institutional backgrounds. In this sense the book is self-contained—a practical, application-oriented survey of key concepts, with enough perspective to assist the user in understanding the framework and the validity of the analytical techniques. In another sense, the book is supplementary to the many full-fledged texts in the field of corporate finance which contain much well-developed conceptual and institutional background.

The evolution of this book began with its First Edition as a collection of what are known as *technical notes* on basic concepts, tools, and techniques made available to students in the MBA program at the Harvard Graduate School of Business Administration. These notes are designed as short briefings on financial analysis, supplementary to the broad reading matter assigned in the finance area. They equip the student with the basic skills and knowledge required to analyze case problems for class discussion and are guides toward more specialized sources of information required in preparation for a management career.

The First Edition of the book, published in 1963, contained selective materials that had been used for some time in the Harvard Business School MBA curriculum and other finance courses and seminars. The concept of publishing a collection of such materials proved successful. In the Revised Edition, published in 1967, all materials were fully updated and three chapters were completely rewritten. The Third Edition, published in 1972, was new throughout, with more emphasis on viewing financial analysis as part of a system of management decisions, and with stress on an integrated concept of investment, operations, and financing. The Fourth Edition, published in 1977, maintained the basic coverage with updating and refinements, as does this revised Fifth Edition. It continues to address both the practitioner and the student. In view of the extensive use the book has found in major corporate and other executive development programs as well as in universities on the graduate and undergraduate levels, both in the United States and in many foreign countries in several translations, the original notion of a straightforward and relatively uncomplicated approach to a complex subject has been maintained. The key thrust is toward explaining the doable and practical—an "executive briefing" concept—and toward building basic ability to grasp financial relationships and issues. The book presupposes only some familiarity with fundamental accounting concepts and financial statement preparation.

I would again like to express my appreciation to my former colleagues in the finance teaching group at the Harvard Business School, and to the administration of that institution—both under former Dean George P. Baker and under Dean Lawrence E. Fouraker—for the opportunity to develop and publish the original materials and for the suggestions and encouragement given me during the various editions. My thanks also go to my colleagues at universities here and abroad, too numerous to mention, for their extensive application of the book and endorsement of its concept, and for their many expressions of interest in further updated editions.

Finally, I would like to express my particular appreciation to the chairman and chief executive of Crown Zellerbach, C. R. Dahl, for the opportunity over the years to apply many of the materials and concepts in the management development programs and the planning processes at Crown Zellerbach.

San Francisco, California   Erich A. Helfert

CONTENTS

INTRODUCTION

The financial manager, analyst, or student must, during analytical efforts for planning or problem solving, rely on a variety of financial analysis techniques which help answer questions of significance. This book provides such tools for use in understanding problems and opportunities of a financial nature, and contains practical examples on which to exercise the application of these skills.

A critical point must be made here: While the tools and concepts exposed in the ensuing chapters are explained and discussed in detail, they cannot be viewed as *ends* in themselves. It is simply not enough to master the techniques! Financial analysis is a process which helps to answer questions properly posed; it is a *means* to an end. We cannot overemphasize the need to view financial analysis only as an aid to the manager in planning for investment, operations, and financing, and to the prospective investor in assessment, valuation, and projection. In each situation the objective must be clearly stated before putting pencil to paper—otherwise, the exercise becomes idle "number crunching." Some have referred to effective management as the "art of asking significant questions"; this is no less true of proper financial analysis, which, after all, is but one aspect of corporate and financial management.

Perspective is also required in choosing the degree of *refinement* to which any financial (or other) analysis should be carried. This book often presents refinements of the methods of analysis, which should, however, be sparingly applied to areas of real significance only. Otherwise, the effort far outweighs the results. There is no need to belabor obvious answers or foregone conclusions.

In applying the tools presented, one should therefore consider and make judgments on the following points *before starting any analysis:*

1. What precisely is the issue to be analyzed and resolved? Has the problem been clearly spelled out?
2. Which factors, relationships, and trends will likely be helpful in analyzing the problem at hand?
3. What ways can be found to get a quick "ballpark" estimate of a possible result?
4. How reliable are the available data, and how is this likely to affect results?
5. How exact does the answer have to be, and how much effort should be expended in refining results?
6. What are the limitations of the tools themselves, and how is this likely to affect results?

Only after having thought through these issues should work proceed on the analysis and the tools be applied. In effect, we are talking not only about good financial analysis but about a rational approach to problem solving. And in the end, this is what decision making in management, operations, financing, and investments is all about.

1 BUSINESS AS A SYSTEM OF FUNDS FLOWS

The starting point of this chapter, and indeed the focus of the whole book, is the concept of business as a series of decisions to deploy resources for profit, that is, for an economic return. Viewed in their broadest sense, these management decisions involve three areas: (1) the *investment* of resources, (2) the *operation* of the business with the help of these resources, and (3) the proper mix of *financing* to provide the resources. While business has infinite variety—we can list, for example, manufacturing, trading, financial, and service institutions of various sizes and with different legal structures—common to all is this theme of management: planned commitments of resources for the purpose of creating, over time, sufficient economic value to recover these resources and a margin of profit beyond. Over the long run, the result of such resource deployment should be a net improvement in the economic position of the owners—including the ability to make further resource commitments. If this is not the case, the economic viability of the business is in question.

The techniques developed in this chapter are designed to assist the student and practitioner in analyzing the pattern of resource deployments in a business over a given time period. The concept used for the purpose is *funds flow analysis,* which is a way of expressing and displaying resource movements in monetary terms, based on the periodic accounting statements of financial condition and profit and loss results. Along with other techniques developed later in this book, this analytical process will provide a basis for judging management effectiveness.

We are interested in funds flow analysis because it allows us to *reconstruct* from accounting statements—which are summaries of the transactions of the period—many important resource decisions made regarding investments, operations, and financing. It is a *comparative* process which identifies shifts in financial condition and the impact of operations. It structures these into a framework of resource (funds) *uses* or applications, and resource (funds) *sources* or provisions. The resulting "decisional" view of business operations provides additional insights beyond the balance sheet, which is a mere static "snapshot" of financial condition at a point in time, and beyond the standard operating statement, which is just a summary of revenue and expenses applicable to the period. Since it does add insight, the inclusion of a funds flow analysis statement has in recent years been made mandatory for the accounting reports of publicly traded companies to obtain a more dynamic picture of management decisions.

Funds flow analysis techniques rest heavily on the understanding of commonly accepted accounting methods, since accounting statements generally have to serve as the raw material for analysis. A thorough funds flow analysis can involve a variety of fairly complex adjustments, as the effect of accounting conventions must be translated into funds movements. Once the basic concepts have been mastered, however, the complexities appear only as variations of the resource deployment theme. In fact, funds flow analysis is a more natural way of characterizing business operations and conditions than the standard accounting statements.

The chapter will contain a gradual buildup of complexities in funds flow analysis. We shall first demonstrate the simple, generally applicable notions and then discuss complications which have to be considered largely because of the *timing* of funds decisions. We shall show that accounting conventions must be analyzed as to their effect on funds movements, since the objective of accounting reports is to achieve first and foremost the reporting of financial condition on a *given date*, and operating profits for a *period*. Finally, we shall discuss the interpretation of the results of funds flow analysis in the attempt to understand and judge the nature of the decisions made by management.

WHAT ARE FUNDS?

In the most basic sense, we think of funds as *cash*, since cash is the easiest form of expressing economic value and is readily convertible into goods and services. Moreover, the fact that most business transactions will eventually involve cash at one time or another leads some to say that "cash is the name of the game." A business operation normally involves a great number of cash transactions over a period of time, as wages are paid, machinery acquired, revenues collected, and so on. If a business were operated strictly on an immediate cash receipt and payments basis, and some simple businesses are, it would be very easy to trace the key commitments and recoveries of cash over a time period. This cash flow pattern would provide a picture of the resource deployments of the business.

Not all resources, however, are committed or obtained on the basis of cash transactions. This introduces a degree of complexity into our analysis. Management has the discretion to grant or obtain credit; and every time this discretion is exercised, an economic resource has been deployed. Eventually such transactions will result in cash changing hands, but in the meantime we cannot ignore the resource commitment. If a business grants trade credit to its customers, for example, its own funds or resources are in effect used by someone else until repayment. If a business obtains trade credit from a supplier, someone else's funds or resources will in effect be employed in the company until repayment is made.

Furthermore, an imprudent management can overcommit an enterprise by taking on too many credit obligations, which represent other people's funds, although no cash will have changed hands. Obtaining merchandise on account would be an example, or acquiring machinery on loans and notes, or trading a piece of land as part payment for a larger property with the difference due some period hence. It would be hard to deny that economic values have been shifted by these noncash management decisions.

The concept of funds, therefore, should be broadly understood to cover *all measurable resources,* including cash. We shall use the term in this wider sense throughout the book. The point of view of the person analyzing funds flow will to some extent influence the precise meaning of the concept. The financial officer worrying about repayments of obligations will have a concept of funds very close to cash and current credit, while the operating executive being judged on return of investment will define as funds all the resources under his command. It should now be clear, however, that cash is only one form of funds; and when referring to cash or cash items in their specific definitions, we shall employ the concept of "cash" or "liquid funds" throughout the book.

SIMPLIFIED VIEW OF A BUSINESS

It may be best to illustrate funds flow analysis by taking a very simplified example of a business and adding realism step by step. For this purpose we shall employ the example of a person operating as a news vendor. Initially our vendor is selling papers on the street corner, without a booth or any equipment. He has invested some of his savings in a working cash fund, which is the only investment required to operate.

The model in Figure 1–1 shows the operations of this very simple business. Financing is provided by the owner in the form of $150 (A), shown as owner's equity and a working cash balance. During the day, $80 (B) of this working cash is spent

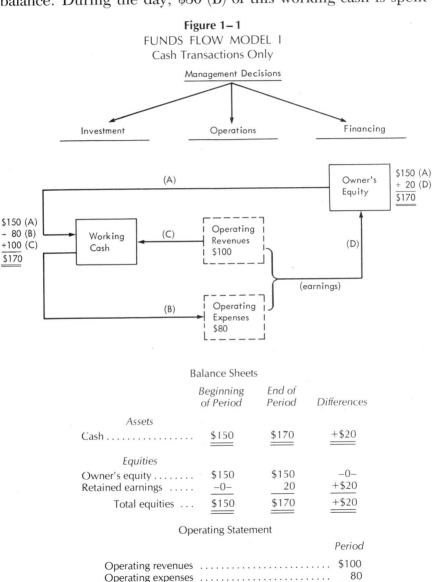

Figure 1–1
FUNDS FLOW MODEL I
Cash Transactions Only

Management Decisions

Investment   Operations   Financing

(A)

Owner's Equity $150 (A)
+ 20 (D)
$170

$150 (A)
− 80 (B)
+100 (C)
$170

Working Cash   (C)   Operating Revenues $100

(D)

(earnings)

(B)   Operating Expenses $80

Balance Sheets

	Beginning of Period	End of Period	Differences
Assets			
Cash..................	$150	$170	+$20
Equities			
Owner's equity........	$150	$150	–0–
Retained earnings	–0–	20	+$20
Total equities ...	$150	$170	+$20

Operating Statement

	Period
Operating revenues	$100
Operating expenses	80
Earnings for period	$ 20

Figure 1–1 (*continued*)

Funds Flow Analysis

a. To start up the business:

Use of funds:
Cash balance established $150

Source of funds:
Owner's investment 150

b. To operate the business for one period:

Use of funds:
Increase in cash balance $20

Source of funds:
Profit from operations (retained earnings) 20

to pay for newspapers, while revenues of $100 (C) are received. The profit or earnings from operations, $20 (D), in effect increases the working cash balance to a net of $170, and this increase is also reflected in owner's equity as earnings. Note that the investment (asset) item, working cash, and the financing (liability and net worth) item, owner's equity, are shown in solid frames, while the periodic operating (profit and loss) items, revenues and expenses, are shown in dashed frames to reflect their temporary nature.

We have drawn up simple balance sheets at the beginning and at the end of the day, showing the effect of these transactions. It is clear that the day's operations have provided a $20 increase in cash and an offsetting increase of $20 in owner's equity. This is the only difference between the two balance sheets. The operating statement for the period reflects the profit of $20.

We can now turn to funds flow analysis, but not before defining our ground. In this instance it is possible to analyze two distinct phases, the establishment of the business and the operation of the business. This distinction does not *have* to be made, but since we are interested in the effects of major decisions, it may be useful to establish the separation. The first analysis, the start-up of the business, shows that our vendor *used* $150 worth of cash to establish his working cash balance. The *source* of these funds was his own private savings. The second analysis, which spans the day's operations, shows that the changes in the funds picture are a *use* of funds of $20, which increased the working cash, and a *source* of funds of $20, which is the profit from operations. As we shall see in later sections of this chapter, the selection of time periods is a critical aspect of funds flow analysis, since the impact of decisions we are trying to picture may be obscured if too long a time period is chosen.

Several things become apparent from this simple illustration. First of all, we find that funds flow analysis is very closely related to the normal decision-making process of the business. In fact, one could carry funds flow analysis to the extreme and display every single transaction that took place during the period in terms of sources and uses. This is unnecessary and impractical for most purposes, since we should be satisfied to reconstruct only the major resource decisions of the period.

Second, we find that funds flow analysis is very closely related to the accounting statements, the balance sheet and the income statement. As pointed out before, funds flow analysis focuses on the differences between periodic statements. While oversimplified here, the process is readily apparent.

Third, as we already pointed out, it is important to recognize that funds flow analysis is related to a time span. We must choose the period over which funds movements are to be observed, and analysis and judgments must be related to those time periods. In this simple case, the only question that comes to mind is the fact that $20 of funds has been committed to an increase in the cash balance. One might ask if it was reasonable to let this cash accumulate, or whether a different, better use for these funds might have been found by the owner.

Let us now introduce some complications in the form of delayed transactions. The model in Figure 1–2 shows the operations of our news vendor on the following day when he decides to sell some news magazines along with his papers. Since the magazines selected are weeklies, he can maintain an inventory for several days. Our vendor decides to invest an

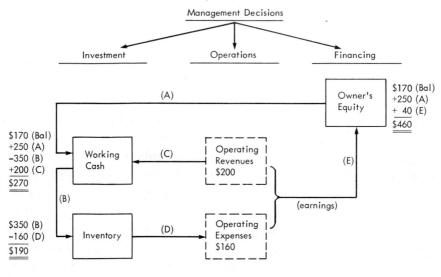

Figure 1–2
FUNDS FLOW MODEL II
Some Delayed Transactions

Balance Sheets

	Beginning of Period	End of Period	Differences
Assets			
Cash	$170	$270	+$100
Inventory	–0–	190	+ 190
Total assets	$170	$460	+$290
Equities			
Owner's equity	$150	$400	+$250
Retained earnings	20	60	+ 40
Total equities . . .	$170	$460	+$290

Operating Statement

	Period
Operating revenues	$200
Operating expenses	160
Earnings for period	$ 40

Figure 1–2 (continued)
Funds Flow Analysis

Period

Uses of funds:
Increase in cash balance $100
Increase in inventory 190

Total uses of funds $290

Sources of funds:
Additional owner's investment $250
Profit from operations (increase in retained earnings) ... 40

Total sources of funds $290

additional $250 (A) from his own savings to increase his working cash balance. He purchases $250 (B) worth of these magazines and also buys the day's supply of newspapers of $100 (B) from his working cash, and the magazines and papers become part of his inventory. Operating revenues for the day $200 (C) are taken in, which represent $160 (D) worth (at cost) of magazines and papers. The profit for the day is the difference of $40 (E), which shows up as earnings in owner's equity.

Balance sheets at the beginning and the end of the period show the differences in the accounts, while the income statement reflects the earnings of $40 for the period. Our funds flow analysis sorts out these differences: an increase in the cash balance of $100 and an increase in inventory of $190 are *uses* of the funds, while the *sources* are the additional owner's investment of $250 and the profit from operations. The main question which arises here is about the wisdom of the decision to provide additional ownership capital to increase both the cash balance and the inventory, and the potential risk of doing so.

Now we are ready to add some long-term perspective to the model in Figure 1–3, which reflects the operations of the ensuing period. Our vendor again invests an additional $450 (A) of his own savings to increase his cash. He uses cash to build his inventory by an additional $400 worth of magazines, and raises it further by the day's requirements of $350, for a total of $750 (B). He also uses cash to prepay required licenses and taxes of $50 (B) for his operation. Furthermore, he decides to have a sheltered newsstand, and a friend and long-term creditor is

12

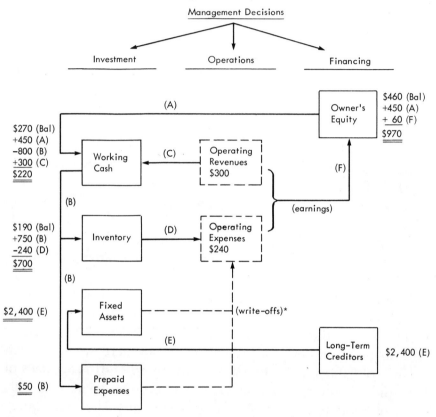

Figure 1–3
FUNDS FLOW MODEL III
Some Long-Term Perspective

* Omitted for purposes of funds flow analysis.

Balance Sheets

	Beginning of Period	End of Period	Differences
Assets			
Cash	$270	$ 220	−$ 50
Inventory	190	700	+ 510
Fixed assets	−0−	2,400	+ 2,400
Prepaids	−0−	50	+ 50
Total assets	$460	$3,370	+$2,910

Figure 1 – 3 (continued)

	Beginning of Period	End of Period	Differences
Equities			
Long-term liabilities ...	–0–	$2,400	+$2,400
Owner's equity	$400	850	+ 450
Retained earnings	60	120	+ 60
Total equities ...	$460	$3,370	+$2,910

Operating Statement

	Period
Operating revenues	$300
Operating expenses*	240
Earnings for period	$ 60

* To be increased by amount of write-offs for *accounting* purposes.

Funds Flow Analysis

Uses of funds:	
Increase in inventory	$ 510
Increase in fixed assets	2,400
Increase in prepaid expenses	50
Total uses of funds	$2,960

Sources of funds:	
Decrease in cash	$ 50
Increase in long-term debt	2,400
Additional owner's investment	450
Profit from operations (increase in retained earnings) ...	60
Total sources of funds	$2,960

providing him with the $2,400 (E) to elevate his operations to a more dignified level. Due to higher sales of $300 (C) against which expenses of $240 (D) are counted, the profit for the day rises to $60 (F), reflected as earnings in owner's equity.

Our balance sheets and operating statements are becoming slightly more complicated, but the differences in the balance sheets at the beginning and end of the period highlight the major funds decisions. The key funds use was, of course, the increase in fixed assets, which has come totally from debt sources. The additional owner's investment provided an increase in inventory, and the Cash account has been reduced by $50 for the first time. As we have more transactions and details to work with, our funds flow analysis begins to provide a basis for asking questions about the size and nature of the resource commitments, the sources which have provided them, and the wisdom of doing so in relation to risk, profitability, and business objectives.

One additional element has been introduced to this picture, the *write-offs* necessary to amortize the fixed assets and prepaid investments over time. From a resource deployment standpoint, the funds commitment was made at the time the fixed assets and prepaids were acquired. Accounting procedures require, however, that book entries be made to show the declining value over time and to charge each operating period with its fair share of this value decline. For funds flow purposes, these write-offs are *not relevant,* however, and thus we have not introduced specifics at this time. From an accounting standpoint, the earnings of $60 shown for the period are, therefore, *overstated* to the extent of any write-offs, but from a funds standpoint (cash flow) the $60 is the appropriate figure. We shall have more to say on this point later.

Next, the model in Figure 1–4 shows the introduction of *accounts receivable* and *trade creditors* in addition to the elements shown in the earlier examples. Our news vendor's operation has now grown to such a size that it reflects the most common transactions we expect of the normal business. No additional ownership investments have been made in this period. On the contrary, $50 (A) of dividends was paid to our owner for the first time, a use shown as a reduction both in owner's equity and in working cash. Also, $100 (G) was used to begin repaying the long-term creditor. Some of the operating revenue of $400 was not received in cash, and is reflected as accounts receivable of $50 (D). The other $350 (C) has found its way into working cash. In the attempt to provide a wider assortment of magazines, our vendor has incurred trade credit of $300 (F), reflected as an increase in inventory of the same amount. The daily operating expense (cost of goods sold) has now risen to $320 (E), which leaves our vendor with a profit of $80 (H) for the day before any accounting write-offs.

From a funds standpoint, the picture is clear and fairly complete when we compare the balance sheets at the beginning and the end of the period. We find that most funds were used in this period for a further increase in receivables and

Figure 1–4
FUNDS FLOW MODEL IV
Most Common Transactions

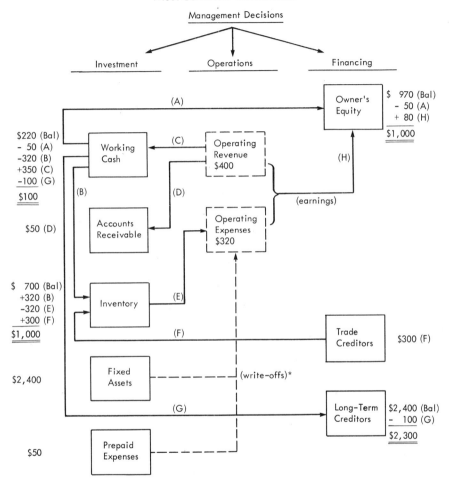

* Omitted for purposes of funds flow analysis.

Balance Sheets

	Beginning of Period	End of Period	Differences
Assets			
Cash	$ 220	$ 100	−$120
Accounts receivable ...	−0−	50	+ 50
Inventory	700	1,000	+ 300
Fixed assets	2,400	2,400	−0−
Prepaids	50	50	−0−
Total assets	$3,370	$3,600	+$230

Figure 1–4 (continued)

	Beginning of Period	End of Period	Differences
Equities			
Accounts payable	–0–	$ 300	+$300
Long-term liabilities ...	2,400	2,300	– 100
Owner's equity	850	850	–0–
Retained earnings	120	150	+ 30
Total equities ...	$3,370	$3,600	+$230

Operating Statement

	Period
Operating revenues	$400
Operating expenses*	320
Earnings for period	$ 80

* To be increased by amount of write-offs for *accounting* purposes.

Funds Flow Analysis

Uses of funds:	
Increase in accounts receivable	$ 50
Increase in inventory	300
Decrease in long-term debt (repayment)	100
Total uses of funds	$450

Sources of funds:	
Decrease in cash	$120
Increase in accounts payable	300
Increase in retained earnings*	30
Total sources of funds	$450

* This could be separated into its components: (a) use—dividend to owner, −$50; and (b) source—profit from operations, +$80.

inventory, a reflection of the growth of the business. Furthermore, funds of $100 were applied to reduce a long-term obligation. The sources for these activities were a sizable decrease in the Cash account and a relatively minor increase in the owner's equity, since more than half of the profit of $80 (before write-offs) was paid out as a dividend to the owner. Trade credit of $300 was required to help support the increase in inventories.

By now it should be obvious that the process of funds flow analysis is nothing more than a sorting out, in resource terms, of the key decisions over a given period—as we said at the start of the chapter. With a little thought given to the differences in financial condition and to the results of operations, a great number of significant questions can be asked about the nature of the management decisions and the strategies implied in these. This will be discussed in more detail in later phases of this chapter, but the reader should recognize that the type of question raised is a *matching* of funds use and source decisions to see if these agree with the risks involved and with the long-term character and plans of the business.

Having dealt with the very simple conditions of our news vendor, we can now turn to a generalized funds flow model, which shows the interrelationships of the key elements of corporate balance sheets and periodic income statements. The model views them in terms of the investment, operations, and financing framework shown in the earlier illustrations. Such a generalized model is represented in Figure 1–5, which shows current assets, fixed assets, and other assets on the investment side; the operations, separated into the temporary accounts of revenues and expenses; and the choices of financing represented by owner's equity, short-term creditors, and long-term creditors. The arrows interconnecting all these segments show the possible funds flows which can be brought about by management decisions. Also shown is the effect of accounting write-offs which are dictated by accounting decisions, but which are irrelevant for funds flow purposes.

We have provided the general rules for funds flow analysis in the form of a quick summary below the model, as applied in the simple illustrations of this part of the chapter. Since we are essentially dealing with changes in balance sheet and profit and loss accounts, the rules for defining uses and sources can be simply broken down into increases and decreases of these accounts. For example, an increase in an asset account means a commitment of resources for that purpose, *a use;* while an increase in a liability reflects the inflow of "other people's" funds, *a source.* The opposite will be true in the case of decreases in assets and decreases in liabilities. Again, the question of accounting write-offs appears, but we will defer this discussion to a later section of this chapter.

Figure 1– 5
GENERALIZED FUNDS FLOW MODEL

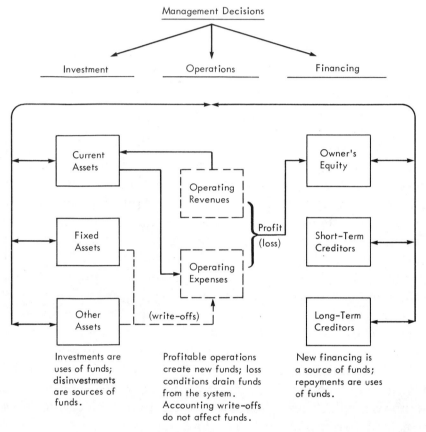

Rules for Funds Flow Analysis

Uses of Funds	Sources of Funds
Increase in asset	Decrease in asset
Decrease in liability	Increase in liability
Decrease in owner's equity	Increase in owner's equity
Loss from operations*	Profit from operations*

* Before accounting write-offs.

The model in Figure 1–6 is another way of showing the dynamic interrelationships of funds flows, this time in a manufacturing setting. This is achieved through representing the cycle of funds flows as a system of reservoirs and pipes through which funds are "pumped," that is, driven by the marketing

Figure 1–6
DYNAMIC FUNDS FLOW MODEL

The figure shows a dynamic funds flow model with the following labeled elements:

Share Capital, Dividends, Stockholders' Funds*, Repayment of Trade Credit, Cash Sales, Collections, Credit Sales, Repayment of L.T. Credit, L.T. Credit Extended, Repayment of Trade Credit, Cash Reservoir, Losses, Accounts Receivable, Disinvestments, Investments, Operating Funds, Trade Creditors' Funds*, Bad Debts, Taxes, Long-Term Creditors' Funds*, Marketing Pump, Fixed Assets, Losses from Disinvestment, Depreciation, Cost of Goods Sold, Use of Materials, Trade Credit Extended, Profits, Raw Materials Inventory, Inventory Losses, Finished Goods Inventory, Inventory Losses, Work In Process Inventory, Inventory Losses, Selling and Administrative Expenses

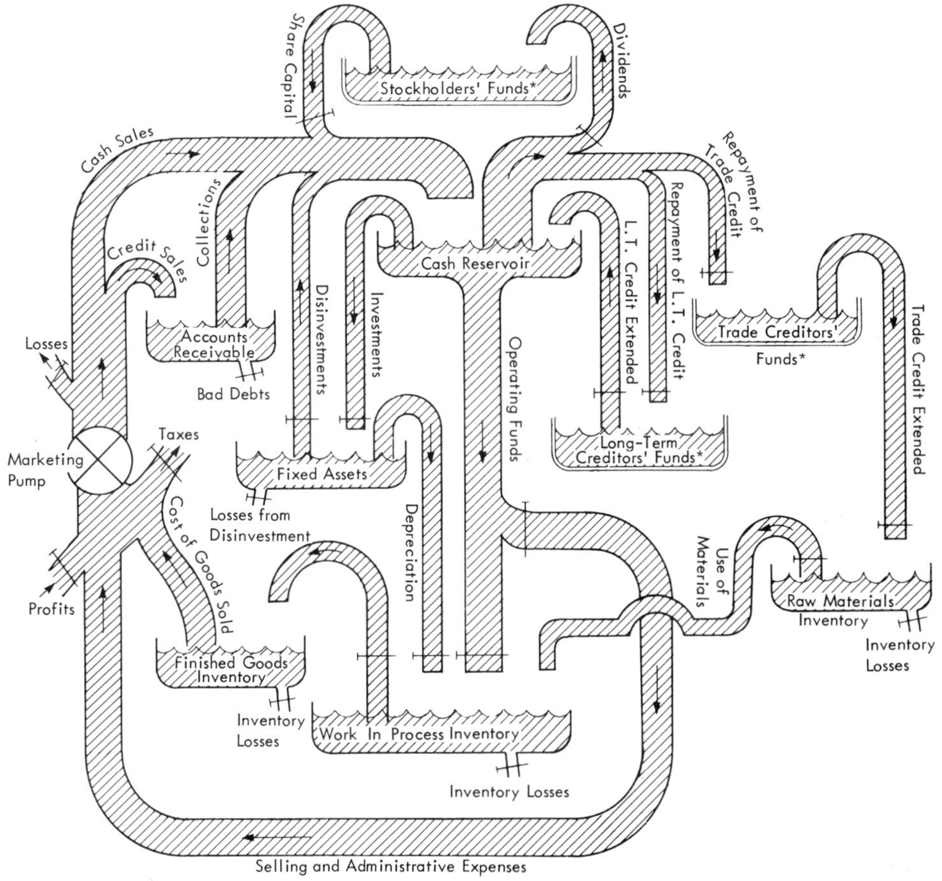

* These represent funds held by others, as contrasted to the resources of the business.

effort, and regulated by management using the various valves at key decision points. In the normal course of business, funds flow clockwise through the system. Various funds sources—stockholders and creditors—are employed to purchase materials. Additional funds, largely cash, are committed to processing and completing the goods. Meanwhile, funds are expended on selling and administrative expenses, in effect driving the "pump," which causes a recapturing of funds through cash and credit sales. Eventually, cash is replenished and the cycle of operations, supported by investment and financing, can begin all over again. Note that in this illustration the reservoirs represent funds owned by the respective parties—trade creditors' funds, for example, are selectively released into the company's funds flow and replenished by repayment. Drawing on these funds is the classic use of "other people's money," while repayment removes these resources from the system. This is true as well for the funds of stockholders and long-term creditors. Note also that profitable conditions will cause a net inflow of funds from operations, while loss conditions will drain the system in part. A balance can be maintained by selective activation or deactivation of funds sources, to cover operating and investment needs. In the end, however, only successful operations over the long term will establish the viability of the resource deployment made by management.

COMPLEXITIES OF REAL OPERATIONS

Having provided the basic concepts of funds flow analysis, we are now ready to turn to an example developed from the published statements of a major corporation. It is critical to remember that the process of funds flow analysis begins with accounting statements which *already contain* a variety of write-offs and other adjustments. These elements did not involve funds movements as we now understand them. While important to the reporting of comparable and consistent results to the financial community, stockholders, and other interested parties, these adjustments are mostly irrelevant for funds flow analysis. Funds movements are related to current decisions, while accounting statements are the combined result of past *and* current decisions. Our approach will be to work back from the published statements and through a variety of refinements attempt to reconstruct the funds movements which took place during the period. Some of these adjustments will be fairly complex and are kept for last in the process.

Figures 1–7 and 1–8 are the condensed balance sheets and operating statements of Crown Zellerbach, one of the world's largest producers of paper, paperboard, packaging, and other

Figure 1– 7
CROWN ZELLERBACH
Condensed Balance Sheets and Changes
December 31, 1978, and 1979
($ millions)

	1979	1978	Change
Assets			
Current assets:			
Cash	$ 9.7	$ 3.2	+$ 6.5
Short-term investments	82.3	159.5	− 77.2
Accounts receivable (net)	280.9	230.4	+ 50.5
Inventories	396.6	305.6	+ 91.0
Prepaid expenses	46.8	30.4	+ 16.4
Total current assets	816.3	729.1	+ 87.2
Properties:			
Timberlands,* buildings,			
machinery, and equipment	2,120.2	1,938.4	+ 181.8
Less: Accumulated depreciation	855.6	786.7	+ 68.9
Net properties	1,264.6	1,151.7	112.9
Investments in affiliated companies	53.0	65.5	− 12.5
Other investments and receivables	5.3	6.2	− 0.9
Deferred charges	21.4	11.2	+ 10.2
Total assets	$2,160.6	$1,963.7	+$196.9
Liabilities and Net Worth			
Current liabilities:			
Accounts payable	$ 174.1	$ 138.2	+$ 35.9
Notes payable	42.3	4.0	+ 38.3
Long-term debt due in one year	25.0	24.3	+ 0.7
Accrued U.S. and foreign taxes	50.7	36.2	+ 14.5
Other accrued liabilities	122.0	106.3	+ 15.7
Total current liabilities	414.1	309.0	105.1
Long-term debt	545.2	559.2	− 14.0
Deferred income taxes†	118.8	96.8	+ 22.0
Other liabilities, reserves‡	16.7	7.5	+ 9.2
Minority interests—Canadian subs	35.2	28.8	+ 6.4
Cumulative preferred stock	—	13.0	− 13.0
Common stock	127.1	127.0	+ 0.1
Other capital	65.7	65.8	− 0.1
Income retained in business	837.8	756.6	+ 81.2
Total liabilities and net worth ...	$2,160.6	$1,963.7	+$196.9

* Shown net of depletion allowance.
 † Result of using different depreciation methods for reporting and federal income tax purposes.
 ‡ So-called surplus reserves are not counted as part of the capitalization or net worth of the company. As a general rule only surplus items not specifically set aside for a definite purpose are so counted, which includes most "contingency" reserves.
 Source: Adapted from 1979 annual report.

Figure 1– 8
CROWN ZELLERBACH
Condensed Operating Statement
For the Year Ending December 31, 1979
($ millions)

Net sales	$2,804.1
Cost of goods sold*	2,286.7
Gross margin	517.4
Selling and administrative expenses	279.2
Operating profit	238.2
Other operating income	7.4
Miscellaneous (net)	19.8
Earnings before interest and taxes	265.4
Interest on debt	46.5
Earnings before taxes	218.9
Federal and foreign income taxes	77.6
Net income before share in earnings of affiliates	141.3
Share in losses of 50% owned affiliates	(7.8)
Net income	133.5
Cash dividends	52.3
Retained income	$ 81.2

* Contains depreciation and amortization of $110.2 million.
Source: Adapted from 1979 annual report.

forest products, for the calendar year 1979. As experienced by the paper and forest products industry and the U.S. economy in general, 1979 was a year of strong activity and resultant profitability before the long expected slowdown of 1980. The results of 1979 were adversely affected, however, by a prolonged regional work stoppage.

The balance sheets contain a column for changes in each of the accounts shown. These changes will be the basis on which we shall develop a funds flow statement, subsequent to which the actual statement published by the company will be shown. Several items are of significant size, and it will be easiest to sort these, initially without refinement, into a statement of balance sheet changes grouped according to sources and uses (Figure 1–9).

The key sources in this picture are an increase in retained income of $81.2 million, a decrease in short-term investments of $77.2 million, an increase in notes payable of $38.3 million, and an increase in accounts payable of $35.9 million. The funds

Figure 1—9
CROWN ZELLERBACH
Statement of Balance Sheet Changes
December 31, 1978, to December 31, 1979
($ millions)

Sources of funds:

Decrease in short-term investments	$ 77.2
Decrease in affiliated companies	12.5
Decrease in other investments and receivables . . .	0.9
Increase in accounts payable	35.9
Increase in notes payable	38.3
Increase in long-term debt due in one year	0.7
Increase in accrued taxes	14.5
Increase in other accrued liabilities	15.7
Increase in deferred income taxes	22.0
Increase in other liabilities, reserves	9.2
Increase in minority interests	6.4
Increase in common stock	0.1
Increase in retained income	81.2
Total sources	$314.6

Uses of funds:

Increase in cash	$ 6.5
Increase in accounts receivable	50.5
Increase in inventories	91.0
Increase in prepaid expenses	16.4
Increase in net properties*	112.9
Increase in deferred charges	10.2
Decrease in long-term debt	14.0
Decrease in cumulative preferred stock	13.0
Decrease in other capital	0.1
Total uses	$314.6

* For a first look, the change in net properties is often sufficient, instead of showing changes in gross property and accumulated depreciation.

thus provided were used for a net increase of $112.9 million in properties, for increased inventories of $91.0 million, and for increased receivables of $50.5 million. Two observations can be made from this limited analysis: (1) a number of financial decisions apparently took place, because of the sizable changes in short-term notes and short-term investments; and (2) the level of investments in properties and working capital elements was significantly increased during the year.

The statement of balance sheet changes does not, however, provide us with a complete picture of major funds flows. Three major classes of adjustments are to be made for this purpose, and all of these will be demonstrated in this example. In each, the analyst has to make a decision as to the level of detail relevant to his purpose, and common sense will have to prevail in the recognition and analysis of individual items. In the extreme case, each transaction might be recognized for its funds implications, as with our news vendor earlier in the chapter. This is clearly impossible and really counterproductive, since we should focus our interest on the significant elements of the funds picture of a business.

The three major classes of adjustments are as follows:

1. The change in *retained income* usually contains at least two elements of interest. The first is net income or loss from operations, as reflected on the operating statement, and the second is dividends paid to the various classes of stockholders. Both normally represent major funds movements, and the picture will be clearer if the net amount shown for them is separated into its components, one a source and the other a use. Moreover, additional adjustments may have been made to the retained income account, and if of significant size, they should be highlighted. Examples of this might be changes in balance sheet reserves, or value adjustments in asset accounts.

2. *Net income* is usually stated after a number of book write-offs, the largest of which is depreciation. Other examples would be amortization of patents, goodwill, and so on, as well as unusual write-offs or reserve adjustments reflected on the operating statement. If any of these are significant, they should be recognized and eliminated from the funds flow picture so that only true funds movements may be recognized.

3. The change in *net property* is a result of a variety of funds and nonfunds movements. It consists of changes in the gross fixed property account, changes in accumulated depreciation, and often the additional effect of nonrecurring asset adjustments from retirements of aged plant and equipment. In most cases, recognition of at least the major elements in this picture will make funds flow analysis more meaningful.

Each of the three classes of adjustments will now be discussed in detail.

CHANGES IN RETAINED INCOME

In our Crown Zellerbach example, an examination of the condensed operating statement in Figure 1–8 will reveal that net income for the period was $133.5 million. Cash dividends paid for the same period were $52.3 million, which left a balance of $81.2 million to be retained. This amount also coincides exactly with the increase in the retained income shown on the statement of balance sheet changes. If this had not been the case, we would have to look for clues in the published information as to any adjustments which caused the difference. Here we can limit ourselves to the two significant elements uncovered, net income for the period and cash dividends paid.

The change in our sources and uses pattern will be as follows. Instead of an increase in retained income, a source for the period, we reflect *two separate* elements: net income as a source of $133.5 million, and cash dividends as a use of $52.3 million. The net effect will, of course, be the same; but a fuller picture has been gained, as is now reflected in Figure 1–10.

In case of a stock dividend, which is in essence a book adjustment reducing the retained income and increasing capi-

Figure 1–10
CROWN ZELLERBACH
Statement of Sources and Uses of Funds
December 31, 1978, to December 31, 1979
($ millions)

Sources of funds:

Net income	$133.5
Depreciation and amortization	110.2
Decrease in short-term investments	77.2
Decrease in affiliated companies	12.5
Decrease in other investments and receivables ...	0.9
Increase in accounts payable	35.9
Increase in notes payable	38.3
Increase in long-term debt due in one year	0.7
Increase in accrued taxes	14.5
Increase in other accrued liabilities	15.7
Increase in deferred income taxes	22.0
Increase in other liabilities, reserves	9.2
Increase in minority interests	6.4
Increase in common stock	0.1
Total sources	$477.1

Figure 1 – 10 (*continued*)

Uses of funds:

Additions to properties	$223.1
Dividends paid	52.3
Increase in cash	6.5
Increase in accounts receivable	50.5
Increase in inventories	91.0
Increase in prepaid expenses	16.4
Increase in deferred charges	10.2
Decrease in long-term debt	14.0
Decrease in cumulative preferred stock	13.0
Decrease in other capital	0.1
Total uses	$477.1

tal stock, we would encounter a special situation. Strictly speaking, no economic values have been shifted; but if the amount is significant enough, the analyst is faced with the choice of making a reversing adjustment (as discussed in the ensuing sections of this chapter) or ignoring the matter entirely.

Had an examination of the company's statements revealed a significant adjustment to retained earnings, such as might have been caused by a change in a major reserve, further analysis might be useful. Let us *assume* that Crown Zellerbach's reserve for self-insurance, which represents a provision against possible losses and which contained a balance of $7.8 million in 1979, had been considered too large and was adjusted by $3 million through an accounting entry. Such a reduction would have resulted in a write-off of $3 million affecting *both* the reserve and retained income, reducing the former and increasing the latter. This $3 million item would be reflected on our statement of balance sheet changes as an additional use of funds of $3 million (decrease in reserves) and an additional source of funds of $3 million (increase in retained earnings).

It could be properly argued that such an item does not represent a funds movement in the full sense of our definition (i.e., no economic values were committed) and should therefore be removed during our analysis. This can be done simply by *reversing* the effect of the accounting adjustment, that is, reducing for funds flow purposes both the change in retained income (a source) and the change in the reserve (a use) by $3 million each. A similar decision could be made for other nonfunds adjustments which affected retained earnings *if* the amounts were material in the analyst's judgment. We must stress again that such refinements should not divert our attention from the key purposes of the analysis.

CHANGES IN NET INCOME

As mentioned before, net income is the combined result of matching current revenue and cost elements. Moreover, it contains a series of accounting write-offs and adjustments intended to reflect the effect on the period of past or anticipated revenue and cost elements. Since funds flow analysis is an attempt to recognize the impact of resource commitments, write-offs such as depreciation or amortization of past expenditures tend to cloud the picture. The true impact of net income on a company's funds must really be measured *before* any such write-offs, as we saw earlier in the case of the news vendor. Reported net income, however, is stated *after* write-offs, and must therefore be adjusted through reversals such as shown in the previous section. The amount of depreciation for the period, the most important item, is normally easily identified, and the adjustment simply amounts to adding back the amount of depreciation as a source and showing an offsetting use by increasing the change in net property. (The details of this latter element are discussed in the next section.)

In our Crown Zellerbach example, the amount of depreciation for 1979 was $110.2 million, which is shown as a source in the funds flow statement (Figure 1–10), with a like amount added to net properties. From this adjustment arises the often cited misconception of depreciation as a "source of funds." Depreciation as such does *not create any* funds, since it is only an accounting entry. To the extent that it has reduced net income, however, it must be recognized and reversed. Common practice has led to labeling the depreciation amount as a source, when in fact net income merely had to be *restored* to its prewrite-off level, to represent funds flow.

Other elements in the net income picture will sometimes be

amortizations and other adjustments of assets and liabilities on the balance sheet. Normally these amounts will not be significant enough to warrant special attention. If they are of material size, however, some analysts will make reversing adjustments of the kind we discussed for depreciation—in effect removing the impact on net income to keep the funds picture "pure." Much discussion has been carried on about the merits of such refinements, and this is not the place to argue for a final answer. The main point here is to establish the principle and to let the analyst decide the relevance of a particular case.

A word should be said about deferred income taxes at this point. This item on the balance sheet is assuming sizable proportions in many companies and is often misunderstood. The deferred income tax is simply the accumulated difference in net income reported for tax purposes as compared to that reported in the financial statements. This difference is due to the use of faster depreciation methods for tax purposes alone, a legal incentive to reduce tax payments early in the life of new investments. Net income reported on the books contains the normal depreciation write-offs, while income taxes were paid based on faster write-offs. This results in a lower tax *payment* actually remitted. The amount of income taxes reported on the operating statement, however, is an *assumed* higher figure than actually paid, with the difference shown as an accumulating reserve on the balance sheet. This "reserve" is built up against the day when the fast write-offs used for tax purposes will run out. It is an attempt to average out the uneven tax effect of fast write-offs. Since most companies continue to invest in fixed assets and thus enjoy fresh accelerated depreciation write-offs, however, the "day of reckoning" is postponed almost indefinitely, and deferred taxes continue to grow.

A simplified example may help to illustrate the points made. Let us assume that a piece of equipment costing $10,000 is depreciated for tax purposes over five years, and for book purposes over ten years. The impact of this dual treatment on a company's annual statements will be as follows, assuming all other conditions unchanged:

	Years 1 to 5		Years 6 to 10	
	Tax Treatment	Book Treatment	Tax Treatment	Book Treatment
Sales	$20,000	$20,000	$20,000	$20,000
Cost of sales	15,000	15,000	15,000	15,000
Depreciation	2,000	1,000	—	1,000
Profit before taxes ...	3,000	4,000	5,000	4,000
Taxes at 50%*	1,500	2,000	2,500	2,000
Net income.........	$ 1,500	$ 2,000	$ 2,500	$ 2,000

* Tax rate of 50 percent assumed for simplicity.

The $1,500 of taxes shown under "tax treatment in years 1 to 5," and the $2,500 in years 6 to 10 are the amounts actually due and payable to the government. The books will assume a *level* tax of $2,000 for each of the ten years, however. The difference of $500 in years 1 to 5 is credited to the Deferred Taxes account in the balance sheet, which will grow to $2,500 in year 5. From year 6 on, the Deferred Taxes account will be reduced by $500 per year, as the actual taxes paid exceed the amount reflected on the books. By the tenth year, the Deferred Taxes account will be zero. As new equipment is added, however, new deferred taxes are accumulated on the balance sheet, a condition found in most going concerns.

From a funds standpoint, no adjustments need be made, but the nature of the item should be recognized for what it is—an income reserve set aside against potential higher tax payments in the future. In that sense it is a proper source of funds for the period, just as was other operating income, and it can be shown together with operating income among the sources. In the case of Crown Zellerbach, the net change in deferred income taxes amounted to a source of $22 million for 1979, including a variety of adjustments too detailed to be discussed here.

Finally, net income is often affected by gains and losses from sale of capital assets. Since the funds effect is normally tied to a combination of circumstances regarding the components of the net property account, the discussion will be taken up in the next section in detail.

CHANGES IN NET PROPERTY

The funds flow pattern behind the change in net property is mostly of significant enough size to warrant some special attention. At the same time, it is also one of the more difficult aspects to understand for most newcomers to financial analysis. Part of the problem is the fact that the account is the *net* of an asset and a reserve account, and another part of the problem is the mystique surrounding depreciation and asset write-offs.

The easiest approach is to lay out the components of the account and to observe the relevance of the figures. Then we can search for clues in other parts of the published statements. Should the clues be missing, we must make any necessary assumptions, since inside information is often involved.

In our Crown Zellerbach example, the two balance sheets in Figure 1–7 provide the following information:

	12–31–79	12–31–78	Change
Gross property	$2,120.2	$1,938.4	+$181.8
Less: Accumulated depreciation	855.6	786.7	+ 68.9
Net property	$1,264.6	$1,151.7	+ 112.9

The task is to identify the relevant funds sources and uses, which in combination amounted to the net use of $112.9 million shown. Quite obviously there was an increase of $181.8 million in gross property, which must have been due to new investments (a use); while accumulated depreciation rose by $68.9 million, which must have been due to current write-offs to begin with (a source, as discussed before). For a first look, this analysis suffices and some analysts will let the matter rest here. Yet we already know, for instance, that depreciation for the period was $110.2 million, which is much more than the change in accumulated depreciation. Thus there must have been other elements, the effect of which has been netted out. This calls for further analysis.

The following questions of significance arise:

1.   What are the relevant elements of funds flow in the accumulated depreciation account, one of which must be the amount of depreciation taken for the year?
2.   What was the total amount of new investment in gross properties—a major element in the management decision process?
3.   Were there any disinvestments (i.e., reduction in gross properties) which significantly affected the company's funds?

The questions are intertwined and can be handled at two levels. The simplest approach is to assume that normally the amount of depreciation taken for the year ($110.2 million in our case) will *equal* the amount by which accumulated depreciation has increased. If this is not the case, in fact, then there must have been some reduction in the accumulated depreciation account which, for simplicity, we can assume to represent the abandonment of *fully depreciated* assets during the period.[1] This simple but often sufficiently creditable approach avoids having to deal with gains and losses on sale of capital items, and leads to the following change in our data:

	(1) 12–31–78	(2) Additions	(3) Deductions	(4) 12–31–79	(5) Change
Gross property	$1,938.4	+$223.1*	$41.3†	$2,120.2	+$181.8
Less: Accumulated depreciation	786.7	+ 110.2	41.3‡	855.6	+ 68.9
Net property	$1,151.7	+$112.9	–0–	$1,264.6	+$112.9

* Derived figure.
† Must be equivalent to accumulated depreciation if fully depreciated assets were abandoned.
‡ Assumed figure to balance the change in the account.

Since we must stay within the net changes of the accounts in the balance sheet, our simple assumption has given us the necessary clues to complete the analysis: we recognize the

---

[1] Fully depreciated assets, when scrapped, are removed by an accounting entry which credits (reduces) assets by the amount of the recorded value and debits (reduces) accumulated depreciation by the same amount.

actual depreciation write-off of $110.2 million as a source (column 2), and a *derived* $223.1 million as new capital investment, a use (column 2). The process relies on the *assumed* write-off of $41.3 million of fully depreciated assets, which under normal accounting practice results in an equal reduction in both asset and accumulated depreciation accounts (column 3). This is reflected in our analysis. We are ignoring possible tax implications which would tend to confuse the issue for little incremental gain.

From a funds point of view, we now have all the elements to separate the sources and uses behind the change in the net property account, as reflected in Figure 1–10:

Source: Depreciation for period ...	$110.2
Use: New investment	223.1
New use	$112.9

It is obvious that this relatively simple adjustment of net balances in the accounts has led to an improved display of one of the most important management decisions—the amount of new asset investment. Figure 1–9 reflected only a fraction of this information. But we are still short of a fully accurate picture because of our simplifying assumption regarding the write-off of fully depreciated assets. A check of the company's annual report shows that the actual capital investment for the period was $215.5 million, a difference of $7.6 million from our derived figure of $223.1 million.

This leads us to the more complex level of analysis in which we try to dig even more deeply into the property accounts and the accounting adjustments which probably occurred in them. Our assumption about fully depreciated assets left out the possibility of gains or losses on sale or abandonment of property and other fixed assets. Normally the amounts involved are relatively minor, as in the current example, but it will be useful nevertheless to have worked through the implications for a fuller understanding.

If in fact there *were* gains or losses on sale of assets—and this can be found from a closer examination of published income statements and balance sheets—there must have been a twofold effect on the company's statements. First, the write-off in the gross property account on the one hand and accumulated depreciation on the other must have been different by the amount of the remaining book value of the disposed assets. This would tend to complicate our basic data slightly.

Second, a gain or loss on sale of assets would normally be reflected in net income. Consequently, the same amount by which gross property had to be adjusted will also affect net income, and we have to ponder the effect on funds flows.

It will be helpful to sort out our basic data again, this time showing all the details now known to us:

	(1) 12–31–78	(2) Additions	(3) Deductions	(4) 13–31–79	(5) Change
Gross property	$1,938.4	+$215.5	−$33.7*	$2,120.2	+$181.8
Less: Accumulated depreciation	786.7	+ 110.2	− 41.3	855.6	+ 68.9
Net property	$1,151.7	+$105.3	+$ 7.6†	$1,264.6	+$112.9

* Derived figure, since both additions are now known.
† Loss on sale of assets, corresponding to the book value.

The funds effect of this refinement is to reflect a slightly lower investment as a source, and to show the offsetting $7.6 million book gain as a use, since in fact net income had been increased by this amount. Consistent with our rules of dealing with changes in net income, the book gain on sale of assets is one of the accounting entries which should be reversed for funds purposes. This is what we have done here, both by actually decreasing the property account (a source) and by in effect decreasing net income (use):

Sources:	Depreciation	$110.2
Uses:	Investment in property	215.5
	Gain from disposal of assets ...	7.6
		223.1
Net change in property		$112.9

Another complication arises if we recognize that some fixed assets were disposed of *for cash* and a gain or loss resulted. Strictly speaking, the proceeds received for the assets should be reflected as a source, with an offsetting use shown as an increase in the Cash account. This refinement would carry the details of analysis back to the transaction stage, however, and few will want to push the analysis this far. The best way to handle the situation is to trace through the details as we did in the previous case, and let judgment prevail.

KEY POINTS OF FUNDS FLOW ANALYSIS

In summary, the series of adjustments shown have followed the concepts of funds movements as discussed at the beginning of the chapter. At all times one should attempt to isolate, in a funds flow sense, significant elements reflecting management decisions on investments, operations, and financing. The key questions to be asked about these refer to the magnitude and type of commitment in relation to the sources from which they were obtained. Have enough long-term funds (retained earnings, new equity, debt) been raised to support major investments? Do temporary loans or other short-term movements constitute the bulk of sources for long-term use? What problems does this suggest for the future? What do changes in working capital suggest about the ability of the business to generate funds? Is business growth outstripping funds generation? Many of these questions will reappear in Chapter 6, where we shall discuss the business as a total system.

In the process of identifying and analyzing funds movements and relating them to each other, the selection of time periods is often quite important. If a business enterprise has a strongly seasonal character, the funds flow analysis should be carefully timed over a period which permits analyzing the swings in the business pattern. Thus, it may be useful to place the boundaries of the analysis on a seasonal high and a seasonal low, instead of straddling the period of seasonality. Again, imagination and feel for a business come in handy—and the analyst must make choices which cannot always be spelled out beforehand.

PRESENTATION OF FUNDS FLOW ANALYSIS

There are two aspects to the problem of presenting the results of funds flow analysis—the development of an analytical framework for internal needs, and the presentation of the key funds movements to the public as part of the total financial disclosure. While not entirely separable, the two aspects do differ, since there is much more flexibility in displaying the data for internal use than in the slowly evolving general format for external publication. Both methods have in common, of course, the desire to show the effect of key management decisions upon the funds picture of the enterprise.

Internal use of the funds flow analysis can and should be tailored to assist top management in assessing past relationships and in planning for future decisions. The amount of detail can be adjusted at will to fit the areas of particular interest and concern. There is an almost infinite variety of ways in which to present funds flow data, and we shall show just one possibility of analyzing the funds flow impact of the decisions made on the three key areas of a business: *operations, financing,* and *investment.* For this purpose we shall employ somewhat more detail than hcrctofore used in our display of funds flows, but at the same time we shall limit the analysis to the data already available in the statements of Crown Zellerbach shown earlier in the chapter. The result of this effort is shown in Figure 1–11, and the reasoning behind the analysis is described below.

The *operational funds flows* are largely contained in the data of the income statement, from which we so far have employed only the net profit and depreciation amounts. It is often useful,

Figure 1–11
CROWN ZELLERBACH
Funds Flow Analysis by Area of Management Attention
For the Year 1979
($ millions)

Operating inflows:
Net sales $2,804.1
Other income (net) 19.4
Increase in accounts payable 35.9
Increase in accrued taxes and other liabilities 30.2
Increase in deferred income taxes 22.0

    Total operating inflows 2,911.6

Operating outflows:
Cost of goods sold, excluding depreciation of $110.2 ... 2,176.5
Selling and administrative expense 279.2
Federal and foreign income taxes 77.6
Increase in inventories 91.0
Increase in accounts receivable 50.5
Increase in prepaid and deferred expenses 26.6

    Total operating outflows 2,701.4

Net operating inflows ....   +$210.2

Financial inflows:
Increase in notes payable 38.3
Decrease in short-term investments 77.2
Decrease in other investments 0.9
Decrease in affiliated companies 12.5
Increase in other liabilities, reserves 9.2
Increase in minority interests 6.4
Increase in common stock 0.1

    Total financial inflows 144.6

Financial outflows:
Decrease in long-term debt* 13.3
Interest paid 46.5
Decrease in preferred stock 13.0
Decrease in other capital 0.1

    Total financial outflows 72.9

Net financial inflows ....   +   71.7

Discretionary outflows:
Additions to properties 223.1
Cash dividends paid 52.3

    Total discretionary outflows ....   − 275.4

Net inflow from operations, financing, and investment ...   +   6.5

Analysis of cash impact:
Beginning cash balance 3.2

Ending cash balance .... $ 9.7

* Net of decrease in long-term debt and increase in current portion of long-term debt.

as we have done here, to take the key variables behind profit, namely, revenues and major costs, and to separate these for funds flow purposes. To display the size of these amounts flowing through the business helps to provide a perspectie for the magnitude of the other flows involved. Furthermore, short-term decisions regarding inventories, receivables, payables, and accrued and deferred income and expense are usually intimately involved with operational concerns such as production schedules, credit policies, and payment practices. Therefore, changes in the current balance sheet accounts can normally be considered as operational, and should be reflected as such. In the case of Crown Zellerbach, the *operational* decisions for the year 1979 resulted in a net inflow from operations of $210.2 million, which under this concept is an amount somewhat less than the normal quick rule of adding net income and depreciation to obtain "cash flow from operations" ($133.5 + $110.2 = $243.7 million). Increases in working capital items (inventories and receivables) in effect caused the difference. Note that in our analysis we have correctly taken into account the depreciation figure by reducing cost of goods sold, to restore essentially a "cash cost" picture.

The *financial* decisions made resulted in a net inflow of $71.7 million, largely due to changes in short- and long-term borrowing, and the liquidation of short-term investments. It would be perhaps more revealing to show the full details behind these financial movements, and additional analysis of readily available data could be used to separate gross borrowings and repayments in our display, for example.

Finally, investments in new properties and equipment represented the largest single outflow of a *discretionary* nature, $223.1 million, followed by dividend payments of $52.3 million during the year. Again, more detail could be shown on the investment side, if desired. Furthermore, the analyst has the choice of presenting in this area other discretionary outlays, such as research and development expenses, advertising programs, or pension contributions, if these are significant. The

Figure 1–12
CROWN ZELLERBACH AND SUBSIDIARIES
Statements of Changes in Financial Position
For the Years Ended December 31, 1978, and 1979
($ millions)

	1979	1978
Cash and short-term investments, January 1	$162.7	$ 90.9
Financial resources were provided by:		
Net income	133.5	112.1
Charges (credits) to income not affecting cash:		
Depreciation, amortization, and cost of timber harvested ...	110.2	104.9
Share in earnings or losses of 50% owned affiliates,		
net of dividends	8.8	(16.7)
Net loss (gain) on disposition of properties	(10.0)	2.0
Provision for deferred income taxes	22.0	14.7
Internal funds generated	264.5	217.0
Increase in long-term debt	20.6	102.3
Proceeds from disposition of properties	15.8	15.1
Decrease in long-term receivables and other investments	0.9	39.7
Decrease in inventories	—	9.0
Increase in notes payable	38.3	—
Increase in accounts payable	35.9	12.3
Increase in accrued income taxes	14.5	5.0
Increase in other accrued liabilities	15.7	7.6
Total financial resources provided	406.2	408.0
Financial resources were used for:		
Additions to properties	215.5	232.6
Long-term debt paid	33.9	38.8
Dividends declared	52.3	48.8
Investments in 50% owned affiliates	—	6.6
Retirement of preferred stock	13.3	0.2
Increase in accounts receivable	50.5	7.2
Increase in inventories	91.0	—
Increase in prepaid expenses	16.4	4.3
Miscellaneous, net	4.0	(2.3)
Total financial resources used	476.9	336.2
Net increase (decrease) in cash and short-term investments	(70.7)	71.8
Cash and short-term investments, December 31	$ 92.0	$162.7

Source: 1979 Annual Report. Shown here without accompanying notes to financial statements.

choices are wide and governed only by the objectives of the analysis.

The *net effect* of funds flows for the year can be brought down to show the ending *cash* balance, which we expected to change by $6.5 million, based on our previous analysis. This approach to displaying funds flows by area of management attention is merely one example of the useful picture which funds flow analysis can provide for the overview and understanding of management decisions. Funds flow is increasingly considered to be a more convenient way to think about a company's operations than review of the accounting statements in their original form. The particular approach used here has employed the key elements of both the balance sheet and the operating statements, and has combined these into a decisional framework from which to ask and begin to answer significant questions, particularly if the review is made over a series of periods.

For *external presentation*, a more accounting-oriented set of data is usually provided. In line with this custom, Crown Zellerbach presented its funds flow picture in an arrangement shown in Figure 1–12. This material has been reproduced from the 1979 annual report, but without the footnotes which explain many of the intricacies. A review and comparison between Figure 1–10 and 1–12 shows that most elements are reflected in the way we would have predicted from our earlier analysis. Only in a few cases does inside knowledge provide extra touches, such as the offset of an increase in long-term debt of $20.6 million by a repayment of $33.9 million for a net decrease of $13.3 million, and the exact information about additions to properties of $215.5 million.

A few more examples of presentations of funds flows analysis to the financial community are given as Figures 1–13 through 1–17. While details and layout vary, all presentations have in common the highlighting of key elements of importance to the respective business, and they all tend to concentrate on major funds movements, with some attention given to nonfunds elements.

Figure 1–13

THE COCA-COLA COMPANY AND SUBSIDIARIES
Consolidated Statements of Changes in Financial Position
For the Years Ended December 31, 1978, and 1979
($000)

	1979	1978
SOURCE OF WORKING CAPITAL		
From operations:		
Net income	$ 420,120	$ 374,692
Add charges not requiring outlay of working capital during the year:		
Provision for depreciation	112,939	94,024
Deferred income taxes	12,298	19,070
Other (principally amortization of goodwill and container adjustments)	29,546	19,549
TOTAL FROM OPERATIONS	574,903	507,335
Increase in long-term debt	7,234	–0–
Decrease in marketable securities—non-current	–0–	20,566
Disposals of property, plant and equipment	25,041	17,127
Proceeds from exercise of stock options	921	1,228
Tax benefit from optioned shares sold	212	318
	608,311	546,574
APPLICATION OF WORKING CAPITAL		
Cash dividends:		
The Coca-Cola Company	242,159	214,344
Presto Products, Incorporated	–0–	298
Additions to property, plant and equipment	329,559	306,022
Acquisitions of purchased companies excluding net current assets:		
Property, plant and equipment—net	51,842	–0–
Other assets including goodwill, net of other liabilities	23,456	–0–
Increase in miscellaneous investments and other assets	13,084	36,843
Increase in marketable securities—non-current	12,139	–0–
Decrease in long-term debt	–0–	72
Other	7,147	3,696
	679,386	561,275
DECREASE IN WORKING CAPITAL	(71,075)	(14,701)
Working capital at beginning of year	492,517	507,218
WORKING CAPITAL AT END OF YEAR	$ 421,442	$ 492,517
INCREASE (DECREASE) IN WORKING CAPITAL BY COMPONENT		
Cash	$ (49,265)	$ 6,780
Marketable securities	(123,655)	(34,879)
Trade accounts receivable	96,788	58,440
Inventories	131,353	96,747
Prepaid expenses	13,820	5,956
Notes payable	(55,573)	(10,962)
Current maturities of long-term debt	1,283	(947)
Accounts payable and accrued accounts	(66,830)	(113,759)
Accrued Taxes—including taxes on income	(18,996)	(22,077)
DECREASE IN WORKING CAPITAL	$ (71,075)	$ (14,701)

Source: Adapted from 1979 Annual Report. Shown here without accompanying notes.

Figure 1–14

PAN AMERICAN WORLD AIRWAYS, INC. AND CONSOLIDATED SUBSIDIARIES
Consolidated Statements of Changes in Financial Position
For the Years Ended December 31, 1978, and 1979
($000)

	1979	1978
Sources of Working Capital:		
Income before equity in income of unconsolidated subsidiaries and associated companies	$ 58,325	$ 97,322
Items not involving working capital—		
Depreciation and amortization	174,491	172,157
Deferred federal income tax (credit)	(2,582)	
Total from operations	230,234	269,479
Disposals of property and equipment	14,698	26,375
Increase in long-term debt	138,581	
Increase in long-term obligations under capital leases		73,793
Secured Equipment Certificates proceeds utilized by trustee		53,000
Conversion of debentures, including accrued interest	1,268	174,178
Deposits returned upon lease or purchase of flight equipment	56,250	
Dividends received from unconsolidated subsidiaries	6,000	
Proceeds from long-term receivables and transfers to current assets	5,500	4,268
Other—net	2,396	8,242
	454,927	609,335
Uses of Working Capital:		
Property and equipment additions	328,486	136,844
Capital lease additions	1,141	70,600
Investment in National Airlines including, in 1979, working capital deficit acquired of $25,802, less minority interest of $85,219	307,472	69,864
Increase in investments in and advances to unconsolidated subsidiaries and associated companies		30,108
Decrease in long-term debt due to conversion of debentures	83	170,558
Reclassification of long-term debt to long-term obligations under capital leases		52,389
Reduction in long-term debt	34,103	61,012
Reduction in long-term obligations under capital leases	31,072	29,035
Advances on aircraft purchase contracts	60,736	46,240
	763,093	666,650
(Decrease) in Working Capital	$(308,166)	$ (57,315)
Summary of Changes in Working Capital:		
Increases (decreases) in current assets:		
Cash and cash investments	$(125,133)	$ 12,461
Receivables, inventories and other current assets	110,622	24,222
Decreases (increases) in current liabilities:		
Notes payable	(40,000)	
Current maturities of long-term debt and obligations under capital leases	7,888	(9,613)
Accounts payable and accrued liabilities	(180,883)	(56,078)
Air traffic liability	(80,660)	(28,307)
(Decrease) in Working Capital	$(308,166)	$ (57,315)

Source: Adapted from 1979 Annual Report. Shown here without accompanying notes.

Figure 1–15
STANDARD OIL COMPANY OF CALIFORNIA
Consolidated Statement Changes in Financial Position
For the Years Ended December 31, 1978, and 1979

	1979	1978*
Sources of Funds		
Net income	$1,784,694,000	$1,089,128,000
Depreciation, depletion and amortization	707,162,000	591,017,000
Deferred income taxes	244,256,000	68,203,000
Undistributed income of affiliated companies	34,426,000	(35,827,000)
Funds Provided by Operations	2,770,538,000	1,712,521,000
Increases in long-term debt	26,988,000	27,724,000
Net book value of properties, plant and equipment		
sold or retired	150,806,000	59,361,000
	2,948,332,000	1,799,060,000
Uses of Funds		
Additions to properties, plant and equipment	1,458,696,000	992,648,000
Cash dividends	494,962,000	434,581,000
Reductions in long-term debt	74,429,000	264,458,000
Other net increase in investments and advances	51,785,000	7,589,000
Decrease (increase) in capital lease obligations	49,014,000	(4,142,000)
Other—net	71,680,000	9,010,000
	2,200,566,000	1,704,144,000
Increase in Working Capital	$ 747,766,000	$ 95,462,000
Analysis of Changes in Working Capital		
Increase (decrease) in current assets:		
Cash and marketable securities	$ (68,978,000)	$ 535,639,000
Receivables	967,150,000	614,143,000
Inventories	242,922,000	(221,310,000)
	1,141,094,000	928,472,000
(Increase) decrease in current liabilities:		
Accounts payable	(332,850,000)	(403,521,000)
Notes and loans payable	6,199,000	7,000,000
Current maturities of long-term debt	216,991,000	(208,239,000)
Federal and other taxes on income	(232,110,000)	(207,098,000)
Other	(51,558,000)	(21,152,000)
	(393,328,000)	(833,010,000)
Increase in Working Capital	$ 747,766,000	$ 95,462,000

Source: Adapted from 1979 Annual Report. Shown here without accompanying notes.

SUMMARY

In this chapter we have laid the foundation for the many techniques to follow in this book. In essence, funds flow analysis is a decisional display of management's disposition of short- and long-term funds available for operations and in-

Figure 1– 16
CARTER HAWLEY HALE STORES, INC.
AND CONSOLIDATED SUBSIDIARIES
Statement of Changes in Financial Position
For the Years Ended December 31, 1978, and 1979
($000)

	1979	1978
Source of funds		
Net earnings	$ 69,720	$ 63,820
Depreciation and amortization:		
Owned properties	42,288	35,648
Leased property under capital leases	9,672	9,844
Deferred income taxes	27,627	17,242
Less equity in undistributed earnings of finance subsidiaries	(8,033)	(4,194)
Working funds provided from operations	141,274	122,360
Properties sold or to be sold under leaseback agreements	66,950	32,935
Issuances of long-term debt	20,528	71,967
Sales of common stock	14,633	11,009
Other sources	11,902	8,415
	255,287	246,686
Use of funds		
Payments on long-term debt	6,788	5,553
Decrease in capital lease obligations	14,453	8,544
Purchases of long-term debt prior to maturity	7,330	4,869
Store property and equipment purchased	143,581	118,554
Net non-working funds acquired in purchase of John Wanamaker, Philadelphia		13,910
Net non-working funds acquired in purchase of Contempo Casuals	13,656	
Investment in finance subsidiaries	24,000	20,000
Cash dividends	31,073	27,289
Other uses	5,436	7,109
	246,317	205,828
Increase in working funds	8,970	40,858
Working funds at beginning of year	432,828	391,970
Working funds at end of year	$441,798	$432,828
Increase (decrease) in working funds by component		
Cash	$ 3,837	$ (1,216)
Short-term investments		(53,000)
Accounts receivable, net	(40,840)	44,677
Reimbursable property costs under sale and leaseback agreements	13,391	
Merchandise inventories	32,598	88,311
Other current assets	3,236	12,745
Current installments on long-term debt and capital lease obligations	200	(1,521)
Accounts payable and accrued expenses	(8,230)	(49,594)
Dividends payable	(833)	(1,112)
Current income taxes	5,611	1,568
Increase in working funds	$ 8,970	$ 40,858

Source: Adapted from 1979 Annual Report. Shown here without accompanying notes.

44

Figure 1–17
BANKAMERICA CORPORATION
Consolidated Statement of Changes in Financial Position
For the Years Ended December 31, 1978, and 1979
($000)

	1979	1978
Sources		
Operations:		
Net income	$ 600,203	$ 497,920
Items included in net income not using funds in the current period:		
Loan loss provision	226,177	176,692
Provision for depreciation and amortization:		
Premises and equipment	84,369	77,549
Lease financing	77,419	83,164
Total from operations	988,168	835,325
Increase in deposits	9,156,702	9,422,665
Increase in funds borrowed in excess of funds sold	2,538,751	2,701,594
Issue of common stock	19,665	4,413
Decrease in securities	119,800	1,497,977
Increase in other liabilities, net	45,713	—
Total Sources	$12,868,799	$14,461,974
Applications		
Increase in cash and deposits	$ 3,938,146	$ 5,785,484
Increase in loans and acceptances	8,008,517	7,962,255
Increase in lease financing	427,470	319,561
Increase in premises and equipment	132,349	206,229
Decrease (increase) in long-term debt	165,708	(37,163)
Increase in other assets, net	—	70,790
Dividends paid	185,157	148,798
Other deductions from capital, net	11,452	6,020
Total Applications	$12,868,799	$14,461,974

Source: Adapted from 1979 Annual Report. Shown here without accompanying notes.

vestment. By tracing through the operations of a simple fictional business, we have shown the funds pattern as the "third dimension" of the reporting of results, as a companion to the familiar balance sheet and income statement. At the same time we have gained more insight into the effects of particular management decisions. Applying the techniques to the statements of a major corporation, we recognized that most of the difficulties in this process stem from the need to translate accounting practices represented in the statement back toward a simple "cash transaction" framework, and that this process is based on commonsense reasoning.

The increasing use of funds flow analysis and the requirement for displaying this approach for publicly held companies is an indication of the importance of the technique. The concepts will appear frequently in part or in total in the later chapters of this book.

SELECTED REFERENCES

Anthony, Robert N., and Reece, James S. *Accounting Principles*. 4th ed. Homewood, Ill.: Richard D. Irwin, 1979.

Hunt, Pearson; Williams, Charles M.; and Donaldson, Gordon. *Basic Business Finance: Text*. Homewood, Ill.: Richard D. Irwin, 1974.

Jaedicke, Robert K., and Sprouse, Robert T. *Accounting Flows: Income, Funds and Cash*. Englewood Cliffs, N.J.: Prentice-Hall, 1965.

Levine, Sumner N., (ed.) *Financial Analyst's Handbook: Portfolio Management*. Chap. 21. Homewood, Ill.: Dow Jones–Irwin, 1975.

Moore, Carl L., and Jaedicke, Robert K. *Managerial Accounting*. 5th ed. Cincinnati, Ohio: South-Western Publishing Co., 1980.

Vancil, Richard F., ed. *Financial Executive's Handbook*. Chap. 40. Homewood, Ill.: Dow Jones–Irwin, 1970.

Van Horne, James C. *Financial Management and Policy*. 5th ed. Englewood Cliffs, N.J.: Prentice-Hall, 1980.

Weston, J. Fred, and Brigham, Eugene F. *Essentials of Managerial Finance*. 4th ed. Hinsdale, Ill.: Dryden Press, 1977.

EXERCISES AND PROBLEMS

1. Develop a funds flow statement from the balance sheets and income statements of the CBA Company shown below for the year 1981. Make appropriate assumptions and comment on the results.

CBA COMPANY
Balance Sheets
December 31, 1980, and 1981

	1980	1981
Assets		
Current assets:		
Cash	$ 39,700	$ 27,500
Marketable securities	1,000	11,000
Accounts receivable (net)	81,500	72,700
Inventories	181,300	242,000
Total current assets	303,500	353,200

CBA COMPANY (*continued*)

	1980	1981
Assets		
Fixed assets:		
Land	112,000	112,000
Plant and equipment (net)	445,200	464,800
Total fixed assets	557,200	576,800
Other assets	13,300	21,500
Total assets	$874,000	$951,500
Liabilities and Net Worth		
Current liabilities:		
Accounts payable	$ 71,200	$ 83,000
Notes payable	50,000	140,000
Accrued expenses	33,400	36,300
Total current liabilities	154,600	259,300
Long-term debt:		
Mortgage payable	106,000	90,800
Net worth:		
Common stock	225,000	230,000
Earned surplus	388,400	371,400
Total net worth	613,400	601,400
Total liabilities and net worth	$874,000	$951,500

CBA COMPANY
Operating Statements for 1980 and 1981

	1980	1981
Net sales	$1,113,400	$1,147,700
Cost of goods sold*	742,500	813,300
Gross margin	370,900	334,400
Expenses:		
Selling expense	172,500	227,000
General and administrative	65,500	71,800
Other expenses	11,200	25,000
Interest on debt	9,700	14,300
Total expenses	258,900	338,100
Profit (loss) before taxes	123,000	(3,700)
Federal income tax	56,600	(1,700)
Net income (loss)†	$ 66,400	$ (2,000)

* Includes depreciation of $31,500 for 1980 and $32,200 for 1981.
† Dividends paid were $30,000 for 1980 and $15,000 for 1981.

2. Work the following exercises:

a. The following data is available about the ABC Company's operations and conditions for the year 1981, from a variety of sources:

```
Depreciation for 1981 ...........................  $ 21,400
Net loss for 1981 ...............................    14,100
Common dividends paid ..........................     12,000
Amortization of goodwill, patents .................    15,000
Inventory adjustment—write-down ...............—     24,000
Investments in fixed assets ......................     57,500
Loss from abandonment of equipment .............     4,000
Balance of earned surplus, 12–31–80 .............    167,300
```

Which of the items above affect earned surplus during 1981 (the only surplus account of the company), and what is the balance of earned surplus at December 31? Which of the items above are funds sources, and which are funds uses? Can depreciation be considered a funds flow item if the operating results are negative? What would be different if the $4,000 loss from abandonment had been a gain from sale of assets instead? Discuss.

b. The following items, among others, appear on the funds flow statement of DEF Company for the year 1981:

```
Outlays for properties and fixed assets ...........  $1,250,500
Profit from operations after taxes ................     917,000
Funds from depreciation .......................   1,613,000
```

The only other information readily available is as follows:

```
Gross property and fixed assets, 12–31–80 .......  $8,431,500
Gross property and fixed assets, 12–31–81 .......   8,430,000
Accumulated depreciation, 12–31–81 ..........   3,874,000
```

Determine the change in the *net* properties and fixed assets accounts from this information, and spell out your assumptions. How significant would be the likely effect on the results if you used some possible alternative assumptions? Discuss.

c. The XYZ Company experienced the transactions and changes listed below, among many others, during 1981, and these affected its balance sheet as follows:

Fixed assets recorded at $110,000 were sold for $45,000 (gain reflected in net income.)

Accumulated depreciation on these specific assets was $81,000.

Accumulated depreciation for the company as a whole decreased by $5,000 during 1981.

Total depreciation charged during 1981 was $78,500.

Balances of gross fixed assets were as follows: 12–31–80, $823,700; and 12–31–81, $947,300.

From this information, determine the amount of new investment in fixed assets for 1981 which should be shown in the funds flow statement. What was the amount of change in the *net* fixed assets account during 1981? Which other items shown above or derived from these should be shown on the funds flow statement? What assumptions are necessary? Discuss.

3. Develop a funds flow statement from the balance sheets, income statements, and earned surplus statements of the FED Company, shown below, for the year 1981. Make appropriate assumptions and comment on the results. If you net out changes in working capital accounts into one figure, will significant information be obscured? Will a format by area of management concern be useful here? Discuss.

FED COMPANY
Balance Sheets, December 31, 1980, and 1981
($000)

	1980	1981	Change
Assets			
Current assets:			
Cash	$ 12	$–0–	–$12
Marketable securities	18	–0–	– 18
Accounts receivable (net)	68	73	+ 5
Notes receivable	30	50	+ 20
Inventories	131	138	+ 7
Total current assets	259	261	+ 2
Fixed assets:			
Land	25	25	–0–
Plant and equipment	268	283	+ 15
Less: Accumulated depreciation	157	160	+ 3
Net plant and equipment	111	123	+ 12
Total fixed assets	136	148	+ 12
Other assets:			
Prepaid expenses	12	14	+ 2
Patents, organization expense	30	27	– 3
Total other assets	42	41	– 1
Total assets	$437	$450	+$13
Liabilities and Net Worth			
Current liabilities:			
Bank overdraft	$–0–	$ 4	+$ 4
Accounts payable	73	97	+ 24
Notes payable	100	70	– 30
Accrued expenses	13	22	+ 9
Total current liabilities	186	193	+ 7
Long-term liabilities:			
Secured notes payable	40	20	– 20

FED COMPANY (*continued*)

	1980	1981	Change
Liabilities and Net Worth			
Net Worth:			
Deferred income taxes	25	27	+ 2
Preferred stock	35	39	+ 4
Capital surplus	90	109	+ 19
Earned surplus	51	51	–0–
Common stock	10	11	+ 1
Total net worth	211	237	+ 26
Total liabilities and net worth ...	$437	$450	+$13

FED COMPANY
Operating Statement for 1980 and 1981
($000)

	1980	1981
Sales	$1,115	$1,237
Cost of goods sold:		
Material	312	345
Labor	274	341
Depreciation	24	26
Overhead	158	210
Cost of goods sold	768	922
Gross profit	347	315
Expenses:		
Selling and administrative expense ...	268	297
Interest on debt	9	7
Total expenses	277	304
Profit before taxes	70	11
Income taxes	32	5
Net income	$ 38	$ 6

FED COMPANY
Statement of Earned Surplus for 1981
($000)

Balance, 12–31–80		$51
Additions:		
Net income from 1981 operations ...	$6	
Gain from sale of fixed assets	4	10
		61
Deductions:		
Preferred dividends	2	
Common dividends	5	
Patent, other amortization	3	10
Balance, 12–31–81		$51

ZYX COMPANY
Balance Sheets by Fiscal Quarters
July 31, 1981, to July 31, 1982
($000)

	1980		1981				1982		
	7-31	10-31	1-31	4-30	7-31	10-31	1-31	4-30	7-31
Assets									
Cash	$ 21	$ 30	$ 74	$ 91	$ 7	$ 28	$ 90	$103	$ 16
Accounts receivable	114	247	319	128	141	293	388	151	103
Inventories	231	417	315	131	271	467	351	98	310
Net plant and equipment	239	233	227	269	262	255	248	291	283
Other assets	15	16	16	15	15	14	18	18	17
Total assets	$620	$943	$951	$634	$696	$1,057	$1,095	$661	$729
Liabilities and Net Worth									
Accounts payable	$ 68	$297	$121	$103	$ 79	$ 314	$ 188	$ 97	$ 84
Notes payable	35	126	294	—	63	178	342	—	80
Mortgage payable	80	80	75	75	70	70	65	65	60
Preferred stock	100	100	100	100	100	100	100	100	100
Common stock	100	100	100	100	125	125	125	125	125
Earned surplus	237	240	261	256	259	270	275	274	280
Total liabilities and net worth	$620	$943	$951	$634	$696	$1,057	$1,095	$661	$729

Other data: (1) sold fully depreciated machinery for $4,000, (2) issued $20,000 of common stock ($1 par) to reduce note payable, and (3) issued $4,000 of preferred stock to outsiders.

4. The ZYX Company, a vegetable packing plant, operates on a highly seasonal basis, which affects its financial results during various parts of its fiscal year and forces a financial planning effort in tune with these fluctuating requirements. From the nine quarterly balance sheets shown in the table, which cover two fiscal years of the ZYX Company, develop a funds flow analysis which will appropriately reflect the funds requirements and sources as balanced by the company management.

Data in addition to the table include (1) purchases of machinery, $48,000 in April 1981 and $50,000 in April 1982; (2) depreciation charged at $6,000 per quarter through April 1981, at $7,000 through April 1982, and at $8,000 through July 1982; and (3) dividends paid at $15,000 per quarter through October 1981 and at $18,000 per quarter through July 1982.

Comment on the various alternative ways this analysis can be developed, and state your reasons for the choices you made. What are your key findings?

2 ASSESSMENT OF BUSINESS PERFORMANCE

So far the discussion has focused on depicting the decision process involved in resource deployment. This has yielded some insights, but also has raised a number of questions which only a more specific analysis can answer. The assessment of business performance is more complex and difficult, since it must deal with the effectiveness with which capital is employed, the efficiency and profitability of operations, and the value and safety of various claims against the business. In these points the reader will again recognize the pattern of the previous chapter—results should be related to the basic decisions on investment, operations, and financing.

Many techniques of analysis—a large proportion based on a variety of *ratios*—exist in performance assessment. Only the most important can be discussed here. It is particularly necessary, however, that the person analyzing business performance have clearly in mind which tests should be applied and for what specific reasons. One must define the viewpoints to be taken, the objectives of the analysis, and possible standards of comparison. The temptation arises in financial ratio analysis to "run all the numbers"—yet normally only a selected few relationships will provide clues for judgment. A ratio can relate any magnitude to any other, such as profit to total assets, or current liabilities to current assets. The choices are wide and numerous, as literally hundreds of relationships can be drawn. The usefulness of any particular one, however, is strictly governed by the objectives of the analysis. Moreover, ratios are not absolute criteria; meaningful ratios serve best to point up changes in direction and patterns of such change, which in turn may indicate risks and opportunities for the business under review.

The analyst must further realize that an assessment of performance deals with *past* data and conditions, from which it may be difficult to extrapolate future expectations. Yet, it is the *future* that can be affected by decisions—the past is gone and cannot be changed.

No attempt to assess business performance can provide firm answers. Only relative insights can be gained, since business conditions vary so much from company to company and industry to industry. Comparisons and standards have been further weakened by the trend of recent years toward multibusiness companies and conglomerates. Differences exist in location, types of facilities, products and services, accounting policies, capital structures, levels of efficiency, and caliber of management, to name but a few. Further complications have been added by the advent of adjustments for inflation in accounting. To develop a rationale for dealing with all of these aspects is far beyond the scope of this book. Nevertheless, they must be kept in mind when we deal with the numerical data available on which performance assessment depends.

We shall discuss the key ratios and measures commonly applied in financial analysis for expressing business performance and characterize each. The chapter will be developed along the major viewpoints which may govern this analysis, and in the end an attempt at integrating the measures will be made.

IMPORTANCE OF POINT OF VIEW

Many persons and groups normally take an interest in the success or failure of a business. The most important are owners (investors), managers, lenders, labor organizations, governmental agencies, and social groups. Depending on their objectives, they will view business results selectively in financial terms, and beyond this will often include intangible values. Since viewpoints and objectives cannot be separated, we shall structure the materials in relation to the major interested parties and those measures most meaningful to them.

Closest to the business from a day-to-day standpoint, but also responsible for long-range plans, is the *management* of the operation—whether composed of professional managers or owner/managers. Managers are responsible for efficiency, current and long-term profit from operations, and effective deployment of capital and other resources in the process. The *owners* of the business in turn are interested in the current and long-term profitability of their equity investment, reflected in growing earnings and dividends and in the rise of the economic value of their "stake" relative to the risk encountered. At the same time, the providers of "other people's money," *creditors and lenders* of short- and long-term nature, are concerned about steady interest payments, the ability of the business to repay the principal, and reasonable specific or residual asset values as a margin of protection for risk. In addition, other groups such as the *government, labor,* and other groupings in *society* will have some specific objectives— reliability of tax receipts, ability to pay wages, or financial strength to carry out social and environmental obligations, for instance.

The ensuing analysis of business operations by means of ratios and other measures will be developed along the first three viewpoints, that is, management, owners, and lenders. The viewpoints are not independent of each other but differ only in focus. The reader is encouraged to consider the applicability of the measures to the interests of the other groups mentioned.

MANAGEMENT'S VIEW OF OPERATIONS

As stated before, management has a twofold interest in the analysis of financial statements—efficient and profitable operations, and effective use of capital entrusted to it. The operational analysis is generally based on the operating (income) statements of the company, while the effective use of capital is usually measured from a combined review of the balance sheet and the income statement. For purposes of illustration we shall again use the sample statements of Crown Zellerbach for 1978 and 1979, which are reproduced as Figures 2–1 and 2–2.

Operational analysis for a business as a whole is generally performed by means of a "common numbers" or percentage analysis of the income statement. The basis against which the ratios are usually developed is *net sales*, that is, gross sales revenues after any returns or allowances. The use of net sales as the base provides a reasonably comparable standard of measurement, which is particularly useful when tracing results over a series of past periods or making intercompany comparisons.

We distinguish among the following types of ratios for operational evaluation:

1. Cost of goods sold and gross margin analysis.
2. Profit (net income) analysis.
3. Operating expense analysis.
4. Contribution analysis.

The purpose of deriving these ratios is both to judge the relative magnitudes of selected key elements and to determine any trends towards improvements or worsening of performance. In this process we must keep in mind the industry

Figure 2–1
CROWN ZELLERBACH
Condensed Operating Statements
Years Ending December 31, 1978, and 1979
($ millions)

	1979		1978	
Net sales	$2,804.1	100.0%	$2,456.0	100.0%
Cost of goods sold	2,286.7	81.5	2,039.0	83.0
Gross margin	517.4	18.5	417.0	17.0
Selling and administrative expenses	279.2	10.0	250.2	10.2
Operating profit	238.2	8.5	166.8	6.8
Other operating income	7.4	0.3	11.1	0.4
Miscellaneous (net)	19.8	0.7	9.5	0.4
Earnings before interest and taxes	265.4	9.5	187.4	7.6
Interest on debt	46.5	1.7	43.8	1.8
Earnings before taxes	218.9	7.8	143.6	5.8
Federal and foreign income taxes	77.6	2.8	49.1	2.0
Net income before share in earnings of affiliates	141.3	5.0	94.5	3.8
Share in earnings of affiliates	(7.8)	0.2	17.6	0.7
Net income	$ 133.5	4.8%	$ 112.1	4.5%
Net income per share of common stock (earnings per share)	$ 5.24		$ 4.39	
Net income	$ 133.5		$ 112.1	
Common dividends	52.1		48.3	
Preferred dividends	0.2		0.5	
Total dividends paid	52.3		48.8	
Retained earnings	$ 81.2		$ 63.3	
Common dividends per share	$ 2.05		$ 1.90	

Source: Adapted from 1979 annual report.

involved and its particular characteristics, as well as the individual trends of the company under analysis. For example, the gross margin percentage of a jewelry store with slow turnover of merchandise and high markups will be much higher (50 percent is not uncommon) than that of a supermarket which depends on low margins and high volume for its success (gross margins of 10 to 15 percent are typical). In fact, the comparison of a particular company's ratios to those of similar companies in its industry *over a period of time* will provide the best clues as to whether the company is improving or worsen-

Figure 2– 2
CROWN ZELLERBACH
Condensed Balance Sheets
December 31, 1978, and 1979
($ millions)

	1979	1978
Assets		
Current assets:		
Cash	$ 9.7	$ 3.2
Short-term investments	82.3	159.5
Accounts receivable (net)	280.9	230.4
Inventories	396.6	305.6
Prepaid expenses	46.8	30.4
Total current assets	816.3	729.1
Properties:		
Timberlands,* buildings, machinery, and equipment	2,120.2	1,938.4
Less: Accumulated depreciation	855.6	786.7
Net properties	1,264.6	1,151.7
Investments in affiliated companies	53.0	65.5
Other investments and receivables	5.3	6.2
Deferred charges	21.4	11.2
Total assets	$2,160.6	$1,963.7
Liabilities and Net Worth		
Current liabilities:		
Accounts payable	$ 174.1	$ 138.2
Notes payable	42.3	4.0
Long-term debt due in one year	25.0	24.3
Accrued U.S. and foreign taxes	50.7	36.2
Other accrued liabilities	122.0	106.3
Total current liabilities	414.1	309.0
Long-term debt	545.2	559.2
Deferred income taxes†	118.8	96.8
Other liabilities, reserves‡	16.7	7.5
Minority interests—Canadian subs	35.2	28.8
Cumulative preferred stock	—	13.0
Common stock	127.1	127.0
Other capital	65.7	65.8
Income retained in business	837.8	756.6
Total liabilities and net worth	$2,160.6	$1,963.7

* Shown net of depletion allowance.
† Result of using different methods of reporting and federal income tax purposes.
‡ So-called surplus reserves are not counted as part of the capitalization or net worth of the company. As a general rule only surplus items not specifically set aside for a definite purpose are so counted, which includes most "contingency" reserves.
Source: Adapted from 1979 annual report.

ing its position. Figure 2–5 contains a selection of representative ratios in a variety of industries.

Cost of Goods Sold and Gross Margin Analysis. One of the most common ratios in operational analysis is the determination of the cost of goods sold as a percentage of net sales. This ratio indicates the magnitude of the cost of goods purchased or manufactured in relation to the margin left over for operating expenses and profit. The ratios for analysis appear as follows:

$$\text{Cost of goods sold} = \frac{\text{Cost of goods sold}}{\text{Net sales}} = \frac{\$2,286.7}{\$2,804.1}$$
$$= 81.55\% \ (1978\text{: } 83.02\%)$$

$$\text{Gross margin} = \frac{\text{Net sales} - \text{Cost of goods sold}}{\text{Net sales}} = \frac{\$2,804.1 - \$2,286.7}{\$2,804.1}$$
$$= 18.45\% \ (1978\text{: } 17.0\%)$$

The cost of goods sold of 81.6 percent and the gross margin of 18.4 percent indicate to us the margin of "raw profit." We must keep in mind that gross margin is the result of the relationship of prices, volumes, and costs. A change in gross margin can be a combination of changes in the price of the product and in the level of manufacturing costs if the product was made by the company. In a trading or service organization, gross margin can be affected by the price of the product or service provided and the prices paid for merchandise or services purchased on the outside. Volume of operations can be significant if, for example, a manufacturing company has a high level of fixed costs (see Chapter 6 for further discussion) or the trading company has less buying power and efficiencies of scale than a large competitor. Complications are found particularly in manufacturing companies, where the nature of the cost accounting system determines the specific costing of products for inventory and for current sale. There can be significant differences between the apparent cost performance of companies using standard full-cost systems and those using direct costing, for example, since the level of charges for a period of operations can be sizably affected by this choice. Inflationary conditions further distort the picture.

A significant change over an appropriate period of time—many businesses have normal seasonal fluctuations, for example—in the cost of goods sold or gross margin would call for further analysis to investigate where the cause of the deviation rests. Thus the ratio is a signal rather than an absolute measure, as we shall find to be true of most of the measures discussed.

Profit Analysis. The relationship of reported net profit (net income) to sales indicates management's ability to operate the business with sufficient success not only to recover from revenues of the period the cost of merchandise or services, the expenses of operating the business (including depreciation), and the cost of borrowed funds, but also to leave a margin of reasonable compensation to the owners for providing their capital at risk. The ratio of net profit to sales essentially expresses the cost-price effectiveness of the operation. As we shall demonstrate later, a more significant ratio in this area is the relationship of total profit to the capital investment employed. The simple calculation for net profit appears as follows:

$$\text{Profit margin} = \frac{\text{Net profit}}{\text{Net sales}} = \frac{\$133.5}{\$2,804.1} = 4.76\% \ (1978: 4.6\%)$$

A variation of this calculation is the use of net profit *before* interest and taxes. This figure represents the operating profit before any compensation is paid to debt holders and before the tax calculations, which are often partly based on a different set of data. The use of this ratio rests on the assumption that it provides a "purer" view of operating effectiveness. Note that in our example the share of earnings from affiliates is not included; in so many cases a decision must be made on the exact items to be counted.

$$\text{Profit margin} = \frac{\text{Net profit before interest and taxes}}{\text{Net sales}} = \frac{\$265.4}{\$2,804.1}$$
$$= 9.46\% \ (1978: 7.6\%)$$

Increasingly one encounters the argument, however, that income taxes should be considered as an ongoing expense of being in business. Another modification of the calculation, therefore, is the use of profits after taxes but before interest— again, to recognize operating efficiency, but leaving out any compensation to the various holders of capital. The formula appears as follows:

$$\text{Profit margin} = \frac{\text{Net profit after taxes, before interest}}{\text{Net sales}}$$

$$= \frac{\$133.5 + \$25.1}{\$2,804.1} = 5.66\% \ (1978: 5.5\%)$$

In the calculation, for convenience, we add back the aftertax cost of interest on debt, which is pretax interest times $(1 - \text{tax rate})$, to the aftertax net profit, assuming a 46 percent incremental corporate income tax rate, thus 54 percent of $46.5, or $25.1. (See Chapter 5 for the specific discussion of the cost of debt.)

Expense Analysis. Various expense categories are commonly related to net sales as a matter of routine. These expense comparisons include such items as administrative expense, selling and promotion expenses, and many other items typical of particular businesses and their industries.

$$\text{Expense ratio} = \frac{\text{Various expense items}}{\text{Net sales}} = \text{Percent}$$

Many trade associations collect such data from their members and publish collections of statistics on expense ratios, as well as on most of the other ratios discussed in this chapter. This is done to provide standards of comparison and the basis for trend analysis to the members of the industry. In order to make the comparisons meaningful, great care is often taken to categorize the businesses by size and other characteristics within the industry, in order to reduce the degree of error introduced by large-scale averaging. A sample of such ratios for the pulp and paper industry is shown at the end of the chapter in Figure 2–4.

Contribution Analysis. Mostly for internal management use, but increasingly for broader financial analysis, we find the attempt to relate to net sales the "contribution margin" of product groups or total businesses. This calculation involves a very selective analysis or estimate of the fixed and variable costs and expenses of the business. Directly variable costs alone are subtracted from net sales to show the margin provided by operations toward fixed costs for the period and profits. Significant differences exist between the contribution margins of different industries, due to different capital investment requirements and cost-volume conditions. Even within a company, various lines of products may contribute rather differently to fixed costs and profits. The calculation of contribution margin appears as follows:

$$\begin{aligned} \text{Contribution to fixed cost} \\ \text{and profit} \end{aligned} = \frac{\text{Net sales} - \text{Direct costs (var. costs)}}{\text{Net sales}}$$

$$= \text{Percent}$$

Contribution margins are useful in gauging the risk characteristics of a business, that is, the degree of leeway management enjoys in pricing and expense control under different economic conditions. Break-even analysis and pricing strategies under different levels of operations are related to the concept, and more will be said on this point in Chapter 6.

Management of Capital. Several ratios are useful in judging the effectiveness of management's employment of capital. These are grouped as various turnover relationships.

The most common of these is the relationship of net sales to gross assets, or net sales to net assets. This ratio provides a clue as to the size of asset commitment required for a given level of sales or, conversely, the sales dollars generated for each dollar of investment. While simple to calculate, the overall asset turnover is a crude measure at best, since the balance sheets of most well-established companies contain a variety of assets recorded at widely different cost levels of past periods. These recorded values often bear little resemblance to current economic values, and the distortion is growing in the inflationary climate of the present times. Nevertheless, the turnover ratio is another of several clues which in combination can point towards favorable or unfavorable performance, especially if over time an improvement or worsening in the situation develops. Here are common ways of calculating turnover ratios:

$$\frac{\text{Net sales}}{\text{Gross assets}} = \frac{\$2,804.1}{\$2,160.6} = 1.30 \text{ times (1978: 1.2)}$$

or

$$\frac{\text{Gross assets}}{\text{Net sales}} = \frac{\$2,160.6}{\$2,804.1} = 0.77 \text{ times (1978: 0.8)}$$

If net assets (total assets less current liabilities, which equals the capitalization of the business) are employed, the calculations appear as follows:

$$\frac{\text{Net sales}}{\text{Net assets}} = \frac{\$2,804.1}{\$1,746.5} = 1.60 \text{ times (1978: 1.5)}$$

or

$$\frac{\text{Net assets}}{\text{Net sales}} = \frac{\$1,746.5}{\$2,804.1} = 0.62 \text{ times (1978: 0.7)}$$

The difference between the two sets of calculations is the choice of the asset total—whether gross assets or net assets. The second concept assumes that current liabilities are available to the business as a matter of course, and therefore the assets employed are effectively reduced through these common trade credit relationships. This reasoning is especially important in trading firms, where current trade payables are quite sizable. In our example the results are quite close, which indicates the forest products companies over time required roughly $1.25 of fixed assets for every $1 of sales—historically a very capital-intensive industry. Due to the rapidly growing cost of new facilities and equipment, incremental sales have to be supported by $2 to $3 of assets today.

Among the assets of a company, inventories and receivables usually receive special attention. The ratio analysis for these categories attempts to establish the relative effectiveness with which inventories and receivables are managed, and aids in detecting signs of deterioration in value or excessive accumulation in these accounts. One generally attempts to relate the amount stated in the account to the best indicator of activity, such as sales or costs of sales, assuming that there should be a close relationship.

Inventories cannot be judged precisely, short of an actual count, verification, and value appraisal. Since this is seldom possible, the next best step is to relate the recorded inventory on the balance sheet to either net sales or cost of goods sold, to see if there is a shift in magnitude over a period of time. Normally, one employs average inventory values (the average of beginning and ending inventories); but it is also desirable at times to deal with ending inventories alone, especially in rapidly growing firms where buildup of inventories may have to occur in support of steeply rising sales. Also, one must be careful to watch the method of costing inventories employed by a company—such as Lifo, Fifo, and other methods, and any changes made in these.

While the relationship of sales and inventories will often suffice as a broad measure, it is usually more precise to relate inventories to cost of goods sold, since only then will both items in the comparison be stated at a comparable cost level. The use of net sales introduces a distortion, since the sales include a markup not recorded in the inventories themselves. In a manufacturing company, we must particularly consider the problem of accounting measurements so often encountered in other tests, since the stated value of inventory in such operations can be seriously affected by the particular accounting system employed.

The method of calculating inventory ratios is as follows:

$$\frac{\text{Average inventory}}{\text{Net sales}} = \frac{\frac{1}{2}(\$305.6 + \$396.6)}{\$2,804.1} = 12.52\% \ (1978: 12.6\%)$$

or

$$\frac{\text{Average inventory}}{\text{Cost of goods sold}} = \frac{\$351.1}{\$2,286.7} = 15.35\% \ (1978:\ 15.2\%)$$

More commonly we find this format, which expresses the number of times inventory has turned over during the period:

$$\frac{\text{Net sales}}{\text{Average inventory}} = \frac{\$2,804.1}{\$351.1} = 7.99 \text{ times } (1978:\ 7.9)$$

or

$$\frac{\text{Cost of goods sold}}{\text{Average inventory}} = \frac{\$2,286.7}{\$351.1} = 6.51 \text{ times } (1978:\ 6.6)$$

The last two calculations reflect the frequency with which the inventory was recouped during the operating period. Generally speaking, the higher this number the better, since low inventory levels are often interpreted to mean a low risk of unsalable stock and efficient use of capital. Yet, inventory turnover out of proportion to industry conditions may signal inventory shortages and poor customer service. The final judgment will depend on the specific conditions.

The analysis of *accounts receivable* again is based on net sales. Here the question arises whether the amount of accounts receivable outstanding at the end of the period closely represents the amount of credit sales we would expect to remain uncollected, assuming normal credit terms. For example, a business selling at n/30 would normally expect to have the last month's sales outstanding. If 40 or 50 days' sales were represented on the balance sheet, one could expect that some customers had difficulty paying or were abusing their credit privileges, or that some sales were made on extended terms. An *exact* analysis of accounts receivable can only be made through an aging process of the accounts on the books of the company. Aging means classifying individual accounts into brackets such as 10 days, 20 days, 30 days, 40 days, and so on, outstanding, and relating these groups to the credit terms applicable in the business. Since this type of analysis requires inside knowledge, financial analysts looking at the business from the outside must be satisfied with the crude or overall approach of expressing accounts receivable in terms of daily sales. This takes the following form:

$$\frac{\text{Net sales}}{\text{Days in the year}} = \frac{\$2,804.1}{360} = \$7,789/\text{day (thousands)}$$

and

$$\frac{\text{Accounts receivable}}{\text{Sales per day}} = \frac{\$280.9}{\$7,789} = 36.06 \text{ days (1978: 33.8)}$$

A complication arises if a company's sales are made to different types of customers under different terms, or if the sales are made partly for cash and partly on account. A separation should be made between cash and credit sales where available. If no detailed information is obtainable on this aspect and on the pattern of terms used, the rough average has to suffice for a broad indication of trends.

A similar process can be applied in judging the company's performance regarding the payment of *accounts payable*. The analysis is a little more difficult, since accounts payable should be specifically related to the purchases made during the operating period. Normally this information is not readily available except in a trading company, where the amount of purchases can be deduced from the change between beginning and ending inventories and the cost of goods sold for the period. In a manufacturing company, purchases of goods and services are buried in the Cost of Goods Sold account and in the inventories at the end of the operating period. A very crude approximation can be made in such a case by relating the accounts payable to the average daily use of raw materials, if this expense element is available. If we can obtain the average daily purchases for the period, we can follow the process demonstrated for the accounts receivable, that is, calculating the number of days of accounts payable outstanding. This figure is then related directly to the normal credit terms under which the company purchases, and serious deviations from that norm can be spotted.

Total assets and *net assets* and the effectiveness of their use by management are analyzed by relating profits, defined in a variety of ways, to the commitment of assets used to generate them. This is one of the more telling analyses, although the character of recorded values will tend to distort the results.

The easiest form of analysis is the ratio of "return on assets," which relates reported net profit (net income) to the total assets on the balance sheet or to the total long-term capital funds, the capitalization. While an indicator of effectiveness, the results can be seriously distorted by changes in the company's capital structure (proportion of debt and equity) and by the federal income tax calculations applicable to the period:

$$\frac{\text{Net profit}}{\text{Assets}} = \frac{\$133.5}{\$2,160.6} = 6.18\% \ (1978: 5.7\%)$$

or

$$\frac{\text{Net profit}}{\text{Net assets (capitalization)}} = \frac{\$133.5}{\$2,160.6 - \$414.1} = 7.64\% \ (1978: 6.8\%)$$

As we stated before, net income is the final operating result after deductions of interest and taxes, and is therefore affected by the proportion of debt capital in the operation. By eliminating both interest and taxes from the ratio, we obtain a somewhat more meaningful result, which takes the following form:

$$\frac{\text{Net profit before interest and taxes}}{\text{Assets}} = \frac{\$265.4}{\$2,160.6} = 12.28\% \ (1978: 9.5\%)$$

or

$$\frac{\text{Net profit before interest and taxes}}{\text{Net assets (capitalization)}} = \frac{\$265.4}{\$1,746.5} = 15.20\% \ (1978: 11.3\%)$$

If we accept the argument that income taxes are a normal part of doing business, the result can be modified to the extent that we use operating income before interest but after taxes. We can employ the adjustment shown on page 61 to add back to net profit the aftertax cost of interest, or if there is reason to believe that income taxes shown have been modified for a variety of reasons and are not an expression of normal conditions, we can use a "normal" income tax rate to arrive at an income figure for the rate-of-return calculation. The first of the two methods was employed here, using a 46 percent tax rate:

$$\frac{\text{Net profit after taxes, before interest}}{\text{Assets}} = \frac{\$133.5 + 0.54(\$46.5)}{\$2,160.6}$$
$$= 7.34\% \ (1978: 6.9\%)$$

or

$$\frac{\text{Net profit after taxes, before interest}}{\text{Net assets (capitalization)}} = \frac{\$158.6}{\$1,746.5}$$
$$= 9.08\% \ (1978: 8.2\%)$$

The various ratios available for judging the business from the point of view of management thus deal with the effectiveness of operations and the effectiveness of capital deployment. All suffer in one form or another from accounting and valuation uncertainties, but together they can provide reasonable clues for further study. We now turn to the viewpoint of the owners, to whom management is responsible, for a discussion of other applicable ratios. So far we have not mentioned the owners, even though it is quite clear that in the timing, execution, and appraisal of business operations management must be fully aware of the owners' viewpoint and expectations of the business, just as it must of the lenders' position.

OWNERS' POINT OF VIEW

The key interest of the owners of an enterprise—the stockholders in the case of a corporation—will be in the returns achieved by management effort on their share of the invested funds, and in the distribution of earnings belonging to them. While there will be an absolute interest in these results, a large portion of the attention paid to these two elements will be focused on the effect these results have upon the value of the ownership investment, particularly in the case of publicly traded shares of stock. The second part of Chapter 5 deals with the key concepts in this area, and we can only briefly mention some of these here.

The first and most common ratio used for measuring the return on owners' investment is the relationship of net profit to net worth (equity). In this case we have to make no adjustments, since net profit has been properly reduced by the interest charges, if any, paid to holders of debt funds. Thus net income represents a residual result belonging totally to the equity holders, common and preferred. The calculation appears as follows:

$$\frac{\text{Net profit}}{\text{Net worth (equity)}} = \frac{\$133.5}{\$1,030.6} = 12.95\% \ (1978: 11.6\%)$$

Some questions arise regarding the handling of deferred income taxes, which, as discussed in Chapter 1, result from the difference between the accounting treatment and the tax treatment of depreciation. Some analysts argue that deferred income taxes are in effect ownership equity set aside against future higher tax levels, while others argue that they represent a form of debt. Often, deferred income taxes are not included in any of the calculations. Many analysts appear to be leaning toward the recognition of deferred income taxes as part of equity, but the point is still in dispute.

A somewhat more refined version of the return calculation is based on earnings ascribed to the common stockholder only, as related to the stated value of the common stockholders' equity. The difference is merely the elimination from earnings of dividends to preferred stockholders and other obligatory payments, such as to minority holders. Also, the preferred equity and any minority elements are removed from net worth to arrive at common equity. The result of this calculation is shown below:

$$\frac{\text{Net profit to common}}{\text{Common equity}} = \frac{\$133.5 - \$0.2}{\$1,030.6} = 12.93\% \ (1978: 11.8\%)$$

The question of accuracy of recorded values and earnings calculations again arises, and adjustments may be necessary if the analyst is aware of major inconsistencies.

The analysis of earnings from the owners' point of view centers on the *earnings per share* result, in the case of a corporate enterprise. This is simply the relationship of net profit (income) to the number of shares of common stock outstanding. Since in many corporations the number of shares changes during the year, either from issuance of new shares (new issues of stock, stock dividends, options, etc.) or retirements of old shares (treasury stock), it is common practice to use the average number of shares outstanding during the year. Earnings per share is a focal concept to which both management and the investor pay a great deal of attention. It looms large in the valuation of common stock (see Chapter 5) and often is the basis for specific corporate objectives and goals in planning for the future.

$$\text{Earnings per share} = \frac{\text{Net income}}{\text{Average number of shares outstanding}}$$

The calculation of earnings per share is normally unnecessary, since earnings per share are announced freely and frequently by corporations large and small. This is done on both a quarterly and an annual basis, and wherever publicly traded shares are involved these are matters of public record.

A great deal of analysis is focused on past earnings per share, both on a quarterly and annual basis. Much of the financial reporting of corporations is built around this figure, and projections are made by the financial community. Fluctuations and trends are watched closely as indicators of strength and weakness. Again, great caution is advised in the interpretation, however, to make allowances for unusual elements both in earnings and numbers of shares. In recent years it has become mandatory to calculate earnings per share also on a "converted" basis if a corporation has outstanding a number of convertible securities which may be turned into common stock in the future. In this fashion an attempt is made to call attention to the dilution effect of such issues. Moreover, any significant change in the number of shares outstanding (such as that caused by stock splits, for example) requires adjustments in past data for comparability.

Cash flow per share is frequently provided as an additional piece of information. This ratio, which represents per share net income plus depreciation and depletion, is an attempt to indicate the potential availability of cash for dividend and other disbursement purposes. Since the use of funds is largely at the discretion of management, however, this figure is at best only a crude indication of the ability to pay dividends. A much more revealing analysis is the funds flow format we discussed in the previous chapter.

Dividends per share are generally declared specifically and directly by the board of directors, and no calculations are necessary. A useful measure, however, is the so-called payout ratio, which represents the proportion of earnings paid in the form of cash during any given year. Since dividend policy quite commonly is oriented toward a fairly stable dividend by most boards of directors, the payout ratio of a company may fluctuate widely over the short term (two or three years) as earnings performance changes. In the long run, the payout ratio can often be used as one predictive device to judge the tendency of the directors to reinvest funds vis-à-vis paying out the earnings to the stockholder. There are no absolute standards for this ratio, but the relationship is significant in characterizing the "style" of corporate management. High-growth companies tend to pay out relatively low proportions of earnings, preferring to reinvest funds, while stable or moderate-growth companies tend to pay out larger proportions. Much more background, of course, must be considered in this as in many other questions of ratio analysis, and the reader is directed to the references at the end of the chapter.

Owners will also be interested in the degree to which their dividends are "covered" by earnings and cash flow. Furthermore, they will be interested in the degree to which the proportions in the capital structure of debt, fixed interest cost, and cash repayment requirements will affect management's ability to achieve reasonably stable and growing earnings and dividends commensurate with their expectations. A variety of "coverage" ratios are calculated, but they hardly differ from the ones we shall take up next in the discussion of the lenders' point of view.

On balance, the judgment about a company's performance by the owner will be based on the return on his "stake," in terms of growth of the value of his capital commitment and the cash rewards in the form of dividends. All of these are related to earnings power and management policies regarding the use of leverage and dividend policy. More details will be provided on these points in Chapter 6.

LENDERS' VIEW

While the main orientation of management and owners is toward the business as a going concern, the viewpoint of the lender of necessity has to be of two minds. He has both an interest in funding a successful business operation and a cautious view toward the possibility of default and liquidation. Sharing none of the rewards of success other than the regular interest and principal payments, the lender must carefully assess the risk of recovering his funds. Part of that assessment must be the value of his claims in case of serious difficulty. The general creditor ranks right after federal tax claims and secured creditors (who lend against a specific asset, such as a building or mobile equipment) in the satisfaction of his claims—and cautious practice dictates the need for a "cushion" against default. Several ratios appeal to this protective motive, while others, particularly coverage of debt service, represent an operational view.

Debt Proportions. The most commonly quoted ratio in appraising the debt exposure represented on a balance sheet is the current ratio, which relates current assets to current liabilities in an attempt to show the safety of the claims of the current debt holders:

$$\frac{\text{Current assets}}{\text{Current liabilities}} = \frac{\$816.3}{\$414.1} = 1.97:1 \; (1978: 2.4:1)$$

Presumably, the larger the ratio the better the position of the debt holders. From the lender's viewpoint, a higher ratio would certainly appear to protect his claim against drastic losses in value in case of liquidation. In that sense, a large excess of current assets over current liabilities would provide for a cushion should inventories have to be liquidated at a forced sale and should accounts receivable contain sizable credit risks. Seen from another angle, however, an excessively high current ratio would indicate slack management practices, since it might signal unused cash, inventories excessive for current requirements, and poor credit management causing overextended accounts receivable. At the same time, the business might not be making full use of its current borrowing power.

A very commonly encountered rule of thumb is the belief that a 2:1 current ratio is "about right" for most businesses, since it would allow a shrinkage of up to 50 percent in value of current assets and still cover current liabilities. The difficulty with this concept is that the current ratio is an essentially static measure which looks on a business as if at the brink of liquidation and does not take the point of view of a going concern, a notion to which management should give top priority. An even more stringent test of static nature is the acid-test ratio, which employs only a portion of current assets—namely cash, marketable securities, and receivables—which are related to current liabilities as follows:

$$\frac{\text{Cash} + \text{Marketable securities} + \text{Receivables}}{\text{Current liabilities}} = \frac{\$9.7 + \$82.3 + \$280.9}{\$414.1}$$
$$= 0.90:1 \; (1978: 1.3:1)$$

As this ratio implies, the whole orientation here is to test the collectibility of current liabilities in case of real crisis, assuming that there will be no value remaining in inventories at all. As drastic tests of ability to pay in the face of disaster, these ratios are quite useful. From an operational standpoint, however, it is better to analyze a business in terms of expected future operating conditions, of which the proportion of current assets to current liabilities will only be a small part.

A more overall way of measuring the riskiness of a business from the lenders' point of view is provided by a variety of ratios dealing with *total debt or long-term debt* in relation to various parts of the balance sheet. These ratios again are an attempt to express the risk exposure of a business in relation to the asset values against which all claims, debt or equity, are held. The first and most overall test is that of relating total debt, current and long-term, to total assets, as follows:

$$\frac{\text{Total debt}}{\text{Total assets}} = \frac{\$414.1 + \$545.2}{\$2,160.6} = 44.40\% \ (1978: 44.2\%)$$

This test merely indicates the proportion of "other people's money" to the total claims against the assets of the business. It is not necessarily a true test of the ability of the business to cover its debt, since, as we already observed, the amounts recorded on the balance sheet are not necessarily indicative of current economic values, or liquidation values.

A more refined version of debt proportion analysis is the relationship of long-term debt to the capitalization of the corporation, the latter again being defined as the total claims against the business, both debt and equity, other than short-term trade and tax obligations. A great deal of emphasis has been placed upon this particular ratio, since many lending agreements in publicly held and private corporations contain covenants regulating maximum debt exposure in these terms.

$$\frac{\text{Long-term debt}}{\text{Capitalization (net assets)}} = \frac{\$545.2}{\$1,746.5} = 31.22\% \ (1978: 33.8\%)$$

As we shall see later, however, recognition is growing that the most relevant aspect of analyzing debt exposure is not so much the proportion in the capital structure but the ability to *service* the debt.

Another version of this relationship is the ratio of total debt, normally all short- and long-term debt, to total net worth (equity). In this ratio, as in some instances before, the question of deferred income taxes is sidestepped by leaving that portion of the capitalization out altogether. The ratio is an attempt to show, in another form, the relative proportions of debt to equity, and again it is used as a measure of debt exposure:

$$\frac{\text{Total debt}}{\text{Net worth (equity)}} = \frac{\$414.1 + \$545.2}{\$1,030.6} = 93.08\% \ (1978: 90.2\%)$$

One specific refinement of this formula uses long-term debt *only*, as related to net worth, while a final refinement calls for long-term debt as a proportion of the total capitalization, in which such elements as deferred income taxes and a variety of other claims might or might not be contained:

$$\frac{\text{Long-term debt}}{\text{Net worth (equity)}} = \frac{\$545.2}{\$1,030.6} = 52.90\% \ (1978: 58.1\%)$$

or

$$\frac{\text{Long-term debt}}{\text{Capitalization} - \text{Long-term debt}} = \frac{\$545.2}{\$1,746.5 - \$545.2}$$
$$= 45.38\% \ (1978: 49.8\%)$$

Regardless of the specific choice of the several ratios just discussed, the debt proportion analysis is essentially a *static* analysis which does not take into account the operational dynamics of the business. The analysis is derived totally from the balance sheet, which in itself is a static snapshot of the financial condition of a business at any one point in time. The relative ease with which the ratios are calculated probably accounts for their popularity. While useful as indicators of trends, when applied over a long period of time, the ratios still do not get at the heart of the analysis of the debt-worthiness of a business, which lies in its ability to repay both principal and interest.

Somewhat more in line with that thinking are the various "coverages" of debt service. One of the very frequently encountered ratios is the relationship of net profit before taxes and interest to the size of the interest payments themselves.

This ratio is developed in the hope that the annual operating profit can be considered a basic source of debt service funds, and that any significant change in the ratio might signal difficulties. No hard-and-fast standards are in existence; rather, after an exhaustive analysis of a business' condition, prospective debt holders might require some covenants concerning the number of times the business is expected to cover its debt service obligations, based on their best judgment.

$$\frac{\text{Net profit before interest and taxes}}{\text{Interest}} = \frac{\$265.4}{\$46.5}$$

$$= 5.71 \text{ times (1978: 4.3)}$$

A somewhat more refined coverage analysis relates to the *cash flow* of the business before taxes and interest to the total of interest and principal repayments, in an attempt to indicate the ability of the business to service its debt. Several problems arise with this particular analysis, since interest payments are tax deductible while principal repayments are not. Care must be taken to develop these figures on a comparable basis.

As indicated before, there is growing interest on the part of the financial community in developing a form of "sensitivity analysis" with which to test the ability of a business to take care of its debt obligations. Lease obligations, which up to the present have not been included in the balance sheet, are analyzed along with debt service requirements if they are significant and available to the analyst. For this purpose, a review is made over an appropriately long period of time to determine the major operational fluctuations which are normal for the type of company and industry. Such past analysis might extend over several years or several seasons, as the case may be, in an attempt to determine characteristic high and low points in earnings and cash flow fluctuations. The pattern of past conditions is then projected into the future, along the lines of the funds flow analysis in Chapter 1 and the earnings projections in Chapter 3, to determine what problems, under presently known conditions, the business might encounter in servicing its debt.

It is often desirable to chart the pretax operating profit, the aftertax operating profit, and the cash flow likely to be encountered over the analysis period, and to draw high and low limits of these conditions from which to judge the maximum debt exposure which might be appropriate for the company. Debt service in this analysis would be defined as the size of the yearly principal repayments, as well as the *aftertax* interest cost encountered on the debt outstanding. If a business is subject to sizable fluctuations in aftertax cash flow, lenders may be more reluctant to provide debt which could not be serviced several times over at the low point. In contrast, when dealing with a public utility or a fairly stable business, the lenders may be satisfied to have a coverage of only one to one and a half times the debt service at the low point of the cyclical experience.

The type of reasoning described here is very much related to the concept of financial modeling touched upon in Chapters 3 and 6, which is nothing more than a simultaneous expression of the key relationships governing a business operation. With the help of computer models it is possible to make projections of a variety of likely conditions, given basic knowledge about the interrelationships of key elements in a company's operating and financial performance. When viewed in this light, mere ratio comparisons or insistence upon a minimum standard in one or two key ratios appears somewhat simplistic. After all, it is to the lenders' advantage, as well as in the management's and owners' interest, to have a business succeed in total, given all of the surrounding conditions. The simulation of a business and the use of such results to judge total debt-worthiness is therefore much more meaningful and has become increasingly accepted in practice.

RATIOS AS A SYSTEM

In recognition of these complexities, many attempts were made in the past to demonstrate the interrelationship of the various ratios discussed in this chapter. One of the first to

Figure 2–3
KEY RATIOS AS A SYSTEM

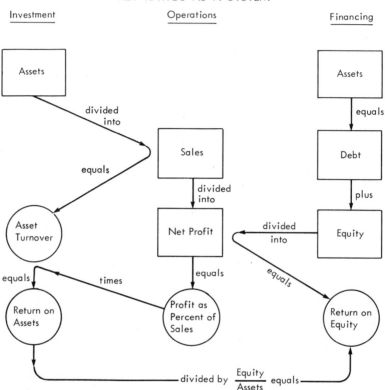

recognize and display the system of ratios was the DuPont company, which in its planning activities developed the "DuPont charts." These illustrate the fact that, for example, asset turnover and net profit as a percentage of sales are related, since the elements contained in them lead to net profit on assets.

A simple formula example shows this mathematical condition, where sales cancel out to provide the new ratio:

$$\underset{\text{(asset turnover)}}{\frac{\text{Sales}}{\text{Assets}}} \times \underset{\text{(percent profit)}}{\frac{\text{Net profit}}{\text{Sales}}} = \underset{\text{(profit on assets)}}{\frac{\text{Net profit}}{\text{Assets}}}$$

Figure 2–3 provides a pictorial display of some of these interrelationships. Here we are using the framework of Chapter 1—the separation of investment, operations, and financing, which of course relates the three viewpoints we have employed in this discussion. There is no particular uniqueness in recognizing that ratios are related—to the extent that they employ common elements they are logically linked together. The main point to remember is that ratios must not be viewed in a static and isolated fashion, as we observed before. As computerized analysis and models have come into use, these and many other interrelationships are quite easily exploited, allowing management to think of the business as a system rather than as a loose combination of checkpoints. We shall return to this systems notion in Chapter 6.

Inflation Impact

Several times so far we have referred to the distortions caused by the inflationary conditions which became a significant issue in the United States beginning with the early 70s. The accounting profession and the Securities and Exchange Commission have expended much effort on new ways to account for and disclose the impact of rapidly changing price levels and changing values of currencies. The intricacies and arguments encountered in this difficult area are beyond the scope of this book.

Yet, since the assessment of business performance rests on analysis of historical accounting and operating data, we must at least recognize the main distortions caused by inflation. Most important is the problem of historical costing, that is, the use of original cost of assets utilized in and charged to operations. Depreciation and amortization reflect lower past, not current, values; and particularly in industries with long-lived capital equipment and physical resources, profits (and taxes) thus tend to be overstated in times of inflation. Comparisons will be hampered between companies with different ages of capital equipment, as an example. Similar, shorter term distortions

Figure 2–4

CROWN ZELLERBACH COMPARED WITH FIVE MAJOR PAPER COMPANIES

Selected Data and Ratios for 1977, 1978, and 1979

($ millions, except per share)

	Crown Zellerbach	International Paper*	Mead	St. Regis	Kimberly Clark*	Scott Paper
Net sales:						
1977	$2,340.1	$3,668.9	$1,821.8	$1,996.3	$1,725.5	$1,520.2
1978	2,456.0	4,018.0	2,322.1	2,300.2	1,910.6	1,724.9
1979	2,804.1	4,533.3	2,569.5	2,498.4	2,218.4	1,908.1
Total assets:						
1977	1,795.2	3,839.6	1,374.0	1,927.4	1,651.3	1,589.5
1978	1,963.7	4,046.2	1,523.8	2,111.2	1,825.8	1,621.8
1979	2,160.6	4,843.4	1,636.5	2,260.8	2,105.0	1,829.6
Net profit:						
1977	111.1	233.7	98.0	106.8	130.7	99.2
1978	112.1	234.2	120.9	126.5	148.8	93.6
1979	133.5	347.8	141.0	158.5	158.0	137.1
Capitalization:						
1977	1,509.2	3,339.7	1,081.2	1,706.4	1,346.8	1,364.3
1978	1,654.7	3,413.7	1,177.6	1,803.6	1,434.9	1,373.6
1979	1,746.5	3,992.2	1,276.3	1,931.2	1,607.1	1,541.4
Gross margin:						
1977	18.8%	16.4%	19.9%	18.4%	29.4%	29.8%
1978	17.0	15.9	18.5	19.0	30.2	32.0
1979	18.4	14.3	18.6	19.3	27.8	33.6
Net profit to sales:						
1977	4.7%	6.4%	5.4%	5.3%	7.6%	6.5%
1978	4.6	5.6	5.2	5.4	7.8	5.4
1979	4.8	7.7	5.5	6.3	7.1	7.2
Net sales to total assets:						
1977	1.30:1	0.96:1	1.33:1	1.04:1	1.04:1	0.96:1
1978	1.25:1	0.99:1	1.52:1	1.09:1	1.05:1	1.06:1
1979	1.30:1	0.94:1	1.57:1	1.10:1	1.05:1	1.04:1

Ending inventory to sales:					
1977	13.4%	9.9%	12.3%	12.3%	11.9%
1978	12.4	10.0	9.7	11.2	10.3
1979	14.1	9.4	8.8	10.9	10.3
Days receivables:					
1977	34.3 days	34.8 days	38.2 days	33.5 days	43.2 days
1978	33.8	32.3	38.8	30.1	46.2
1979	36.1	32.4	38.0	29.3	38.4
Net profit to capitalization (before interest):					
1977	8.8%	8.4%	10.4%	9.4%	8.4%
1978	8.2	7.6	11.8	8.2	8.0
1979	9.1	9.7	12.5	7.3	9.8
Net profit to shareholder's equity:					
1977	12.4%	11.8%	16.1%	10.3%	11.5%
1978	11.6	10.4	17.7	11.3	10.1
1979	13.0	13.0	18.1	12.9	13.3
Current ratio:					
1977	2.3:1	2.2:1	1.7:1	3.4:1	1.5:1
1978	2.4:1	1.9:1	1.6:1	2.8:1	1.4:1
1979	2.0:1	1.9:1	1.6:1	2.7:1	1.5:1
Long-term debt as percent of capitalization:					
1977	33%	30%	40%	30%	32%
1978	34	27	38	28	27
1979	31	25	35	27	27
Earnings per share (before extraordinary items):					
1977	$4.35	$4.73	$4.10	$3.36	$2.56
1978	4.39	4.72	5.12	3.94	2.41
1979	5.24	7.25	5.42	4.87	3.52
Price-earnings ratio—range:					
1977	10–7×	14–8×	6–4×	12–9×	13–8×
1978	9–7×	10–7×	7–3×	9–6×	8–5×
1979	8–6×	7–5×	5–4×	7–6×	6–4×

* Both International Paper and Kimberly Clark had major nonrecurring earnings additions in 1979. The data shown are *before* these items.
Source: Adapted from company annual reports.

Figure 2–5

SELECTED RATIOS FOR MANUFACTURING COMPANIES

1979 Composites

(upper quartile, median, and lower quartile)

Line of Business	No. of Concerns	Current Assets to Current Debt (times)	Net Profits on Net Sales (percent)	Net Profits on Tangible Net Worth (percent)	Net Sales to Tangible Net Worth (times)	Collection Period (days)	Net Sales to Inventory (times)	Current Debt to Tangible Net Worth (percent)	Funded Debts to Net Working Capital (percent)
Blast furnaces and steel mills	99	2.54	6.92	34.22	7.62	50	15.5	125.5	191.8
		1.74	3.96	15.87	4.36	43	8.6	59.3	136.9
		1.43	2.23	7.67	2.89	35	5.5	39.7	86.3
Book publishing	270	5.93	14.42	36.97	5.16	90	10.0	108.2	100.4
		2.58	6.60	17.70	2.62	49	4.6	40.0	43.8
		1.58	3.18	6.99	1.19	28	2.8	12.8	9.8
Chemicals: Alkalies and chlorine	5	2.17	5.04	21.96	6.71	59	44.88	127.6	697.3
		1.62	1.80	11.25	3.46	53	14.1	72.5	273.7
		1.31	0.73	2.65	2.62	43	7.7	38.2	113.9
Concrete block and brick	149	3.35	8.10	27.52	5.04	54	16.1	85.6	161.4
		2.15	4.88	15.55	3.35	40	9.0	48.5	72.8
		1.48	2.32	5.75	2.31	28	6.0	22.4	15.1
Converted paper and paperboard products	89	3.78	6.30	41.83	7.00	48	17.0	99.2	113.3
		2.38	3.64	20.09	5.12	36	11.0	41.5	57.6
		1.56	1.61	11.47	2.70	29	4.4	21.3	8.8
Electric transformers	77	4.28	6.61	41.49	7.61	71	11.5	116.6	84.4
		2.59	4.80	17.69	4.23	57	6.6	54.9	34.9
		1.64	1.95	11.42	2.73	37	4.2	27.5	8.4
Engineering and scientific instruments	152	4.98	8.70	30.99	5.31	84	8.7	109.1	69.6
		2.74	5.70	20.92	3.50	55	5.3	49.8	43.3
		1.80	3.04	10.85	2.12	39	3.4	20.4	17.5
Farm machinery and equipment	401	3.66	7.96	36.58	7.48	52	8.2	180.0	107.6
		2.05	4.57	20.98	4.37	34	4.9	76.9	60.4
		1.34	2.47	9.67	2.86	18	3.1	30.7	20.8

Line of Business									
Footwear; men's except athletic	58	3.09	5.48	22.45	7.91	65	6.1	147.3	71.3
		2.39	3.27	13.26	4.47	44	4.8	62.3	35.6
		1.86	1.76	5.92	3.29	24	3.4	35.8	15.2
Industrial buildings and warehouses	1,563	2.41	6.67	50.00	13.90	70	290.1	220.4	78.9
		1.55	3.11	24.72	8.12	44	98.8	109.5	30.0
		1.24	1.46	12.42	4.37	23	26.9	43.3	8.1
Machinery, except electrical: Pumps and equipment	80	4.28	9.46	30.56	5.63	59	9.1	96.7	66.6
		2.98	5.98	18.91	2.77	47	6.6	42.4	29.4
		1.87	3.00	9.12	2.15	29	3.8	24.2	14.1
Meat packing plants	234	3.91	2.61	26.95	21.07	19	55.1	127.9	195.2
		1.79	1.04	13.75	11.06	14	32.9	58.6	83.2
		1.25	.43	4.39	5.96	9	18.1	20.6	16.7
Motor vehicle parts and accessories	335	3.61	8.71	43.69	6.25	53	13.4	98.7	79.6
		2.21	4.94	24.03	4.09	39	7.4	52.7	45.8
		1.47	2.48	12.78	2.88	25	4.8	28.6	13.7
Office computing and accounting machines	276	3.13	10.50	40.67	6.73	89	10.1	146.6	94.2
		1.98	6.24	21.38	3.50	64	5.0	68.5	50.3
		1.51	2.62	11.73	2.16	38	3.3	31.4	18.9
Paper mills, except building paper	49	2.93	9.57	24.64	6.43	50	11.9	72.9	181.6
		1.97	6.34	17.10	3.62	34	9.7	38.9	94.6
		1.52	3.10	12.40	2.15	26	6.2	27.0	51.5
Petroleum refining	74	1.85	6.73	49.49	11.74	59	21.7	188.2	206.0
		1.36	4.32	26.34	5.95	39	15.2	94.5	61.2
		1.14	2.12	18.87	4.26	27	8.0	61.1	17.8
Plastics, materials, and resins	99	2.84	6.46	37.26	8.14	62	14.9	129.4	118.1
		1.98	4.31	19.68	4.76	50	10.0	68.0	42.6
		1.37	2.46	14.51	3.10	33	6.9	28.0	15.6
Women's and misses' suits and coats	232	2.79	4.64	37.56	13.95	62	14.9	234.5	68.4
		1.72	2.22	16.97	8.68	40	7.9	122.0	33.7
		1.34	.87	9.01	4.80	19	5.5	49.3	11.3

Source: "Key Business Ratios." Reprinted with the special permission of *Dun's Review*, November 1980. Copyright 1980, Dun & Bradstreet Publications Corporation.

Figure 2–6

SELECTED RATIOS FOR RETAILING COMPANIES, 1979 Composites (upper quartile, median, and lower quartile)

Line of Business	No. of Concerns	Current Assets to Current Debt (times)	Net Profits on Net Sales (percent)	Net Profits on Tangible Net Worth (percent)	Net Sales to Tangible Net Worth (times)	Collection Period (days)	Net Sales to Inventory (times)	Current Debt to Tangible Net Worth (percent)	Funded Debts to Net Working Capital (percent)
Auto and home supply stores	3,072	4.96	8.54	39.91	8.47	40	7.8	149.3	111.7
		2.41	4.35	20.33	4.82	21	5.0	63.7	56.2
		1.52	1.08	8.65	2.61	9	3.4	22.1	19.2
Department stores	845	5.40	4.69	18.11	5.97	52	6.2	87.4	78.5
		2.99	2.14	9.46	3.70	24	4.5	43.8	41.1
		1.97	.79	3.49	2.37	5	3.2	18.9	13.9
Family clothing stores	2,132	8.04	11.01	31.26	5.26	31	5.2	79.0	93.8
		3.82	5.27	16.05	2.93	12	3.3	31.2	51.5
		2.06	1.92	6.43	1.58	3	2.2	11.1	21.0
Furniture stores	7,051	6.30	9.39	33.88	6.78	72	7.1	115.3	87.1
		2.96	4.48	15.51	3.38	31	4.5	45.5	43.0
		1.71	1.81	6.43	1.78	13	3.1	15.7	14.8
Gasoline service stations	2,976	7.26	7.50	64.84	18.92	16	40.0	86.3	207.5
		2.96	3.60	29.07	8.95	7	22.6	30.6	71.7
		1.49	1.46	11.85	3.82	2	12.0	9.7	20.6
Grocery stores	4,293	6.78	5.00	40.26	18.08	7	21.8	93.1	205.3
		2.81	2.05	19.49	9.90	7	15.0	37.9	91.6
		1.50	.87	8.85	4.74	2	10.0	12.1	31.0
Hardware stores	3,159	8.95	9.65	30.49	5.66	28	4.8	90.2	109.4
		3.88	4.63	16.11	3.20	15	3.3	37.0	57.9
		2.06	1.97	7.23	1.84	7	2.4	12.4	23.0
Jewelry stores	2,298	8.10	14.12	36.36	4.32	53	3.5	106.7	71.6
		3.64	7.47	18.84	2.50	26	2.4	46.4	37.6
		2.08	3.45	9.61	1.45	10	1.6	16.0	15.3
Lumber and other building materials dealers	3,739	4.45	6.24	32.49	8.02	51	10.3	116.8	99.6
		2.50	3.49	17.08	4.60	35	6.2	54.1	47.2
		1.62	1.62	7.89	2.68	20	4.1	22.5	17.0
Motor vehicle dealers	6,191	1.69	2.12	26.68	21.14	9	8.0	354.2	87.9
		1.37	1.03	13.60	13.75	5	6.0	210.5	41.7
		1.20	.32	4.86	8.85	3	4.5	116.9	14.7

Source: "Key Business Ratios." Reprinted with the special permission of *Dun's Review*, November 1980. Copyright 1980, Dun & Bradstreet Publications Corporation.

Figure 2-7

SELECTED RATIOS FOR WHOLESALING COMPANIES, 1979 Composites (upper quartile, median, and lower quartile)

Line of Business	No. of Concerns	Current Assets to Current Debt (times)	Net Profits on Net Sales (percent)	Net Profits on Tangible Net Worth (percent)	Net Sales to Tangible Net Worth (times)	Collection Period (days)	Net Sales to Inventory (times)	Current Debt to Tangible Net Worth (percent)	Funded Debts to Net Working Capital (percent)
Automotive parts and supplies	3,340	4.88	6.75	33.65	7.99	40	7.7	120.7	78.2
		2.73	3.55	18.06	4.81	28	5.1	54.3	39.6
		1.73	1.71	9.10	2.96	18	3.6	24.9	13.6
Beer, wine, and alcoholic beverages	490	4.23	4.72	40.96	12.18	18	19.4	104.3	148.0
		2.10	2.91	23.25	7.87	8	13.6	48.4	63.7
		1.48	1.40	10.67	4.67	1	9.7	17.2	16.3
Clothing and furnishings, men's and boys'	560	3.84	6.83	39.40	12.91	60	11.0	227.1	63.1
		1.94	2.94	19.91	6.75	34	6.2	102.9	35.5
		1.40	1.16	9.18	3.43	17	3.7	38.2	10.2
Drugs, drug proprietaries, and sundries	412	3.31	5.27	28.90	12.24	49	11.2	208.3	78.4
		1.96	2.21	14.05	6.75	31	7.1	96.1	39.5
		1.43	.73	5.91	3.59	18	5.0	40.2	17.5
Electronic parts and equipment	936	4.33	7.11	44.15	11.02	56	15.5	160.6	73.3
		2.30	3.73	22.46	5.91	38	7.1	69.3	30.1
		1.47	1.55	11.12	3.28	23	4.7	25.0	9.7
Groceries, general line	874	3.50	2.75	26.01	21.68	27	18.5	183.5	109.0
		2.04	1.10	12.92	11.34	15	12.1	76.8	49.0
		1.40	.41	5.73	6.16	8	8.1	33.0	16.1
Hardware	824	4.42	5.99	37.47	8.70	52	10.3	138.0	66.9
		2.52	3.21	18.70	5.15	38	6.2	60.0	27.9
		1.66	1.64	8.80	3.08	26	3.9	28.4	10.5
Metals service centers and offices	747	3.10	6.23	41.30	13.78	62	16.6	225.4	73.0
		1.80	2.91	19.08	6.30	45	7.7	98.8	32.8
		1.27	1.25	10.22	3.78	29	5.0	39.4	11.7
Printing and writing paper	133	3.66	5.23	35.17	12.13	51	14.6	160.5	73.6
		2.32	2.53	20.41	5.76	40	9.8	59.2	37.8
		1.61	1.22	6.24	3.46	26	7.1	30.4	8.9
Tobacco and tobacco products	313	3.97	1.91	20.11	21.22	18	20.2	139.7	57.8
		2.47	.95	11.70	12.46	13	13.8	65.7	26.0
		1.67	.36	5.70	7.93	9	9.4	34.5	7.0

Source: "Key Business Ratios." Reprinted with the special permission of *Dun's Review*, November 1980. Copyright 1980, Dun & Bradstreet Publications Corporation.

Figure 2–8
CROWN ZELLERBACH AND SUBSIDIARIES

Effect of Changing Prices

In the financial statements, our cost of raw materials, supplies and equipment is based on their prices when originally acquired. Because of the time span between purchase and consumption, their prices have increased dramatically, particularly in recent years. One of the major contributors to this upward trend is a rise in the general price level (or a decline in the dollar's purchasing power), commonly known as inflation.

In the schedule below we have calculated the company's net income as it would appear if its cost of goods sold and depreciation, amortization and cost of timber harvested had been adjusted to dollars which reflect 1979 purchasing power, using the Consumer Price Index. For some costs, such as raw materials, the increase is not significant because of their frequent turnover. For others, for example our pulp mill installations, inflation would cause a fivefold increase in depreciation expense. While this method of adjustment has flaws, one being that the Consumer Price Index does not accurately portray the price movements of the specific commodities we buy, it does show that a large portion of the company's income results from holding goods and facilities in periods of increasing prices. If those goods and facilities had to be bought at today's prices, net income would shrink to less than one fourth of the reported amount.

Because of the rise in the general price level, the equivalent purchasing power required to repay net monetary obligations incurred in prior years is reduced. The net gain resulting from the reduction of this outflow of purchasing power was $78.1 million.

For the Year Ended December 31, 1979
(in millions of average 1979 dollars, except per share amount)

Income from continuing operations:		
Net income as reported		$133.5
Less:		
Additional cost of goods sold	$32.7	
Additional depreciation, amortization		
and cost of timber harvested	69.5	102.2
Income from continuing operations adjusted for general inflation ($1.22 per share		$ 31.3

Shareholders' equity at December 31, 1979, adjusted for general inflation, is $1,731.5 million.

Figure 2–8 (*continued*)

Selected Supplementary Financial Data
Adjusted for Effect of Changing Prices
(in millions of average 1979 dollars, except per share data)

	1979	1978	1977	1976	1975
Net sales	$2,804.1	$2,733.5	$2,803.4	$2,710.6	$2,406.2
Other information					
Cash dividends declared					
per common share	2.05	2.11	2.22	2.30	2.43
Market price per common share					
at December 31	43½	34½	40¾	57⅜	48
Average level of the					
Consumer Price Index					
(1967 = 100)	217.4	195.4	181.5	170.5	161.2

We refer you to Crown Zellerbach's Annual Report on Form 10-K (a copy of which is available on request) for information with respect to the estimated replacement cost of inventories and properties at December 31, 1979, and the related estimated effect of such costs on cost of goods sold and depreciation, amortization and cost of timber harvested for the year then ended.

are caused by inventory values changing rapidly, and various methods of costing are used to provide a consistent basis for analysis. Other issues involve the impact of inflation on borrowing, since declining values of the currency will reduce the economic burden of repayment to the borrower, while reducing the attractiveness of the loan to the lender. Current operations are also affected by differential price movements both in the goods and services sold, and in the factor costs of the operations carried out.

The sample ratios shown in Figure 2–4 for six major paper companies are based on historical accounting procedures, however, as are the selected industry ratios in Figures 2–5 through 2–7. While internally consistent, these sample results are distorted by these inflationary impacts which have not been taken into account.

Replacement cost accounting, new forms of inventory valuation methods, and partial or full periodic restatement of financial reports are among the many attempts to deal with the complex inflation issue. In fact, inflation has turned the simple accounting principle of matching costs and revenues into an economic and intellectual challenge. At the end of this chapter are shown a few examples of disclosure of the impact of inflation as found in the 1979 annual reports of some of the companies whose funds flow statements were displayed at the end of Chapter 1 (Figures 2–8 through 2–11). These efforts are an early version of what is likely to become a much expanded feature of corporate financial statements. The 1980s will hopefully bring, after much experimentation, a set of fairly consistent techniques in common use which will permit assessment of business performance both in current and inflation-adjusted terms.

SUMMARY

In this chapter we have shown that the assessment of business performance is inseparable from the viewpoints of the persons or groups analyzing this performance. We have chosen to talk about only three major viewpoints—management, owners, and lenders—leaving out detailed discussions of other interested groups. The various analyses displayed lead one very quickly to recognize that in the end the crucial test is the economic return on the investment employed in the business and its attendant effect on the value of ownership. All three parties are concerned about the success of the operation, each from its own standpoint; but it is management's duty to bring about stability, growth, and reliability of earnings performance relative to the investment entrusted to it by the owners. All the ratios are intertwined and are best interpreted when viewing the business as a system of interconnected conditions. To this end, modeling and computerized simulation are increasingly becoming useful, since many ratios are by their nature only fairly static tests which cannot do justice to the dynamics of a business operation.

Figure 2– 9

STANDARD OIL COMPANY OF CALIFORNIA
Inflation Adjusted Data
(unaudited)

1979 Statement of Income*
(millions of dollars)

	As Reported	Constant Dollars
Revenues	$31,755	$31,755
Costs and Expenses		
Cost of products sold and operating expenses	25,769	25,785
Depreciation, depletion and amortization	707	1,167
Taxes other than on income	2,188	2,188
Interest and debt expense	156	156
Provision for income taxes	1,150	1,150
Net income	$ 1,785	$ 1,309

	1979	1978	1977	1976	1975
Five Year Summary (1979 constant dollars)†					
Revenues	$31,755	$27,367	$26,637	$26,220	$24,507
Net Income	1,309	732	765	725	614
Net Assets	14,666	13,619	13,145	12,635	12,204
Unrealized gain from decline in purchasing power of net amounts owed	226	219	206	162	186
Per Share Data‡					
Net Income: As Reported	$ 10.44	$ 6.38	$ 5.82	$ 5.16	$ 4.60
In Constant Dollars	7.66	4.29	4.49	4.27	3.61
Cash Dividends: As Reported	2.90	2.55	2.35	2.15	2.00
In Constant Dollars	2.90	2.84	2.81	2.74	2.70
Market Price @ 12/31: Per NYSE	56	47	39	41	29
In Constant Dollars	56	52	47	52	39
Effective Tax Rate: As Reported	39.2%	42.7%	43.5%	37.9%	45.0%
In Constant Dollars	46.8%	55.2%	54.4%	48.5%	58.4%
Average Consumer Price Index	217.4	195.4	181.5	170.5	161.2

* "As Reported" refers to the data presented in the audited financial statements of the Annual Report. Adjustments to reflect "Constant Dollar" reporting have been made for consolidated companies only.
  † Prior year constant dollar amounts adjusted to average 1979 dollars for comparative purposes.
  ‡ Per weighted average number of shares issued.

Figure 2–10

THE COCA-COLA COMPANY AND SUBSIDIARIES
Statements of Income Adjusted for Changing Prices
Year Ended December 31, 1979
(in thousands except per share data)

	As Reported in the Primary Financial Statements	Adjusted for General Inflation
Net sales	$4,961,402	$4,961,402
Cost of goods sold (excluding depreciation)	2,733,621	2,773,027
Depreciation and amortization	114,151	154,275
Other operating expenses	1,393,525	1,393,525
Net of other income and deductions	(22,087)	(22,087)
	4,219,210	4,298,740
Income before income taxes	742,192	662,662
Provision for taxes on income	322,072	322,072
Net income	$ 420,120	$ 340,590
Net income per share	$ 3.40	$ 2.76
Effective income tax rate	43.4%	48.6%
Purchasing power gain from holding net monetary liabilities during the year		$ 20,740

Five-Year Comparison of Selected Supplemental Financial Data
Adjusted for Effects of Changing Prices
(in average 1979 dollars)

	Year Ended December 31 (in thousands except per share data)				
	1979	1978	1977	1976	1975
Net sales	$4,961,402	$4,826,322	$4,335,825	$4,011,391	$4,018,055
Cash dividends declared per common share*	1.96	1.94	1.84	1.69	1.55
Market price per common share at year-end*	32.67	47.01	43.52	49.27	53.76
Average Consumer Price Index—Urban used in developing these data	217.4	195.4	181.5	170.5	161.2
Net assets at year-end	$2,377,186				

The actual market price of the common stock of The Coca-Cola Company at December 31, for the years 1975 to 1979 (adjusted for stock split) was $41.125, $39.50, $37.25, $43.875 and $34.50, respectively.

* Adjusted for 1977 stock split.

Figure 2–11

PAN AMERICAN WORLD AIRWAYS, INC.
AND CONSOLIDATED SUBSIDIARIES
Supplemental Financial Information—(Continued)
Statement of Income from Continuing Operations
Adjusted for Changing Prices

	Year Ended December 31, 1979 (Unaudited) (in thousands)		
	Historic Statements	Adjusted for General Inflation (Constant $)	Adjusted for Changes in Specific Prices (Current Costs)
Operating revenues	$2,484,709	$2,484,709	$2,484,709
Depreciation and amortization expense	174,491	276,887	280,972
Other operating expense	2,231,838	2,231,838	2,231,838
Other expenses	20,055	20,055	20,055
Equity in income of unconsolidated subsidiaries and associated companies	17,803	17,803	17,803
Income (loss) from continuing operations	$ 76,128	$ (26,268)	$ (30,353)
Gain from decline in purchasing power of net amounts owed		$ 112,251	$ 112,251
Effect of increase in general price level			$ 250,776
Increase in specific prices of property and equipment owned and leased during the year*			222,349
Excess of increase in general price level over increase in specific prices			$ 28,427

* At December 31, 1979, owned and leased property and equipment, stated at current cost, net of accumulated depreciation was $2,685,788,000 compared with historic value of $1,947,824,000. Property and equipment acquired by purchase of National Airlines is stated at fair value.

SELECTED REFERENCES

Anthony, Robert N., and Reece, James S. *Accounting: Text and Cases.* 6th ed. Homewood, Ill.: Richard D. Irwin, 1979.

Bernstein, Leopold A. *Financial Statement Analysis: Theory, Application, and Interpretation.* Rev. ed. Homewood, Ill.: Richard D. Irwin, 1978.

Graham, Benjamin. *The Interpretation of Financial Statements.* 3d ed. New York: Harper & Row, 1975.

Hunt, Pearson; Williams, Charles M.; and Donaldson, Gordon. *Basic Business Finance: Text.* Homewood, Ill.: Richard D. Irwin, 1974.

Levine, Sumner N., ed. *Financial Analyst's Handbook: Portfolio Management.* Chap. 22. Homewood, Ill.: Dow Jones–Irwin, 1975.

Robert Morris Associates. *Annual Statement Studies.*

Troy, Leo. *Almanac of Business and Industrial Financial Ratios.* Englewood Cliffs, N.J.: Prentice-Hall, 1976.

Van Horne, James C. *Financial Management and Policy.* 5th ed. Englewood Cliffs, N.J.: Prentice-Hall, 1980.

Viscione, Jerry A. *Financial Analysis—Principles and Procedures.* Boston: Basic Books, 1976.

Weston, J. Fred, and Brigham, Eugene F. *Essentials of Managerial Finance.* 4th ed. Hinsdale, Ill.: Dryden Press, 1977.

EXERCISES AND PROBLEMS

1. Work the following exercises:

   a. A company has achieved a 1981 net profit which represents 11.4 percent of net sales. What is the company's return on net worth if asset turnover is 1.34 and the capitalization is 67 percent of total assets? How would a faster asset turnover affect the result?

   b. A company's gross margin on sales for 1981 is 31.4 percent. Total cost of goods sold amounted to $4,391,300, and net profit was 9.7 percent of sales. What are the company's total assets if the ratio of sales to assets is 82.7 percent? What is the return on capitalization if current liabilities are 21 percent of total assets?

   c. What is the change in a company's current ratio of 2.2:1 (current assets are $573,100) if the following actions are taken individually? Also, how does each item affect working capital?

      1. Pays $67,500 of accounts payable with cash.
      2. Collects $33,000 notes receivable.
      3. Purchases merchandise of $41,300 on account.
      4. Pays dividends of $60,000, of which $42,000 had been shown as accrued.
      5. Sells machine for $80,000, on which book value is $90,000 and accumulated depreciation, $112,000
      6. Sells merchandise on account which cost $73,500. Gross margin is 33 percent.
      7. Writes off $20,000 from inventory as scrap and amortizes $15,000 of goodwill.

   d. From the following data calculate the outstanding days' receivables and payables for a company, using the methods shown in the chapter. What is the inventory turnover, calculated in different ways? Discuss your assumptions.

Sales for three months	$437,500
Cost of sales	298,400
Purchases	143,500
Beginning inventory	382,200

Ending inventory	227,300
Accounts receivable	156,800
Accounts payable	69,300
Normal sales terms	2/10,n/30
Normal purchase terms	n/45

2. From the following financial statement of the ABC Company for 1980 and 1981, prepare the ratios and measures discussed in this chapter.

a. Ratios from the viewpoint of management.

b. Ratios from the viewpoint of owners.

c. Ratios from the viewpoint of lenders.

Comment on the changes shown between the two years, and discuss the significance of the results from the three points of view. Indicate which additional kinds of comparison you would like to make for this company, a manufacturer of electronics, and the type of information you would need.

ABC COMPANY
Balance Sheets
December 31, 1980, and 1981
($ millions)

	1980	1981
Assets		
Current assets:		
Cash	$ 82.7	$110.9
Accounts receivable (net)	92.6	146.2
Inventories	88.8	129.5
Prepaid expenses	2.8	6.2
Advances from government	5.3	2.8
Total current assets	272.2	395.6
Property, plant, and equipment	215.2	283.4
Less: Accumulated depreciation	101.2	119.6
Net Property	114.0	163.8
Other assets	3.1	4.2
Total assets	$389.3	$563.6
Liabilities and Net Worth		
Current liabilities:		
Accounts payable	$ 43.4	$ 62.9
Accrued income tax	36.7	44.0
Accrued pension and profit sharing	27.1	38.4
Other accruals	21.9	31.2
Current portion of long-term debt	2.1	—
Total current liabilities	131.2	176.5
Debentures (9% due 1989)	—	94.0
Other long-term debt	7.8	4.1
Deferred income tax	5.2	7.6
Common stock ($1 par)	10.1	10.2
Paid-in surplus	25.1	27.2
Earned surplus	209.9	244.0
Total liabilities and net worth	$389.3	$563.6

ABC COMPANY
Operating Statements for 1980 and 1981
($ millions)

	1980	1981
Net sales	$655.1	$872.7
Cost of goods and services*	460.9	616.1
Gross profit	194.2	256.6
Selling, general, and administrative expenses	98.3	125.2
Employee profit sharing and retirement	26.9	38.7
	125.2	163.9
Operating profit	69.0	92.7
Other income	1.1	1.8
	70.1	94.5
Interest paid	1.0	7.4
	69.1	87.1
Provision for income taxes	31.8	40.1
Net profit†	$ 37.3	$ 47.0

	1980	1981
* Depreciation and amortization	$28.2	$38.5
† Common dividends paid	5.5	6.0

3. Select a major manufacturing company, a retailing firm, a public utility, a bank, and a transportation firm. From an information source like Moody's or Standard and Poor's, develop an historical analysis of key measures you consider significant to appraise the effectiveness of management, the return to the owners, and the position of the lenders. Develop significant industry comparisons and comment on the relative position of your chosen company. Also comment on some of the assumptions and choices you have to make on the selection of specific accounts and data to work the analytical techniques.

3   PROJECTION OF
BUSINESS PERFORMANCE

Our discussion so far has dealt with an appraisal and judgment of the results of *past* business decisions about investments, operations, and financing. This chapter will be the first of three chapters to deal with a forward look toward likely future conditions—the projection of operating and financial performance and the analysis of various alternative plans under different conditions. The projection of financial performance is only part of the business planning process in which management positions its future activities relative to the expected economic, competitive, technical, and social environment. During the total planning effort, management sets objectives and goals, with strategies for achieving desired short-run, intermediate, and long-term results. In the specific, narrower analysis of financial projections, the manager or analyst can employ the useful ratios illustrated in Chapter 2 to the extent that they apply, in addition to various statistical techniques. Regardless of the techniques employed, however, financial projections are an essential part of the planning structure.

The scope of this book permits us to focus only on major specific methods and formats of financial projection, without explicitly taking into account the broader planning framework. Also, discussion of the increasingly popular use of statistical projection techniques through easy access to time-shared computer systems will be left out because of space limitations. Such specialized techniques are adequately covered in the common textbooks on statistics and the specific descriptive materials available from time-sharing service companies. The reader is also referred to planning literature at the end of Chapter 6 for a broader framework within which to view the process discussed here.

The main techniques of financial projection fall into three categories—operating budgets, financial (cash) budgets, and pro forma financial statements. Operating and cash budgets are projections dealing with key sections and elements of the business operation, while pro forma financial statements represent a forward look for the business as a whole, in the form of the usual balance sheet and income statements. In all three cases we are talking about an arrangement of basic physical and financial data as the starting point for planning activities. These efforts are not only necessary for the short run but also become a basis for truly strategic long-range thinking. Each of the three areas will be dealt with specifically in this chapter, and the most important techniques will be highlighted. At the end of the chapter the concept of financial modeling will be related to these techniques, since such models can provide a fully integrated set of concepts for projection.

OPERATING BUDGETS

The most frequently encountered type of projection, and the one with the greatest variability, is the operating budget. As an expression of ongoing operations, the operating budget is linked closely to the organizational structure of the business and to its performance measurement. Most managements will attempt to structure the total company into manageable parts, for each of which a manager or executive is held responsible. This separation may take the form of a functional organization—that is, one person is responsible for sales, another for production, a third for purchasing resources, and so on. In other cases, the organization may be composed of a set of smaller "profit centers," each of which is expected to provide a profit contribution to the corporation.

While there are countless variations of organizational structure and performance evaluation, the principles of financial projection are quite simple. Projection of operating results must take a form which expresses the scope of the business unit involved. It must be related to the elements under the control of the responsible manager, and should be the basis on which the manager's performance is measured. These criteria quite obviously require that operating budgets be carefully structured to fit the particular unit's conditions and the management style of the company as a whole. This means that there will be a great deal of difference in the approaches taken by various companies, even within the same industry, and differences will have to be recognized also within a given company. A growing body of literature on the concept of responsibility accounting has recognized these aspects.

To illustrate the principles within the scope of our discussion, let us take two simple examples of the process: (1) the sales manager of all product groups of XYZ Corporation is asked to establish a quarterly sales budget for the year 1981, which is to show his contribution to corporate profits; and (2) the manager of a factory of XYZ Corporation is asked to prepare his operating budget for the third quarter of 1981, which is to show the output expected and the total costs incurred in the process.

Our sales manager first must project the level of unit sales he expects in the territories served, by major product line. He most likely will build this up from his and his people's judgments about the expected demand from his major current and potential customers, based on the strategies he and his competitors are likely to follow. Next, he has to estimate the price levels under which he will have to operate. This will commonly be a function of industry pricing practices, the competitive environment, and to some extent the cost performance of his company's manufacturing operations. Furthermore, he must estimate the cost of the products transferred internally or purchased from the outside. In addition, he must project the manpower requirements for his sales activities, the travel and entertainment expenses, and other direct sales support costs. Another element will be delivery expense to the customer, if borne by the company. Finally, estimates of sales support costs provided by the company, general marketing and advertising expense, and the share of corporate overhead ascribed to his operations will normally be projected.

In all of these estimating efforts, our manager can make use of past relationships and selected ratios, tempered by his best judgment of changes in future conditions. The operating budget for his organization may take shape as shown in Figure 3–1. In this sample, both basic data and dollar elements have been set out by four quarters and for the total year 1981. There is nothing unique about the format selected here, since many arrangements of the information are possible. Generally, a company will prescribe formats for its managers to follow, both to maintain a certain amount of uniformity and to ease the accounting problem of consolidation. From a financial projection standpoint, the sales and contribution data shown in the example are pieces of raw material which go into making up the total operating plan of the company.

Another example of an operating budget is the factory budget shown in Figure 3–2. This time, the data are displayed in a monthly format highlighting three months of the year and a quarterly total. Again, the format selection must suit the particular needs and preferences of the organization. In this case we have chosen to show, in the arrangement of the data and headings, the fact that certain items of cost are under the control of the local manager. Other costs will be transferred in from corporate headquarters and are thus only to a very limited extent under his control. This type of structuring becomes

Figure 3–1
XYZ CORPORATION
Sample Quarterly Sales Budget
Year Ended December 31, 1981

	First	Second	Third	Fourth	Total
			Quarter		
Basic data:					
Unit sales (number of units):					
Product A	2,700	2,900	3,000	2,800	11,400
Product B	8,000	8,500	10,000	8,000	34,500
Product C	17,500	18,500	21,000	16,000	73,000
Price level (per unit):					
Product A	$ 145	$ 145	$ 150	$ 150	—
Product B	92	92	95	95	—
Product C	74	74	74	74	—
Number of salespersons	25	25	25	26	—
Operating budget ($000):					
Sales revenue	$2,423	$2,572	$2,954	$2,364	$10,313
Less: Returns, allowances	25	26	28	24	103
Net sales	2,398	2,546	2,926	2,340	10,210
Cost of goods sold	1,916	2,051	2,322	1,868	8,157
Margin before delivery	482	495	604	472	2,053
Delivery expense	56	60	68	54	238
Gross margin	426	435	536	418	1,815
Selling expense (controllable):					
Salespersons' compensation	94	94	94	98	380
Travel and entertainment	32	32	32	33	129
Sales support costs	23	23	26	24	96
Total selling expenses	149	149	152	155	605
Gross contribution	277	286	384	263	1,210
Departmental period costs	18	18	18	18	72
Net contribution	259	268	366	245	1,138
Corporate support (transferred):					
Staff support	23	25	25	27	100
Advertising	50	50	75	50	225
General overhead	63	63	63	63	252
Total corporate support	136	138	163	140	577
Profit contribution (before taxes) ...	$ 123	$ 130	$ 203	$ 105	$ 561

useful if the operating plan as displayed is to serve as a control device on which to measure the performance of the unit during the projected time period.

In both the sales and manufacturing operating budgets, it is possible to include additional columns in which to record the actual experience. Also, variance columns can be provided to

Figure 3–2
XYZ CORPORATION
Sample Factory Budget
For the Quarter Ended June 30, 1981

	April	May	June	Total
Basic data:				
Number of shifts (5-day week)	3	3	3	3
Days worked	20	21	22	63
Hourly employees per shift	33	33	33	33
Number of machines	35	35	34	—
Unit production:				
Product A	1,000	1,050	1,100	3,150
Product B	2,400	2,510	2,640	7,550
Capacity utilization	94%	94%	96%	95%
Down time for repairs (hours)......	–0–	36	–0–	36
Operating budget:				
Direct costs (controllable):*				
Manufacturing labor	$ 57,600	$ 60,500	$ 63,400	$181,500
Raw materials	53,800	56,400	59,200	169,400
Operating supplies	6,500	6,900	7,300	20,700
Repair labor and parts	7,300	12,400	6,500	26,200
Power, heat, light	4,200	4,500	4,800	13,500
Total direct costs	129,400	140,700	141,200	411,300
Period costs (controllable):				
Supervision	5,500	5,500	5,500	16,500
Support labor	28,500	28,500	28,500	85,500
Insurance, taxes	8,700	8,700	8,700	26,100
Depreciation	20,500	20,500	20,500	61,500
Total period costs	63,200	63,200	63,200	189,600
Total controllable costs ...	192,600	203,900	204,400	600,900
General overhead				
(allocated)	72,000	72,000	72,000	216,000
Total cost	$264,600	$275,900	$276,400	$816,900

* Where appropriate, unit costs can be shown.

measure deviations from the plan. We shall not go into such refinements, since the purpose of showing the example is to highlight the type of analysis and projection that takes place, formally or informally, in parts of an organization, preparatory to developing a financial plan.

CASH BUDGETS

Of more specific interest to the financial analyst and the financial manager within a company is the detailed projection of cash requirements, which normally takes the form of a cash budget. In contrast to the activity plans highlighted in the earlier section, which are a reflection of selling or manufacturing operations as they will be recorded through the accounting system, the cash budget is an attempt to focus very specifically on the *incidence of cash* receipts and payments. Our sales manager or factory manager was not overly concerned as to when the actual payment for the expenses incurred by him would be made, or when collection for sales on credit would take place. The accounting system under which he is measured concentrates on recording the transactions for revenues and expenses *as they are committed,* with the accrual method ascribing to each time period the appropriate amounts, irrespective of cash movement.

In contrast, our financial manager is very much concerned with observing the activity in the Cash account, which he must maintain at a level high enough to allow timely payment of amounts due. As a consequence, he must develop a cash *activity plan* which reflects the very specific timing of the inflows and outflows of cash in response to the operational and investment activities planned.

The process of cash budgeting is quite simple when one always remembers the need to estimate cash incidence. The approach is similar to personal budgeting, where bills due are matched with receipts from paychecks, dividend checks, bank interest payments, and so on. The purpose of the effort is, of course, to determine funds requirements which will be reflected by changes in the cash balance available for payment. This balance may fluctuate from day to day, week to week, or month to month. If a company's collections from credit sales tend to lag for weeks while wages and purchases must be paid for currently, serious cash shortages can occur. Similarly, cash payments for nonperiodic commitments such as capital equipment can cause temporary problems which must be met by a cash provision. It is necessary, therefore, to lay out a *time schedule* of the estimated receipts and payments of cash, and to observe the net effect of projected activity. The selection of the time period depends on the nature of the business and the trade terms under which it operates. If daily fluctuations are likely to be large, as in some parts of the banking business, daily projections will be helpful; in other cases, weekly, monthly, or even quarterly projections will suffice.

In the example used by way of illustration, Figure 3–3, we have chosen to show a monthly cash budget for XYZ Corporation which covers the quarter ended December 31, 1982. The process begins with a presentation of the basic data of the company's operations regarding sales, production, and purchases. Two months' activities prior to the quarter analyzed are shown, since under the sales and purchase terms assumed here the cash effect from these months will lag into this period. This condition is clearly reflected in the first item of cash receipts, the collection of receivables. If we can assume that the company's customers will continue to pay within the 30-day terms, then the cash receipts of any one month should be the sales of the *previous* month. A 60-day collection would mean receipts of sales of *two* months prior. Any change in expected customer behavior, or in the credit terms themselves, would have to be reflected in a different receipts pattern. For this purpose, it is often helpful to draw a time scale on which the days or months of sales activity are marked off. Any assumed collection experience can then be simulated by "staggering" the receipts by the appropriate number of days. Our example shows other cash receipts according to the best estimate of incidence.

Another lag is reflected in the payment for purchases, on the assumption that normal payment terms of 45 days will be observed by XYZ Corporation. This means a lag in payment by 45 days, and part of August and September purchases will, therefore, be paid for in October, with a similar lag observed for November and December. Again, it is helpful to draw a time pattern to make sure that the amounts are properly staggered.

Since the last quarter is projected as a seasonal low in sales and manufacturing activities, the effect of the timing pattern is to shift somewhat higher cash receipts and payments into a period of low operating activity. In contrast, a rising volume of operations would have resulted in lower cash incidence, as the current budget would partly reflect earlier low-level conditions because of the time lag. This observation points out the critical need for cash budgeting in a business where operating levels and payment conditions may vary widely from period to period.

Other cash disbursements are listed on the assumption that payments for the expenses and obligations are made within the time period they are incurred. This practice could be slightly incorrect in the case of payroll disbursements and certain manufacturing expenses. Such items could lag by one or two weeks. The degree of precision to be employed will have to be judged against the seriousness of any indicated cash problems. Note also that production-related payments are based on the *operating* plan, which calls for an inventory reduction (see "Basic data"). This is a major difference from the income statement for the period, where cost of goods sold will be based on *selling* activities—a commonly encountered point in cash budgeting.

The result of the cash budget is a picture of the cash effect of the various operating plans on which the budget is based. In this case, the first two months of the quarter show sizable net cash disbursements, while the third month provides a slight cash surplus. The period began with a cash balance of $1.45 million, which therefore is reduced each month until December. Overall, a net cash outflow of $1.6 million is indicated. Further analysis of the effect on the corporate cash balance shows a funds requirement building up from about $0.6 million to $1.4 million, with a slightly larger requirement in November. This is based on an assumed requirement for a minimum cash balance of $1.25 million. Obviously, any other such minimum level established would change the funds need. It is further possible to show the total corporate borrowing requirement by adding any outstanding loans to the funds requirement of each period.

It is important to remember that the monthly picture shown here could indeed hide some more serious cash shortages during certain days or weeks of the quarter. Only a more

Figure 3–3

XYZ CORPORATION
Sample Cash Budget for the Quarter Ended December 31, 1982
($000)

	August	September	October	November	December	Total
Basic data:						
Unit sales	48,000	46,000	42,000	36,000	33,000	111,000
Unit production	50,000	50,000	35,000	34,000	31,000	100,000
Change in inventory	+2,000	+4,000	−7,000	−2,000	−2,000	−11,000
Sales volume (on credit)	$4,450	$4,250	$3,850	$3,350	$3,050	$10,250
Purchases (on credit)	760	740	520	500	460	1,480
Cash receipts:						
Collection of receivables—prior months' sales; normal terms of 30 days assumed			$4,250	$ 3,850	$ 3,350	$11,450
Proceeds from sale of stock options			–0–	250	–0–	250
Proceeds from sale of used machines at book value (original cost, $1,500)			–0–	–0–	550	550
Total cash receipts			4,250	4,100	3,900	12,250
Cash disbursements:						
Payment for purchases*			750	630	510	1,890
Production payroll (from operating budget)			560	545	490	1,595
Manufacturing expenses (from operating budget)			1,265	1,260	1,235	3,760
Selling and delivery expenses (from sales budget)			350	345	335	1,030

General overhead expenses				
(from administrative budget)	200	200	200	600
Interest payment on debt	-0-	-0-	175	175
Principal payment on note payable	1,500	-0-	-0-	1,500
Federal tax payment	400	-0-	-0-	400
Payments on construction of new plant	-0-	2,000	900	2,900
Total cash disbursements	5,025	4,980	3,845	13,850
Net cash receipts (disbursements)	(775)	(880)	55	
Cumulative net cash flow	$ (775)	$(1,655)	$(1,600)	$ (1,600)
Analysis of cash requirements:				
Beginning cash balance	$1,450	$ 675	(205)	$ 1,450
Net cash receipts (disbursements)	(775)	(880)	55	(1,600)
Ending cash balance	675	(205)	(150)	(150)
Minimum cash balance	1,250	1,250	1,250	1,250
Cash requirements	$ 575	$ 1,455	$ 1,400	$ 1,400

* Normal terms of 45 days assumed. Payments represent one month's purchases prior to last 1.5 months (e.g., half of August and half of September paid during October).

detailed analysis would reveal these. Also, any change in the assumptions about receipts and collections could seriously affect the picture. The advantage of such a format, on the other hand, is that one can test the likely effect of significant changes by working through the figures under different assumptions. The cash budget thus becomes a financial planning tool on the basis of which arrangements can be made for future cash needs.

PRO FORMA STATEMENTS

So far we have dealt only with segments of the projection needs of XYZ Corporation. The most comprehensive look at likely future conditions for a company, however, can be taken by developing a set of pro forma statements. These statements are but an income statement and balance sheet extended into the future, and in that sense present an "operating plan" of the company as a whole. They are prepared by taking the most readily available estimates of activity and projecting, account by account, the expected results and conditions. This is one of the most widely used quick ways of estimating future profitability and financial condition, and is particularly in favor with bank loan officers, who must assess the credit-worthiness of the client company from the total financial picture.

It is not really necessary to have all the detailed plan segments (sales budgets, manufacturing and service plans, etc.) available in order to build up the pro forma statement—although this would increase the degree of precision—since a heavy use of ratios can produce statements that are entirely satisfactory as a first look. As will be shown later, pro forma balance sheets can also be used to find total *funds requirements* necessary to support operations as of the projected balance sheet date—that is, at one point in time.

Having worked with key planning segments of XYZ Corporation earlier in this chapter, let us now develop a set of pro forma statements for the last quarter of 1982. We begin with the income statement, Figure 3–4, since the profit (retained

Figure 3–4

XYZ CORPORATION   Pro Forma Income Statement for the Quarter Ended December 31, 1982 ($000)

	Actual Quarter Ended 9-30-82		Pro Forma* Quarter Ended 12-31-82		Remarks
Units sold	137,000		111,000		Last quarter is seasonal low (see sample sales budget).
Net sales	$12,650	100.0%	$10,250	100.0%	Projected from sales plan.
Cost of goods sold:					Expected to reflect low volume inefficiencies —rise of 1%.
Labor	2,210		1,810		21.5% of cost of goods.
Materials	2,045		1,680		20.0% of cost of goods.
Overhead	5,685		4,660		55.5% of cost of goods.
Delivery	305		250		3.0% of cost of goods.
Cost of goods sold	10,245	81.0	8,400	82.0	
Gross Margin	2,405	19.0	1,850	18.0	
Expenses:					
Selling expense	875	6.9	825	8.1	From sales plan, essentially fixed.
General and administrative expenses	585	4.6	600	5.9	From administrative budget.
Total expenses	1,460	11.5	1,425	14.0	
Operating profit	945	7.5	425	4.0	Shows effect of fixed costs.
Interest	190	1.5	175	1.7	Based on outstanding debt.
Profit before taxes	755	6.0	250	2.3	
Income taxes	347	2.7	115	1.1	Projected at 46%.
Net income	408	3.3	135	1.2	
Dividends	100	0.8	-0-	-0-	No payment of dividends scheduled.
Retained earnings	308	2.5%	135	1.2%	Carried to balance sheet.
Depreciation added back	575		600		From overhead plans.
Cash flow after dividends	$ 883		$ 735		Rough measure of cash from operations (should add back any dividends for completeness).

* All projections are rounded off.

earnings) will have to be reflected in the pro forma balance sheet. The starting point is a unit and dollar projection of sales. We already know from the sales plan that the last part of 1982 is a seasonal low. Price and product mix are assumed unchanged for this example, although more specific analyses could be made in many cases. For example, in an inflationary period as at present, projections of future prices and costs should be made with the best possible judgments of expected higher price levels applicable to these. Costs of goods sold is projected by using a modified ratio approach, which assumes that a lower volume of production will result in inefficiencies and will cause a one percentage point rise in cost. The breakdown into cost elements is based on ratios experienced in the past. If no details were available, the projection might have been made on broad cost-to-sales assumptions.

Selling and general and administrative expenses in XYZ Corporation are assumed to be essentially fixed. The projection therefore shows a higher percentage of costs relative to sales than in the previous quarter. If detailed knowledge about such elements were not available, a more arbitrary judgment might have to suffice. An unchanged ratio of selling expenses to sales might be used, for example. In any case, the analyst must use the best possible judgment. Should there be no historical pattern as a guide to the future, an attempt must be made to estimate the expected conditions using knowledge of the industry or of similar businesses. Interest expense is based on outstanding obligations, while taxes are projected at 46 percent. For ease of calculation, a tax rate of 50 percent is often assumed.

The results of the projections provide a net income figure for the period, which is only one third of that of the previous quarter. This is largely a reflection of the lower operating rate. Also shown, for illustration, is the so-called cash flow, which is a quick estimate of cash provided by operations, but which has to be viewed in connection with other cash movements to be truly meaningful. It is obvious that a cash budget, if available, would be much more precise for judging the cash flow pattern during the period.

We can now turn to the pro forma balance sheet which has been constructed in Figure 3–5. We note that each account has been changed in anticipation of known or expected conditions. The analyst has relative freedom to assume various conditions, since the desired result of the analysis is not to have a completely balanced statement in the accounting sense, but rather to gauge the approximate funds needs and the overall financial condition. Consequently, the projection process can be built on a variety of assumptions about key items, such as accounts receivable, inventory levels, payable periods, and so on, as long as *consistency* is observed between the assumptions used for the operating statement and the balance sheet.

For example, the assumptions about accounts receivable outstanding at the end of the period should tie to the pro forma operating statement, since the normal process will be to consider outstanding an appropriate number of days' sales of recent months. If there is a significant rise or fall in sales during the period projected, care must be taken to reflect a realistic accounts receivable balance in correspondence with this sales pattern.

In a similar fashion, the assumptions about inventories should represent the projected operating pattern of the business. In a trading company, the projection of inventories is relatively simple, since the two main elements to be watched are purchases and sales, with ending inventories a net result. In a manufacturing company, however, we must think through the effect of the level of production as well as the pattern of sales and materials purchases. For high precision, it will be necessary to develop the projected operating plan typified in the factory budget in Figure 3–2, except that the analysis must cover the business as a whole. The type of cost accounting used will have a major impact here, and a reasonable attempt should be made to simulate the pattern expected. Nevertheless, if only quick and overall results are desired, a rough assumption about the inventory balance will suffice.

In keeping with our rule of consistency, note that the sale of machinery reflected earlier in the cash budget reappears in the pro forma balance sheet. The Plant and Equipment account is

Figure 3–5

XYZ CORPORATION, Pro Forma Balance Sheet as of December 31, 1982 ($000)

	Actual 9–30–82	Change	Pro Forma 12–31–82	Remarks
Assets				
Current assets:				
Cash	$ 1,450	–$ 200	$ 1,250	Cash set at minimum balance.
Accounts receivable	4,250	– 1,200	3,050	Represents 30 days' sales
Raw materials	1,500	–0–	1,500	Safety level; purchase requirements as needed.
Finished goods	4,050	– 760	3,290	Reduced production, per plan.
Total current assets	11,250	– 2,160	9,090	Reflects seasonal pattern.
Fixed assets:				
Land	2,500	–0–	2,500	No change assumed.
Plant and equipment	20,800	– 1,500	19,300	Sale of machines with original cost of $1,500, accumulated depreciation of $950 (per cash budget). Depreciation for period $600, per income statement.
Less: Accumulated depreciation	8,350	350	8,000	
Net plant and equipment	12,450	– 1,150	11,300	
Total fixed assets	14,950	– 1,150	13,800	
Other assets	1,250	–0–	1,250	No change assumed.
Total assets	$27,450	– 3,310	$24,140	
Liabilities and Net Worth				
Current liabilities:				
Accounts payable	$ 1,120	–$ 410	$ 710	45 days' purchases, per plan.
Notes payable	3,000	– 1,500	1,500	Repayment as required.
Due contractor	3,400	– 2,900	500	From payment schedule.
Accruals	1,250	– 285	965	Tax payments (–$400) and accrual (+$115).
Total current liabilities	8,770	– 5,095	3,675	Reflects heavy current repayments.
Long-term liabilities	8,500	–0–	8,500	No change.
Common stock	4,250	+ 250	4,500	Sale of stock under option.
Retained earnings	5,930	+ 135	6,065	Retained earnings per income statement (no payment of dividends).
Total liabilities and net worth	$27,450	– 4,710	22,740	
Funds required		+ 1,400	1,400	"Plug" figure representing financing need as of 12–31–82, the same as in Figure 3–3.
		–$3,310	$24,140	

reduced by the original cost of $1,500, while accumulated depreciation is reduced by $950, the net being the book value.

Assumptions chosen will finally reflect themselves on the balance sheet in the resulting funds need or surplus—the "plug" figure which is the difference between the projected asset and liability accounts. This last item on the pro forma balance sheet will show the *funds condition* on the specific date of the balance sheet. Any intervening peaks and valleys of cash requirements would have to be found by intermediate balance sheets or by developing cash budgets as shown in the previous section of this chapter. In fact, the pro forma balance sheet masks the rapid buildup of the funds need in October and November which were so clearly evident on the cash budget in Figure 3–3. Only the final results are the same.

In the example of XYZ Corporation, we have shown the set of assumptions which matches those underlying the earlier analyses. Therefore, the plug figure of $1.4 million is *exactly* that shown in the detailed cash budget. One of the keys in this case is the recognition that lower production plans will result in a reduction in finished goods inventory of three quarters of a million dollars. This drop was reflected both in the cash projections and on the balance sheet. If a more cursory approach to pro forma analysis had ignored this fact, the funds need (plug figure) would have risen to over $2 million. The assumption could have been simply that production levels would match sales levels, and thus the inventory would not have been reduced. Similarly, different projections could be made for other accounts, with resultant effects on the funds requirements. The main caution is to observe reasonable consistency between the pro forma income statement and the balance sheet—otherwise, too much deviation may occur. It is sometimes helpful to prepare funds flow statements from the projected balance sheets, if this format of projections is of interest. Together, the set of pro forma statements summarizes in a convenient form the effect of planning assumptions, and provides a basis for judging the viability of the projected operations, trend in key ratios, the financial requirements on specific dates, and the effect of alternative plans.

INTERRELATIONSHIP OF FINANCIAL PROJECTIONS

It should be obvious by now that the various analyses presented in this chapter are closely related. If all three types of analyses—operating budgets, cash budgets, and pro forma statements—are based on the *same* set of assumptions about operating rates, receipts and collections, payment rates, inventory levels, and so on, they will all fit precisely together in the fashion illustrated in Figure 3–6. Differences in the plans arise only if such assumptions are allowed to differ between the analyses, particularly between the cash budget and the pro forma statements. It is quite easy to reconcile cash budgets and pro forma statements, however, by carefully thinking through the operational assumptions, one by one, and by laying out formats with sufficient detail on background conditions.

The diagram in Figure 3–6 shows how the various operational budgets flow into a combined cash budget, which is reinforced by information from the investment and financing plans. The combination of this information goes into making up the pro forma statements. The picture also shows that pro forma statements, at the top of the figure, are the all-encompassing expression of the conditions of the period ahead. Thus if pro forma statements alone are developed, they in effect imply assumptions about all the other elements in the diagram.

We have not yet specifically mentioned *staff budgets,* which are spending plans based on operating various service functions. These budgets find their way into the total financial picture in the same fashion as other expense budgets. *Investment plans* are the projection of spending on new land, plant, equipment, and related working capital, or reduction in any of these. In the case of XYZ Corporation, we had assumed a minor reduction in investment through the sale of used machines (see cash budget and pro forma balance sheet). The obligation for the construction of a new plant had already been reflected in the current liability "due contractor" on the actual

Figure 3–6
INTERRELATIONSHIP OF FINANCIAL PROJECTIONS

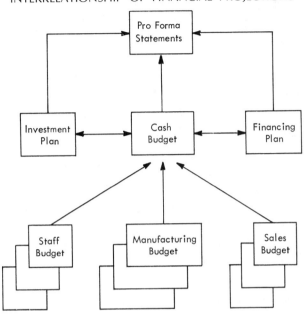

balance sheet as of September 30, 1982, and only the payment due was properly included in the cash disbursements. The *financing plan* is an expression of the proposed future additions or reductions in obligations and equity funds contemplated by a company. In the case of XYZ Corporation, we left the specific nature of future financing open and only developed the cash requirements as shown in the cash budget and the pro forma balance sheet.

FINANCIAL MODELING

The capabilities of the computer and the increasing application of its computational speed to financial analysis have in recent years lead to the concept of financial modeling. In principle, this approach is no more than a mathematical representation of the key operational and financial relationships peculiar to a company and is basically similar to the process of analysis demonstrated here. A financial model will contain such items as key accounting procedures, tax calculations, depreciation schedules, debt service and repayments, financial restrictions and covenants, inventory policies, and so on. The computer will calculate from these relationships the projected results of the conditions to be encountered by the company, given the assumptions made by management.

The major difference between the projection techniques discussed in this chapter and financial modeling is only the degree of automation of the process. A cash budget done by hand is essentially a model of the cash flow pattern of the company wherein the analyst must refer to corporate accounting, tax, and other procedures and policies. By incorporating into computer programs the concepts and logic applied in developing such a cash budget, it is possible to run many different financial plans with ease and speed. Moreover, the computer is capable of simultaneously tracking all interrelationships seen as important.

The nature of financial models ranges all the way from a simple calculation of condensed pro forma statements to a highly sophisticated full representation of a company's accounting system, to which are often added projectional capabilities. In such cases, the model will contain routines which use various statistical methods for projecting past trends in key accounts, while observing interrelationships. The use of this kind of model enables the management of a firm to calculate, on paper, a variety of operating conditions and financing options and to gauge the impact of different alternatives before making a real commitment. Some companies have proceeded to develop models which not only, in a deterministic sense, will calculate the results of specified assumptions but also include "optimizing routines" which will indicate the most desirable alternative investment patterns, as well as financing arrangements based on criteria submitted to the model. Most service companies offering computer time-share packages are incorporating financial modelling capabilities into their catalog of services.

It is clearly beyond the scope of this book to treat in detail the vast number of concepts and specialized techniques involved in computerized models. Figure 3–7 depicts the nature of the relationships of a full computer model, the central element of which consists of the various computer programs in the middle of the diagram. The reader should keep in mind, however, that financial projection at almost any level of complexity is a "modeling" effort. The main advantage of sophisticated financial models is that they are able to analyze and

Figure 3– 7
FINANCIAL MODELING
An Overview of Relationships

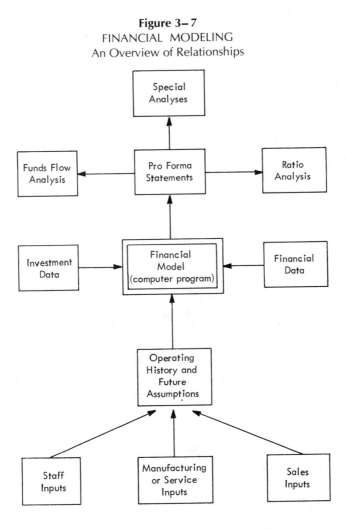

relate simultaneously a great number of variables affecting a business, and to indicate the results of different possible actions with high speed and accuracy of calculation.

SUMMARY

The principles of financial projection discussed in this chapter revolve around the use of budgets and pro forma statements. We have observed that financial projection is one part of business planning which is expressed in the familiar form of financial statements and specifically tailored budget formats. The process is simple as it represents an orderly way of sorting out the financial impact of operational, investment, and financing decisions. The process is difficult in that the nature of the judgments about *future* conditions is fraught with uncertainty—as any planning must be. It is here that the calculation of alternative assumptions can narrow the range of uncertainty, and computerized financial models can be of material assistance.

SELECTED REFERENCES

Anthony, Robert N., and Reece, James S. *Accounting: Text and Cases.* 6th ed. Homewood, Ill.: Richard D. Irwin, 1979.

Gershefski, George W. *The Development and Application of a Corporate Financial Model.* Sun Oil Co. Oxford, Ohio: Planning Executives Institute, 1968.

Horngren, Charles T. *Cost Accounting, a Managerial Emphasis.* 4th ed. Englewood Cliffs, N.J.: Prentice-Hall, 1977.

Hunt, Pearson; Williams, Charles M.; and Donaldson, Gordon. *Basic Business Finance: Text.* Homewood, Ill.: Richard D. Irwin, 1974.

Johnson, Robert W. *Financial Management.* 4th ed. Boston: Allyn & Bacon, 1971.

Rivett, Patrick. *Model Building for Decision Analysis.* Chichester (Eng.); New York: J. Wiley, 1980.

Vancil, Richard F., ed. *Financial Executive's Handbook.* Part VI. Homewood, Ill.: Dow Jones–Irwin, 1970.

Van Horne, James C. *Financial Management and Policy.* 5th ed. Englewood Cliffs, N.J.: Prentice-Hall, 1980.

Viscione, Jerry A. *Financial Analysis—Principles and Procedures.* Boston: Basic Books, 1976.

Weston, J. Fred, and Goudzwaard, Maurice B. *The Treasurer's Handbook.* Homewood, Ill.: Dow Jones–Irwin, 1976.

EXERCISES AND PROBLEMS

1. Work the following exercises, based on these selected data about a company. Consider each exercise separately.

Total assets on 12–31–81	$2,750,000
Sales for the year 1981	9,137,000
Current assets on 12–31–81	1,315,000
Long-term debt on 12–31–81	210,000
Current ratio on 12–31–81	2.4:1
Cost of goods sold for 1981	83% of sales
Purchases during 1981	$5,316,000
Depreciation for 1981	174,000
Net profit after taxes for 1981	131,000
Taxes on income for 1981	112,000

   a. Currently the company's accounts receivable outstanding are 18 days' sales. In order to meet competitive pressures in 1982, the company will have to extend credit to an average of 40 days' sales to maintain operations and profits at the 1981 levels. No other changes are contemplated for the next year, and sales and operations are expected to continue at 1981 rates. What is the impact of this change in credit policy on corporate funds needs? Will the company have to borrow? What if credit had to be extended to 60 days? Discuss.

   b. The inventory levels maintained by the company have averaged $725,000 during 1981, with little fluctuation. If turnover were to slow to seven times (average inventory in cost of goods sold) due to a switch to a consignment policy, what would the financial impact be? Assume no change in sales levels. What likely other changes would take place, and how would these affect the company's financial stance? What if turnover rose to 11 times? Discuss.

   c. Payment for purchases has been made under normal trade terms of 2/10, n/30 with discounting done as a matter of policy. Suppliers anxious for business are beginning to offer 2/15, n/45 terms, which will become universal during the coming year. What would the financial impact of this change be if the company were to follow its policy of discounting purchases? What trade-off has to be considered? Discuss.

d. If the company is planning capital expenditures of $125,000 and simultaneously is planning to pay dividends at the rate of 60 percent of net profits, what are the financial implications, assuming all other elements are unchanged?

e. If sales are expected to grow 10 percent for the following year, with all *normal* relationships under (a) through (c) unchanged, what financial considerations arise? How would the intentions of (d) look then? Discuss.

2. In September 1982, ABC Company, a manufacturing firm, was laying budget plans for the 12 months beginning November 1, 1982. The projected sales volume was $4,350,000, as compared to an estimated $3,675,000 for the fiscal year ended October 31, 1982. The best estimates of the operating results for the current year were as follows:

ABC COMPANY
Estimated Operating Statement
For the Year Ended October 31, 1982
($000)

	Amount		Percent
Net sales		$3,675	100.0
Cost of goods sold:			
Labor	$919		25.0
Materials	522		14.2
Overhead	743		20.2
Depreciation....................	133	2,317	3.6 63.0
Gross profit......................		1,358	37.0
Selling expense	305		8.3
General and administrative expenses ...	323	628	8.8 17.1
Profit before taxes		730	19.9
Income taxes		336	9.1
Net income		$ 394	10.8

The projected increase in volume of operations was expected to bring improvements in efficiency, while at the same time some of the cost factors would continue to rise absolutely, in line with past trends. The following were the specific working assumptions with which to plan financial results for the next year:

Manufacturing labor would drop to 24 percent of direct sales, since volume effciency would more than offset higher wage rates.

Materials cost would rise to 14.5 percent of sales, since some price increases would not be offset by better utilization.

Overhead costs would rise above the present level by 6 percent of the 1982 dollar amount, reflecting higher costs; and additional variable costs would be encountered at the rate of 11 percent of the incremental sales volume.

Depreciation would increase by $10,000, reflecting the addition of some production machinery.

Selling expenses would rise more than proportionately, by $125,000, since additional effort was expected to move to higher sales volume.

General and administrative expense would drop to 8.1 percent of sales.

Income taxes were estimated at 46 percent of pretax profits.

Develop a pro forma operating statement and discuss your findings.

3. In December 1982 the DEF Company, a distributor of stationery products, was planning its financial needs for one year ahead. As a first indication, the firm's management wished to have a pro forma balance sheet as of December 31, 1983, to gauge the funds needs at that time. The estimated financial condition as of December 31, 1982, was reflected in this balance sheet:

DEF COMPANY
Estimated Balance Sheet,
December 31, 1982

Assets

Current assets:

Cash	$ 217,300
Receivables	361,200
Inventories (pledged as security)	912,700
Total current assets	1,491,200

Fixed assets:

Land, buildings, trucks, and fixtures	421,500
Less: Accumulated depreciation	217,300
Total fixed assets	204,200
Other assets	21,700
Total assets	$1,717,100

Liabilities and Net Worth

Current liabilities:

Accounts payable	$ 612,300
Note payable—bank	425,000
Accrued expenses	63,400
Total current liabilities	1,100,700
Term loan—properties	120,000
Capital stock	200,000
Paid-in surplus	112,000
Earned surplus	184,400
Total liabilities and net worth	$1,717,100

The operations for the ensuing year were projected with the following working assumptions with which to plan the financial results:

Sales were forecasted at $10,450,000, with a gross margin of 8.2 percent.

Purchases were expected to total $9,725,000, with some seasonal upswings in May and August.

Accounts receivable would be based on a collection period of 12 days, while 24 days' accounts payable would be outstanding.

Depreciation was expected to be $31,400 for the year.

Term loan repayments were scheduled at $10,000, while bank notes payable would be allowed to fluctuate with the seasonal needs.

Capital expenditures were scheduled at $21,000 for trucks and $36,000 for warehouse improvements.

Net profits after taxes were expected at the level of 0.19 percent of sales.

Dividends for the year were scheduled at $12,500.

Cash balances were desired at no less than $150,000.

Develop a pro forma balance sheet and discuss your findings.

4. In September 1982 the XYZ Company, a department store, was planning for cash needs during the last quarter of 1982 and the first quarter of 1983. The Christmas buying season always meant a considerable strain on finances, and the first planning step was the development of a cash budget. The following data were available for this purpose:

Projected sales (half for cash, half charged on 90-day account):

October	$ 770,000	January	$650,000
November	690,000	February	580,000
December	1,010,000	March	720,000

Projected purchases (half on n/45; 40 percent on 2/10, n/30; 10 percent for cash):

October	$610,000	January	$320,000
November	535,000	February	450,000
December	290,000	March	480,000

Projected payments on purchases as of 9–30–82:

Due by October 10 (2% discount)	$ 60,000
Due by October 31 (net 45)	257,000
Due by November 15 (net 45)	113,000
Total	$430,000

Projected collections of receivables as of 9–30–82:

Due in October	$215,000
Due in November	245,000
Due in December	265,000
Total (bad debts negligible)	$725,000

Projected financial data:

Minimum cash balance required	$75,000
Beginning cash balance (October 1)	95,000
Mortgage payments (monthly)	7,000
Cash dividend due December 31	40,000
Federal taxes due January 15	20,000

Projected operations: salaries and wages average 19 percent of sales, cash operating expenses average 14 percent of sales.

Develop a monthly cash budget to show the seasonal funds requirements. Discuss your findings.

5. A newly formed space technology company, the **ZYX Corporation**, was in the early stages of planning for the first several months of operations. The initial capital put up by the founders and their associates amounted to $250,000 shares of $1 par value stock. Furthermore, patents estimated to be worth $50,000 were provided by two of the principals in exchange for 50,000 shares of common stock. Equipment costing $175,000 was purchased with the funds, and organization expenses of $15,000 were paid. Operations were to start February 1, 1983.

Orders already in hand were for $1,400,000 of electronic devices, which, at an estimated monthly output of $400,000 (sales value), represented almost four months' sales. More orders were expected from contacts made. Monthly operating expenses and conditions were estimated as follows:

Manufacturing labor	$ 60,000
Rent for building	18,500
Overhead costs	76,000
Depreciation	6,000
Write-off of patents	500
Selling and administrative expenses	55,000
Purchases of materials, supplies	125,000
Sales terms	n/30
Collection experience expected	45 days
Purchase terms	n/30
Raw materials inventory level	$ 60,000
Finished goods inventory level	145,000
Prepaid expenses (average)	12,000
Accrued wages	1 week's
Accrued taxes (40% effective rate)	As incurred

If the company desired to maintain a minimum cash balance of $40,000, what would the financial situation be after six months' operations? Develop pro forma statements and discuss the likely timing of any funds needs. How are the next six months likely to affect this picture? Discuss your findings.

6. The ABC Supermarket's management expected the next six months from January 1, 1983, through June 30, 1983, to bring a variety of cash requirements beyond the normal operational outflows. A monthly cash budget was to be developed in order to trace the specific funds needs within close timing. The following projections were available for the purpose:

   a. Cash sales projected:

January	$200,000	April ...	$200,000
February ...	190,000	May	230,000
March	220,000	June	220,000

   b. Cost of goods sold averages 75 percent of sales.

   c. Purchases closely scheduled with sales volume. Payments average a 15-day lag behind purchases. December purchases were $168,000.

   d. Operating expenses projected:
   1. Salaries and wages at 12 percent of sales, paid when incurred.
   2. Other expenses at an average 9 percent of sales, paid when incurred.
   3. Rent of $3,500, paid monthly.
   4. Income tax payments of $2,000 due in January, March, and June, and $3,500 due in April.
   5. Cash receipts from sale of property at $6,000 per month due in March, April, and May.
   6. Payments on note owed local bank due as follows: $3,000 in February and $5,000 in May.
   7. Repayments of advances to principals of the firm due at $3,000 each in January, March, and May.
   8. New store fixtures of $48,000 acquired, and four payments of $12,000 each due in February, March, April, and May.
   9. Old store fixtures with a book value of $4,500 scrapped, to be written off in January.
   10. Rental income from a small concession granted on the premises to begin at $300 per month in March.

   Develop a cash budget as requested and show the effect of the operations and other elements described above on the beginning cash balance of $42,500. The principals of the firm would like to keep a cash balance of not less than $20,000 at any one time. Will additional funds be required, and when? Discuss your findings.

7. The XYZ Company, a fast-growing manufacturing operation, found its inventories growing in 1982 at a rate faster than its growth in sales. As additional territories and customers had been developed, production schedules were stepped up in an effort to provide excellent service levels. Also, the collection experience had deteriorated, and the company's receivables represented two months' sales compared to normal 30-day terms. Since both conditions caused considerable pressures on the company's finances, a change to a level production schedule was considered beginning October 1, 1982, to allow inventories to be worked off while still providing employment to the company's full-time workers. Also, more effort on collections would be expended. A six-month trial of the new policy was to be analyzed financially in September before implementation, and the following assumptions and data were provided:

a. Current sales and forecast:

August	$1,925,000	December	$2,450,000
September (est.)	2,050,000	January	2,625,000
October	2,175,000	February	2,750,000
November	2,300,000	March	2,850,000

b. Current purchases and forecast (terms n/45):

August	$750,000	December	$650,000
September (est.)	675,000	January	650,000
October	650,000	February	650,000
November	650,000	March	650,000

c. Collection period, current and forecast:

August 31	63 days	December 31	40 days
September 30 (est.)	60	January 31	40
October 31	50	February 28	40
November 30	50	March 31	40

d. Materials usage beginning October: $825,000 per month.

e. Wages and salaries, beginning October: $215,000 per month, paid as incurred.

f. Other manufacturing expenses, beginning October: $420,000 per month, paid as incurred.

g. Depreciation: $43,000 per month.

h. Cost of goods sold has consistently averaged 70 percent of sales.

i. Selling and administrative expenses: October and November, 15 percent of sales; December and January, 14 percent of sales; and February and March, 12 percent of sales.

j. Payments on note payable: $750,000 each in November and February.

k. Interest due in January: $300,000.

l. Dividends payable in October and January: $25,000 each.

m. Income taxes due in January: $375,000.

n. Most recent balance sheet (estimated):

XYZ COMPANY
Estimated Balance Sheet
For September 30, 1982
($000)

Assets

Current assets:

Cash		$ 740
Accounts and notes receivable		3,975
Inventories:		
Raw materials	$ 2,725	
Finished goods	6,420	9,145
Total current assets		13,860
Plant and equipment	12,525	
Less: Accumulated depreciation	5,315	7,210
Other assets		1,730
Total assets		$22,800

Liabilities and Net Worth

Current liabilities:

Accounts payable	$ 1,050
Notes payable	4,120
Accrued liabilities	2,875
Total current liabilities	8,045
Long-term debt	5,250
Preferred stock	1,750
Common stock	5,000
Earned surplus	2,755
Total liabilities and net worth . . .	$22,800

From the data given, develop a cash budget for the six months ended March 31, 1983, and pro forma statements for the quarters ended December 31, 1982, and March 31, 1983. Assume income taxes to be 50 percent, do not detail cost of goods sold, and assume no changes in accounts not specifically analyzed or projected here. What funds needs arise, and when? What if the collection speedup effort were unsuccessful and receivables stayed at 60 days? Discuss your findings about the policy changes being considered.

4 ANALYSIS OF CAPITAL INVESTMENT DECISIONS

In the previous chapters we have dealt with the basic operational aspects of a business—the analysis of results and the projection of expected operating conditions. In both cases we had to assume that the decisions to invest and to finance these operations had been made in an appropriate fashion to obtain profitable results. In this chapter, we shall concentrate on the analytical techniques which are used to support business investment decisions. We shall assume that management has the capability to operate the new facilities and other investments, and that the necessary capital can be provided to finance the investments under review.

The process of investment in land, productive equipment, buildings, working capital, raw materials deposits, and other assets for future economic gain is particularly difficult and calls for careful analysis. Decisions in this area usually commit a business enterprise for a considerable time period to an activity, line of business, or geographic region. As one of the three basic areas of decision making—investment, operations, and financing—the investment process has the longest time horizon and rests most heavily on careful forecasts and detailed assumptions about the likely future conditions which must provide the economic gain to justify the contemplated outlay of funds.

Before we turn to the specific concepts and methods of analysis, it should be emphasized that in this book we are viewing the capital investment problem (a part of capital budgeting) in a narrow sense. The critical task of management is first to establish the general objectives and specific goals of the enterprise, which we shall assume to have been done. On the basis of these and the known strengths and limitations in administrative talent, manpower, technical know-how, market standing, financing possibilities, and so on, management must next formulate appropriate strategies which we shall again assume to exist. Many objectives and related strategies call for the commitment of long-term capital investments—and at times also for the opposite, capital disinvestment. Thus every time a capital outlay is considered, it should take place within the framework suggested in Figure 4–1.

Capital budgeting has been the subject of learned dispute for many years. Ideally, it would be a simple process of listing all investment opportunities against all sources of financing. The theoretical economist's argument would then be to accept all investments up to the point at which incremental benefits equal incremental cost. In reality, it is not possible to see ahead to all investment opportunities, since management is faced with a revolving planning horizon over which opportunities keep appearing. Even if it were possible to view all investments at any one time, it would be difficult to make all the "right" decisions, since there are many restrictions on a company's ability to take care of surges of investment opportunities. In reality, management must seek to enhance the idea flow throughout the organization and hope that in the long run the results from a continuous process of accepting and

Figure 4–1
INVESTMENT ANALYSIS IN PERSPECTIVE

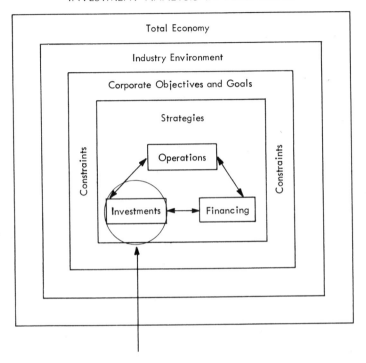

rejecting investment opportunities will outperform the competition.

The capital budgeting process also distinguishes among many types of investment opportunities. There are such critical needs as replacing a washed-out railroad bridge, where any detailed economic analysis would be waste motion. The decision is obvious. Other investments may be caused by governmental requirements, such as environmental protection. At the other extreme, there are many investment opportunities which involve implications far beyond the detailed and rational economics that can be expressed in numbers. Management's obligation is to provide sufficient profitable investment opportunities to carry the load of those investments which may be necessary for a variety of reasons other than pure economic return.

In this book we shall assume this framework and concentrate on the *technical* approach to investment analysis, namely, the specific tools which determine the relative attractiveness of projects. We shall also set aside the question of financing, which is the subject of Chapter 5. Given these conditions, we must stress again that calculation and methodology are only the underpinning for the broader questions involved.

THE FRAMEWORK FOR DECISION

Our specific focus on analytical techniques still requires the thoughtful establishment and observation of a series of ground rules to ensure consistent and meaningful results. These ground rules have to do with the nature of the data and estimates employed, with careful definition of the problem to be solved and any alternative actions available, and with economic reasoning based on incremental conditions. Also, there is the need to define truly relevant costs and revenues, and the distinction between accounting data and cash flows. Each of these will now be discussed briefly.

Careful *definition of the problem* and the alternatives under analysis is critically important to ensure appropriate results of any investment analysis, yet is often overlooked and even ignored. While apparently an obvious matter, the stress on proper problem definition cannot be overdone. For example, the replacement of a machine nearing the end of its useful life is not a simple problem. As a general rule, there are several alternatives, and the specific circumstances could mean an even greater number. The most obvious alternative is to do nothing and to continue to patch up the machine until it falls apart. Such an ongoing cost pattern often is the basis for comparison with a replacement; yet it may be useful to ask the not-so-obvious question of whether the company should stop making the product altogether. "Go out of business" is an alternative which, though often painful, should at least be considered before new resources are committed. For example, the improved efficiency of a new machine or plant may raise the product's profit performance from poor to average; yet there may be different alternatives elsewhere to use the funds more profitably. Even if the decision to replace has been made, there exist still other alternatives. Replacement with the same machine, or with a larger, more automatic model, or with one employing a different manufacturing process are some of these choices.

The picture of these alternatives can be represented in the simple decision tree shown in Figure 4–2. This basic illustration of the options in one type of investment should demonstrate the need to think through the many alternatives usually present with any major or even minor capital outlay. It is crucial to select the *appropriate* alternatives for analysis and to structure the problem in such a way that the power of the analytical tools is brought to bear on the real decisional issue.

Next, it is critical for us to recognize that the economic calculations to justify, say, a new machine, the replacement of an outmoded factory, or the acquisition of a plot of land for

Figure 4–2
OPTIONS FOR REPLACEMENT DECISION

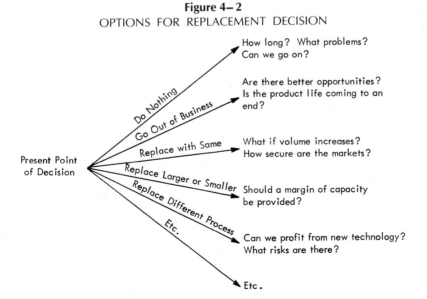

development must rest on projections and forecasts of *future revenues and costs*. It will not do simply to assume that past operating costs of a machine will go unchanged, or that past experience with land development will be applicable to a new venture. While this may seem obvious, the temptation exists in practice to *extrapolate* past conditions instead of carefully *forecasting* likely developments. The past is at best a rough guide to future events, and at worst irrelevant. Investment analysis, with time horizons of 5, 10, or even 25 years, deals entirely with future conditions and the uncertainty surrounding them. It will therefore behoove the analyst to gauge as much as possible the relative uncertainty surrounding the estimates, and perhaps to run the analysis under different assumed conditions if the uncertainty is too great. Such an approach can be used to test the "sensitivity" of the result to changes in particular variables such as product prices, raw materials costs, and so on. The uncertainty of future conditions represents for management the *risk* of investments in capital assets—the degree of risk being a function of the relative uncertainty of the key variables of the project. Careful estimates and research are often warranted to narrow the margin of error in the predicted conditions put into the analytical framework.

The *economic reasoning* connected with any capital outlay is based on the conditions which will *change* because of the action taken. Thus the questions to be dealt with are as follows: What *additional funds* will be required to carry out the alternative chosen? If the investment proposal results in the sale or other disposition of assets, as well as the addition of new ones, it is the *net* outlay that counts. What *additional revenues* will be created over and above any existing ones? If new revenues are brought about but some existing ones are lost, it is the *net* impact of the action which is relevant for economic analysis. What costs will be added or removed from the business operation? The *relevant* elements of cost will be those which go up or down because of the decision—anything that remains the same before and after the investment decision is *not relevant* for the purpose. Thus the economic reasoning is based on *incremental changes*—a relative rather than absolute approach, which is tied closely to carefully defined alternatives. The specific data developed are therefore *differential* funds commitments, revenues, and costs caused by the decision.

Finally, a distinction must be drawn between *accounting data* and *relevant revenues and costs*. While our analysis will often be based on data taken from the accounting system, particularly in the case of cost elements affected by the investment decision, we must differentiate between those items which *do vary* with the change brought about by the investment and those which only *appear* to do so. The latter are accounting *allocations* which may change in size but do not necessarily represent a true change in cost incurred. For example, a new machine with greater output than the old may be charged with a larger proportion of general overhead (plant manager's salary, administrative costs, insurance, etc.) if the allocation is based on operating volume. While overhead costs thus have risen for the specific operation, there has likely been no change in total general overhead, since we have merely substituted one machine for another. The analysis thus requires a judgment whether in the overall divisional or corporate picture there has been a change in *true* outlays and revenues, *not* whether the accounting system is *redistributing* the existing costs differently. The emphasis is always on *cash in* and *cash out*, as affected by the decision—an *economic cash flow framework*. Since federal and state income taxes are a common "expense" of doing business, we are talking about the *aftertax cash effect* of a decision on the business, and all analytical effort should point in this direction.

METHODS OF ANALYSIS: BASIC CONCEPTS

The investment of capital is, in its simplest form, made for one basic reason: to obtain sufficient economic returns over a future period to warrant the original outlay, that is, enough cash receipts to justify the cash spent. The method of analysis should take into account in one way or another this *trade-off* of current cash outflow versus future cash inflow. This section of the chapter will deal with an often-used simple framework for analysis and its advantages and shortcomings, while also spelling out the key elements needing attention. The next section will deal with more advanced but increasingly common methods, which employ present value concepts—the adjustment for the timing of cash flows and the recognition of economic opportunity costs.

Let us now demonstrate the components of investment analysis on the basis of a simplified example. An investment of $100,000 in facilities for a new product is expected to provide aftertax cash flow benefits of $25,000 over a period of six years, without significant annual fluctuations. Although the equipment will not be fully worn out after six years, it is unlikely that more than scrap value will be obtained due to technical obsolescence. The cost of removal is expected to offset this scrap value. Depreciation over the six years ($16,667 per year) has been appropriately reflected in the $25,000 figure, along the principles of Chapter 1, where we defined cash flow as the sum of aftertax profits and depreciation. Inflation is ignored here.

To judge the attractiveness of this investment we thus face three elements: the *investment*, the *operating benefits*, and the *time period* over which these benefits are expected to prevail. Our analysis must relate these three elements to provide a clue whether the investment is worthy of consideration or not. These basic conditions are true of all investment proposals. For the remainder of the chapter, we shall therefore use the following economic terminology:

Net investment refers to the net outlay which consists of gross capital requirements less any capital recovered from trade or sale of existing assets, after adjustment for applicable taxes. If there are any substantial recoveries of capital at the end of the analysis period, some allowance will have to be made for this later in our analysis. Similarly, if additional capital outlays during the period are necessary for the project, this will have to be considered in the net investment figure, as we shall see later on. For our simple example, the net investment is $100,000.

Operating cash flows are the net economic benefits, period for period, which are caused by an investment. They are such elements as operating savings caused by a machine replacement, the additional profits earned by a new product line, the profit increase from plant expansion, or the profits created by developing a natural resource. These economic benefits are normally experienced as an aftertax cash flow, which includes the tax savings from any depreciation charges. In our example, the annual operating cash flow after taxes is $25,000, representing new product profits of $8,333, adjusted for depreciation of $16,667. As we shall see later on, the pattern of annual or periodic cash flows can influence our measures of analysis significantly. Level periodic flows are easiest to deal with, and as we shall see later the more common uneven flows encountered in practice add to the complexity of our analysis.

The *economic life* of a project is the time period over which one can expect to obtain the benefits of the investment proposition. This is the third element of the investment process. It is very important to distinguish this relevant time period from the *physical* life of any equipment involved or the *technological* life of a particular process. Even though physically a building or piece of equipment may be perfectly usable, the investment's economic life has ceased if the market for the product or service has expired. It will be necessary to redirect resources still usable, or to dispose of them at that point. Technology likewise must be related to economic use—the best process is useless if the product can no longer be sold. The *depreciation life* for accounting or tax purposes is similarly suspect as a clue to the project's true life span, since such write-offs are normally based on standard accounting and tax guidelines, not the particular economic circumstances. In our example, the economic life is six years, the period over which the product is expected to be sold.

How do we relate the three basic elements—investment, operating cash flow, and life—to find the project's attractiveness? Three simple methods are often employed for this purpose: the *payback* or payout, the *return on investment*, and the *average return*. All of these measures are in essence rules of thumb, which under most conditions provide only an approximation of the economic desirability of a project, and at times can be misleading. Nevertheless, their use is so widespread that they should be discussed here.

Payback

The payback measure is a simple relationship of the annual benefit of a project to the investment required.

$$\text{Payback} = \frac{\text{Net investment}}{\text{Average annual operating cash flow}} = \frac{\$100,000}{\$25,000} = 4 \text{ years}$$

The result of the calculation is the number of years required to achieve repayment of the original outlay. When related to the economic life, the payback figure is used as an indication of whether the investment will be repaid within the economic life span. This is true in our simple example, where payback is achieved in four years versus an estimated life of six years.

While the payback period is easy to calculate—which probably accounts for its popularity—some difficult questions arise in its use. First of all, the concept measures the return of the original investment on, so to speak, the installment basis. "How long will it be until I get my money back?" is the implied query. From an economic viewpoint this is not enough, of course, since one would hope to earn a profit on the funds invested. An analogy can be drawn to a savings account in which $100 is invested and from which $25 is withdrawn at the end of each year. After four years the principal would have been repaid. The saver would be very upset if the bank told him that his account was now depleted. He expected to earn at least 5 or 6 percent per year on the declining balance in his account, and would demand the accumulated interest due him.

In the case of our investment example, the payback period is insufficient to allow for any economic return on the amount of the investment. We must look to the years *beyond* the payback to provide some profit. In fact, if economic life and payback were to coincide precisely, an *opportunity loss* would have been suffered, since the same funds invested elsewhere would presumably have earned some return. Table 4–1 illustrates these points. If we assume that a normal return earned in our hypothetical company was 10 percent after taxes, our simple example could be represented in the amortization schedule shown, which takes into account the opportunity of earning a normal 10 percent.

For simplicity, we have assumed that earnings are calculated on the beginning balance and operating cash flows are received at the end of the period. From the calculation it is quite obvious that a payback of four years could mean an opportunity loss of about $30,400, if the project ended at this point. If the economic life were five years, the opportunity loss vis-à-vis alternative earnings opportunities at 10 percent would be reduced to about $8,400, while at six years the gain vis-à-vis alternative earnings opportunities would be a quite favorable $15,700.

This brief illustration points up one of the major drawbacks of the payback calculation; namely, that it is relatively insensitive to the economic life span and thus is not a truly meaningful and comparable criterion of earnings power. The speed with which money is repaid is not a convenient way to think

Table 4–1
AMORTIZATION OF $100,000 INVESTMENT AT 10 PERCENT

Year	Beginning Balance	Normal Earnings, 10 Percent	Operating Cash Flow	Ending Balance to Be Recovered
1	$100,000	$10,000	$(25,000)	$85,000
2	85,000	8,500	(25,000)	68,500
3	68,500	6,850	(25,000)	50,350
4	50,350	5,035	(25,000)	30,385 (payback)
5	30,385	3,039	(25,000)	8,424
6	8,424	842	(25,000)	(15,734)

about profitability because without further analysis, all we can say about our example is that the project pays out in four years, with two "extra" years for profit. Moreover, on other similar projects with a five-year or a ten-year life the payback measure would show the same results, namely, four years plus something extra, even though the projects are clearly superior.

Another drawback of the payback measure is its inability to handle projects with varying cash flow patterns. Since the measure assumes level average annual operating cash flows, a project with rising or declining cash flow patterns cannot be handled properly. A new product, for example, may show slowly rising cash inflows over time, leveling out and sharply declining in the late stages of its economic life. A machine replacement proposal will normally show rising savings as the existing machine deteriorates. Moreover, any additional investment during the period or capital recoveries at the end will cause distortions in this rule of thumb. Table 4–2 illustrates the insensitivity of the payout concept to variations in cash flow:

Table 4–2
PAYBACK RESULTS UNDER VARYING CONDITIONS

	Project 1	Project 2	Project 3
Net investment	$100,000	$100,000	$100,000
Average annual operating cash flow ...	25,000	25,000	33,333
Economic life	6 years	8 years	3 years
Payback	4 years	4 years	3 years
Cash flow pattern (years):			
1	$ 25,000	$ 20,000	$ 16,667
2	25,000	30,000	33,333
3	25,000	50,000	50,000
4	25,000	40,000	–0–
5	25,000	30,000	–0–
6	25,000	15,000	–0–
7	–0–	10,000	–0–
8	–0–	5,000	–0–
Total	$150,000	$200,000	$100,000
Cumulative first four years	$100,000	$140,000	n.a.
Average first four years	$ 25,000	$ 35,000	n.a.

n.a. = not applicable.

If we assume similar risks for each project shown in Table 4–2, we would choose project 2 over project 1 since over its life it will return $50,000 more than project 1. Yet the payback is the same. Project 3, on the other hand, appears to be the most favorable if judged only on the payout criterion of three years. Yet it is obvious that the project involves an opportunity loss, as discussed earlier—it merely repays the original capital without any economic return. The difference in cash flow patterns of projects 1 and 2 is also masked by the payout criterion. If we cumulate the first four years of operation, we find that project 2 is far superior to project 1, with average cash flows of $35,000 versus $25,000—since project 2 provides heavy operating cash flows in the early years.

By now it should be clear that the payback device must be used with considerable caution. Only if the cash flow patterns of alternative projects are similar *and* if their economic lives are equal or close will the measure provide a proper ranking. If these conditions do not hold, which is quite common, the measure must be supported by further analysis of the kind just shown, and even then the answers are blurred. Average annual cash flows and extra years of life are concepts which are simply too crude to deal with except under very limited circumstances.

A modification of payback involves the use of average *accounting profit after taxes* in the denominator of the formula. The rationale is that accounting profit, which contains a depreciation allowance (see Chapter 1), is a better measure, since it implicitly provides for both a return of principal and a profit. The depreciation charge is assumed to simulate the return of the principal. In our simple example we had employed aftertax *cash flows* of $25,000, which are represented by an accounting profit of $8,333 plus depreciation of $16,667 ($100,000 over six years). On the new basis, the modified payback would appear as follows:

$$\frac{\text{Net investment}}{\text{Average annual aftertax profit}} = \frac{\$100,000}{\$8,333} = 12 \text{ years}$$

This answer obviously is a distortion of the economic picture, since it in no way represents the cash-in, cash-out reasoning underlying investment analysis. One should be careful not to let accounting profits and depreciation write-off rules take the place of *economic trade-offs*, since each is designed for a valid but different purpose. In Table 4–1 we saw that the project was desirable if its economic life was five years or better. Thus a 12-year payout simply does not appear reasonable. Depending on the circumstances, particularly variations in the economic life span, the degree of distortion introduced by the use of accounting profits will vary—and one cannot hope for any consistency in this measure. The reader is invited to test the effect of varying the key elements in our simple example.

Simple Return on Investment

This measure is an outgrowth of the payback reasoning, and in fact it represents the inverse of the payback formula. It is an attempt to express the economic desirability of an investment project in terms of a percentage return on the original outlay. The method shares all of the shortcomings of the payback criterion, however, since it again relates only two of the three aspects of a project, net investments and operating cash flows, and leaves out the life span:

$$\text{Return on investment} = \frac{\text{Average annual operating cash flow}}{\text{Net investment}}$$

$$= \frac{\$25,000}{\$100,000} = 25\%$$

With no reference to economic life and with no recognition of the fact that, just as in a savings account, regular cash withdrawals will reduce the principal balance, all the measure indicates is that $25,000 happens to be 25 percent of $100,000. Note that the same answer would be obtained if the economic life were 1 year, 10 years, or 100 years. In fact, the return shown would be true in an economic sense only if the investment provided $25,000 per year in perpetuity; only then could we speak of a true return of 25 percent. The conceptually superior devices of the next section will provide better economic answers. As in the case of the payback device, meaningful comparisons can be made only of alternatives quite similar in life and cash flows.

A modification of the return on investment is the use of accounting profit as the numerator:

$$\frac{\text{Average annual aftertax profit}}{\text{Net investment}} = \frac{\$8,333}{\$100,000} = 8.3\%$$

Apart from economic criteria, this is an attempt to simulate the effect the project would have on corporate financial statements. As a very crude approximation it will give such a reading, at least for the early part of the project's life. The measure is still subject, however, to the shortcomings discussed earlier.

Average Return on Investment

For completeness, it will be necessary to mention the third common measure, which employs the average net investment related to average operating cash flows or accounting profit:

$$\text{Average return} = \frac{\text{Average operating cash flow}}{\text{Average net investment}} = \frac{\$25,000}{\$50,000} = 50\%$$

or:

$$\text{Average return} = \frac{\text{Average accounting profit after taxes}}{\text{Average net investment}} = \frac{\$8,333}{\$50,000}$$
$$= 16.7\%$$

The latter figure is, under some conditions (simple projects of medium life), a fair approximation of the economic return. It is still subject to serious distortion when complexities are present in a project, and must therefore be used with extreme caution.

METHODS OF ANALYSIS: ADVANCED CONCEPTS

The Time Value of Money

We have described investment analysis as involving a *trade-off* between current dollar outlays and future benefits over a period of time. Common sense tells us that the investor cannot be indifferent between otherwise exactly comparable propositions in which the timing of benefits varies widely. More immediate benefits will be preferable to benefits to be obtained further out in time, even if risk and uncertainty are comparable. The reason for this, of course, is the opportunity for an individual or a corporation to invest funds at profit—in a savings account, a government bond, or any of a great variety of other economic propositions. If one has to wait for a period of time to obtain a sum of money instead of having the same sum of money presently, the obvious choice will be to take the immediately available funds and to invest them at a profit commensurate with the risk preferences of the investor. To wait would mean an *opportunity cost* in terms of lost earnings. Conversely, common sense dictates that the choice between an expenditure now versus the same expenditure some time hence will be to defer the outlay, since normally the opportunity exists to earn a profit on the funds in the meantime. Stated another way, money has value directly related to the timing of its receipt or disbursement, and this value is determined by the opportunity to earn a profit from a normal investment.

A simple example will illustrate the point. If an investor normally uses a savings account which provides interest of 5 percent per year, $1,000 invested today will grow to $1,050 one year hence (we ignore daily or monthly compounding, as is practiced by many banks). If our investor were forced to wait one year before receiving his $1,000, he would have lost the opportunity to earn $50. Without question, a sum of $1,000 offered to him one year hence will be worth less to him than the same amount offered him today. Specifically, the value of the delayed \$1,000 will be related to his earnings power of 5 percent, and we can calculate the present value of the \$1,000 as follows:

$$\text{Present value} = \frac{\$1,000}{1.05} = \$952.38$$

Quite obviously, \$952.38 must be the amount which, invested at 5 percent today, will be worth \$1,000 at the end of one year from now. The trade-off is thus determined by the *length of time* and the *earnings power* available. Ignoring risk for the moment, our investor should be willing to pay \$952.38 for a contract for \$1,000 to be delivered in one year if he normally earns 5 percent on his money.

Similarly, a lengthening in the time period to receipt or disbursement will reduce the present value of a sum of money. A sum of \$1,000 to be received in five years will be worth only \$783.50 today, since that amount invested today at 5 percent would grow to \$1,000 five years hence. The figure was derived from the following calculation:

$$\frac{\$1,000}{1.27628} = \$783.53$$

which relates \$783.53 to its compounded value at 5 percent five years hence, shown in the denominator as 1.27628, which is 1.05 raised to the fifth power. We refer to the calculation of present value as discounting, which is nothing more than the reverse of the familiar compound interest process applied to an investment's growth in value due to periodic interest receipts which are reinvested. Through this reasoning process, we are able to fix at any point in time the value of a receipt or disbursement, once the opportunity rate of earnings has been stipulated.

The process of compounding and discounting is as old as moneylending and has been in use in financial institutions since time immemorial, although the application of the process to business investment analysis is of more recent interest. The transformation of cash flows into present values is eased considerably through the use of present value tables, a set of which is provided at the end of the chapter. The tables are based on the concepts discussed earlier. There are two tables, the first of which (Table 4–10) displays the results of discounting a sum of money received or disbursed at the end of any period, using interest rates applied to these periods. The general formula is:

$$\text{Present value} = \frac{1}{(1 + i)^n}$$

where i is the applicable interest (discount) rate and n the number of discount periods. For any number of periods up to 60 years and discount rates from 1 to 50 percent, we can find the present value of a sum of money by simply multiplying the amount involved by the appropriate factor in the table:

$$\text{Present value} = \text{Factor} \times \text{Amount}$$

Note that our savings example on page 140 can be found in Table 4–10 in the 5 percent column, lines 1 and 5.

Table 4–11 is a variation of Table 4–10 and is helpful for calculating more complex patterns. For example, we may be faced with analyzing the present value of a series of equal receipts or payments over a number of years. It would be possible to make the calculation by using Table 4–10, repetitively multiplying the annual amounts with the appropriate sequence of factors, and adding the results. Table 4–11 eases the task, however, by providing a set of *additive* factors from those of Table 4–10. Thus a single multiplication of the annual amount (annuity) with the appropriate factor will provide the present value of the whole series of *equal* receipts or disbursements:

$$\text{Present value} = \text{Factor} \times \text{Annuity}$$

These basic tables can be used for practically all normally encountered investment problems. Many variations and refinements could be introduced, such as more frequent discounting (monthly, weekly), or the assumption could continuously be made that the amounts received or disbursed will occur in weekly or monthly increments rather than at the end of the period. This forward shift in timing would provide slightly higher present values, both for single sums and annuities. The continuous pattern would represent a closer approximation of operating changes such as labor reductions, material savings, and other daily, weekly, and monthly disbursements and receipts.

For practical purposes, such refinements are not critical to the process, since the relatively small impact of greater precision is easily outweighed by the imprecise nature of most of the estimates employed. The references at the end of this chapter contain sets of tables which can be used for achieving any mathematical precision desired. Now let us turn to the use of these principles in investment analysis.

NET PRESENT VALUE

The basic idea of net present value is simply to find the balance of the trade-off between investment outlays and future benefits, in terms of time-adjusted present value dollars. The analysis assumes that a company's management has determined a normal opportunity rate or standard at which funds can and should be employed in the business. This rate is often referred to as the "cost of capital," that is, the weighted average of the compensation for all long-term funds provided to the company (see Chapter 5). Others prefer to use an estimate of future rates of return at which funds can likely be invested in the company, an "opportunity rate" approach.

Given such a standard, it is possible to determine the present value of all outlays and the present value of all inflows over the economic life of the project, and to *net* these against each other. The result is a positive or negative (net inflow or net outflow) figure which indicates whether the project, over its life, is meeting or falling short of the earnings standard built into the calculation. Since present value dollars are dependent on timing and earnings opportunity, a positive net present value indicates that over the economic life the project will return the original capital outlay (as well as any required future ones), earn the standard return on the outstanding balance, and provide a "cushion" of excess value. Conversely, a negative figure indicates that the project is not achieving the built-in earnings standard and will cause an opportunity loss. Obviously, the timing of cash flows is critical, as is the volume pattern of the flows.

Our simple project on page 132 will serve as an illustration here. It is best to present the information in a time scale format, which permits easy calculation and serves to visualize the problem in a time perspective. When we use a time scale, the present is normally point "0," with periods marked off in positive steps into the future, and negative steps into the past, where applicable. This format is used in Table 4–3.

The result of the calculation is a net present value of almost $16,000, if the company considers 8 percent a normal earnings standard. All of the investment will have been recovered over the six-year period, and 8 percent after taxes will have been earned on the declining outstanding balance during the project life. Moreover, a cushion of $15,575 of extra dollars in present value equivalents can be counted on *if* the project lives out its economic life and the cash flow estimates are correct. We note a similarity to the simple payback concept discussed earlier,

Table 4– 3

PRESENT VALUE ANALYSIS BY PERIOD AT 8 PERCENT

Time Period	Investment (outlays)	Benefits (inflows)	P.V. Factors at 8 Percent*	Present Values	Cumulative P.V.
0	$100,000	—	1.000	−$100,000	−$100,000
1	—	$ 25,000	0.926	+ 23,150	− 76,850
2	—	25,000	0.857	+ 21,425	− 55,425
3	—	25,000	0.794	+ 19,850	− 35,575
4	—	25,000	0.735	+ 18,375	− 17,200
5	—	25,000	0.681	+ 17,025	− 175
6	—	25,000	0.630	+ 15,750	+ 15,575
	$100,000	$150,000		+$ 15,575	

* To illustrate use of Table 4–10, assuming that benefits occur at year-end. We could instead use, from Table 4–11, 4.623 times $25,000, since the annual inflows are equal. The result for the total present value of the inflows is identical. Note that the factors for years 1 through 6 add to a total of 4.623.

which also referred to a recovery of the investment and "something extra." The critical difference, however, is that the net present value concept has a built-in economic earnings requirement beyond the recovery of the principal, and thus the cushion of a positive net present value is truly an economic gain beyond satisfying a normal earnings standard.

If a higher earnings standard had been required, say 12 percent, the result would appear as shown in Table 4–4. The net present value remains positive, but the size of the cushion has decreased to $2,800, which we would expect, since we have raised the required earnings hurdle. At a 14 percent discount rate, the net present value shrinks to a similar, slightly negative result ($25,000 × 3.889 − $100,000 = --$2,775). We observe the sensitivity of the net present value measurement to changes in the required earnings rate. From the last columns in Tables 4–3 and 4–4 we also note the importance of economic life. As the earnings requirement increases, the time required for the net present value to turn positive is lengthened. At 8 percent it took a life of about five years to do so, while at 12 percent most of the sixth year of life was necessary. The net present value measure thus appears to reflect properly the trade-off of cash outlays and cash inflows over time, and it also recognizes both principal recovery and earnings rate. The reader is invited to calculate the notable impact of a different cash flow pattern, such as one rising, say,

Table 4–4
PRESENT VALUE ANALYSIS AT 12 PERCENT

Time Period	Cash Flows	P.V. Factors at 12 Percent*	Present Values	Cumulative P.V.
0	−$100,000	1.000	−$100,000	−$100,000
1	+ 25,000	0.893	+ 22,325	− 77,675
2	+ 25,000	0.797	+ 19,925	− 57,750
3	+ 25,000	0.712	+ 17,800	− 39,950
4	+ 25,000	0.636	+ 15,900	− 24,050
5	+ 25,000	0.567	+ 14,175	− 9,875
6	+ 25,000	0.507	+ 12,675	+ 2,800
	+$ 50,000		+$ 2,800	

* As in Table 4–4, we could instead use 4.112 times $25,000 from Table 4–11.

from $15,000 to $40,000, and one falling from $40,000 to $15,000, in each case to total $150,000 over six years.

The best use of net present value is as a screening device with which to ascertain whether, over the economic life, a minimum earnings standard can be obtained. When net present value is positive, there is earnings potential in excess of the standard; when net present value is close to or exactly zero, the earnings requirement has just been met, given that the earnings estimate and length of life are quite certain. When the net present value is negative, the minimum earnings standard and capital recovery cannot be achieved with the estimated cash inflows during the economic life.

The concept of net present value by itself, however, does not answer all our questions, many of which have been implied in the discussion just concluded. Given a corporate return standard, the evaluation of the size of the "cushion" is a little difficult when comparing projects, particularly if the investments are of significantly different magnitude. Moreover, the degree to which one must rely on the project living out its estimated economic life is often a significant problem. Further, we are interested in quantifying the amount of error we can afford in our estimates of cash inflows. Finally, a valid question often asked is: What level of "true" return will the project provide if all estimates can be expected to materialize? Net present value must be fortified with several other measures for us to be able to make these judgments. The most common measures of this nature are the *present value index*, the *present value payback*, the *annualized net present value*, and the *yield*. They will be taken up in this order.

Present Value Index

If the analyst, after calculating net present values, is faced with a choice among several alternative investments of different size, he cannot be indifferent to the fact that even though their net present values may be equal or close, the amount of investment required by the various projects varies widely. In other words, it makes quite a difference whether an investment proposal promises a net present value of $1,000 for an outlay of $10,000, or whether another investment requires $25,000 for the same net present value, even if we assume equivalent lives and equivalent risk. In the first case, the cushion is a much larger fraction of the commitment than in the second.

A formal way of expressing this relationship is the following ratio:

$$\text{Present value index} = \frac{\text{Present value of operating inflows}}{\text{Present value of net investment}}$$

The present values in this formula are the same amounts we used earlier to derive the net present value, by subtracting one from the other. In this case the question is simply: How much in present value benefits is created per dollar of net investment? The two cases just cited would appear as follows:

$$1. \ \text{Present value index} = \frac{\$11,000}{\$10,000} = 1.10$$

$$2. \ \text{Present value index} = \frac{\$26,000}{\$25,000} = 1.04$$

As expected, the first project is much more favorable if we assume all other aspects to be reasonably comparable. The higher the index, the better the project. If the index is 1.0 or less, the project is just meeting or missing the minimum standard built into the derivation of the present values. The example in Table 4–3 has an index of $115,575 \div 100,000 = 1.16$ at 8 percent, and 1.03 at 12 percent. While the measure provides some further insight, it still leaves several points unanswered, and there are theoretical issues involved which should be studied further in the references provided at the end of the chapter.

Present Value Payback (minimum life)

In Table 4–3, we provided a column for cumulative present value. This column was useful for deriving the time required until the net present value turned positive—that is, the point in its life when the project became attractive. This test is nothing more than an answer to finding the minimum economic life required for the project to meet the return standard, given the level of cash inflows projected. At the point in time when the trade-off of cash outflows and inflows is even in present value terms, the project will achieve a payback or payout of the investment *plus* an economic return on the outstanding balance at the return standard (opportunity rate) used for the present value analysis.

If a project has uneven and complicated cash flows, as we shall demonstrate shortly, the analysis to find the minimum life requires a year-by-year accumulation of the present values, positive or negative, as was done in Table 4–3. If a project is straightforward in the simple terms used for many of our examples—that is, a *single* net investment at point zero and *level* annual operating cash inflows—use can be made of the annuity factors of Table 4–11 to find a quick answer. For this purpose, the relationship

$$\text{Present value} = \text{Factor} \times \text{Annuity}$$

can be exploited, as we are looking for the condition at which the present value of the outflows is exactly equal to the present value of the inflows. Since the net investment (outflow) is one of these equal amounts (it has to be recovered by the inflows), we can change the formula to:

$$\text{Net investment} = \text{Factor} \times \text{Annuity}$$

And since the annuity (annual operating cash flows) is known, we can find the factor which satisfies the condition:

$$\text{Factor} = \frac{\text{Net investment}}{\text{Annuity}}$$

For our investment example, we calculate the following results: $100,000 ÷ $25,000 = 4.0, and we can look for the closest factor in the 8 percent column of Table 4–11. The answer lies almost exactly on period 5 (3.993), which indicates that the minimum life of the project must be five years to achieve 8 percent. At 12 percent, the life is approximately 5⅔ years, using an interpolation between 3.605 and 4.112.

The test for present value payout or minimum life thus becomes one more step in assessing the margin for error in the project estimates, and is one method of displaying the risk involved. It sharpens the understanding of the relationship of economic life and acceptable performance—a much improved version of the simple payback and a companion to the net present value.

Annualized Net Present Value

The net present value calculation normally results in an excess or deficiency of present value benefits over the net investment. If positive, the amount can be viewed as a cushion against estimating error in future cash inflows. Unless a project has highly irregular annual flows, it is often useful to transform the net present value cushion into an *equivalent annuity* over the project's economic life. These annual equivalents representing a margin of error can then be directly compared to the raw annual cash inflow estimates, since the net present value has in effect been "reconstituted" into future cash flows. To illustrate, we can transform the net present value in Table 4–3 of $15,575 into an annuity over the six-year life by simply again exploiting the present value relationship:

$$\text{Present value} = \text{Factor} \times \text{Annuity}$$

Since we are interested in finding the annuity represented by the net present value, over a known economic life and a set discount rate (the opportunity rate employed in the present value calculation in the first place), the annuity formula is transformed as follows:

$$\text{Annuity} = \frac{\text{(Net) present value}}{\text{Factor}}$$

In our example the result is as follows:

$$\text{Annuity} = \frac{\$15,575}{4.623} = \$3,369$$

The annual operating cash inflows were originally estimated at $25,000. The result above indicates that over the six-year life the actual experience can be lower by about $3,400 per year (a 13 percent reduction of the total cash flow, but a 40 percent reduction in the aftertax profit of $8,333!) and the project will still meet the minimum return standard of 8 percent.

There are two additional aspects to the process of annualization. As we shall see later, the process can be used to compare the annual net benefits of alternatives with different lives. Moreover, in a general framework, the annualizing process is a very practical and quick method to turn the investment analysis process around for a rough test of the desirability of an investment. This is a useful way to find the approximate annual operating cash flow required to justify an investment if the capital outlay itself is known (e.g., the cost of a machine) but the operating benefits have not yet been established. Given an economic life estimate and an opportunity rate of return, the formula,

$$\text{Operating cash flow} = \frac{\text{Net investment}}{\text{Factor}}$$

can be employed to find a level annual *target cash flow*. Care must be taken to modify this figure by the depreciation adjustment to arrive at the *minimal pretax operating improvement* necessary. This simply involves working backward through the analysis, recognizing that cash flow consists of aftertax operating profit with depreciation added back. The concept is a useful tool for a first judgment of the chance of an investment's being "in the ballpark." We can apply the example from Table 4–3 as follows:

First, we find the level target cash flow over six years at 8 percent:

$$\frac{\$100,000}{4.623} = \$21,631$$

Next we transform this aftertax cash flow into its equivalent pretax operating improvement:

Aftertax cash flow $21,631
Less: Depreciation 16,667

Aftertax profit	4,964
Tax at 46% of pretax profit	4,229
Pretax profit...........................	9,193
Add: Depreciation	16,667
Minimal pretax operating improvement ...	$25,860

Thus our investment has to provide a minimum of almost $26,000 in direct operating improvement such as lower costs, incremental revenues, and so on. It is a quick way of checking the potential of the investment considered.

Yield (discounted cash flow return)

The concept of a "true" return on an investment over its economic life (often referred to as DCF return) has already appeared in the discussion of the previous measures. The yield of a project is simply that rate of discount which, when applied to cash outflows and inflows over the economic life, provides a *zero net present value*—that is, the present value of the inflows is sufficient to provide an exact trade-off with the present value of the outflows. Stated another way, the principal of the investment can be amortized over the economic life, earning the exact return implied by the discount rate. Naturally, the yield will vary with changes in economic life and cash flow patterns. While heretofore we had employed a specified opportunity rate to find present values, the yield analysis turns the problem around to find a rate of discount, given equality of inflows and outflows. Again we can employ our simple formula (Present value = Factor × Annuity) if the project has a single current investment outflow and level annual cash inflows. The formula can be turned around as follows:

$$\text{Factor} = \frac{\text{Present value (investment)}}{\text{Annuity}}$$

This is the same approach employed earlier to find the present value payback (minimum life), and we again use the factor to check the result in Table 4–11 for investments with period-end cash flows. This time, however, the economic life is given and we look for the rate of discount instead. Our investment example had a factor of 4.0 ($100,000 ÷ $25,000), and we find that on the six-period line of Table 4–11 the factor 4.0 lies almost exactly between 12 percent (4.112) and 14 percent (3.889). Approximate interpolation indicates that the result is 13.0 percent. Had we assumed continuous receipt, instead of year-end, the result would be slightly higher.

When a project has a more complex cash flow pattern we must employ a trial-and-error approach to find the yield. Successive application of different discount rates to all cash flows over the economic life must be made until a close approximation to a zero net present value has been found. With some experience, usually no more than two trials are necessary, since the first result will indicate the direction of rate selection. A positive net present value indicates the need for a higher discount rate, and vice versa. We observed this process in Tables 4–3 and 4–4.

As a ranking device, the yield is reasonably accurate and much superior to the simple payback and return on investment. It is not without problems, however. Apart from the many conceptual and mathematical arguments possible, one should recognize that the use of yield alone is not necessarily accurate. For example, alternative projects of greatly different magnitudes may have yields inverse to the size of the investment. A $10,000 investment with a 50 percent yield cannot be directly compared to an outlay of $100,000 with a 30 percent yield, particularly if risks are similar and the company normally looks to a 15 percent opportunity rate as acceptable. It may be better to employ the larger sum at 30 percent than the smaller sum at 50 percent, unless both projects can be undertaken.

Similarly, length of life is important here. It may be more advantageous to employ funds at the lower rate for a longer period of time than to have a short high yield, if a choice has to be made between the two investments. The problem with yield is that a unique rate is found for each project, which *implies* that the cash flows returned over time can be reinvested at that same rate—which may not be possible. This argument is frequently used against the yield concept. Net present value analysis, on the other hand, employs a long-run opportunity rate which represents a judgment as to the normal earnings power of funds in the enterprise, and the reinvestment problem thus is not an issue. In addition, it is mathematically possible to have two or even more solutions for the yield in a complex project—which adds to the problem of interpretation. Increasingly practitioners prefer the net present value as a concept of investment selection over the discounted cash flow return (yield), although the yield has had ready acceptance as a deceptively simple figure to understand. The reader is invited to turn to the references at the end of the chapter for a more exhaustive analysis of the many theoretical and conceptual arguments.

COMPLICATIONS AND REFINEMENTS

So far we have limited ourselves to simple examples with which to illustrate the methodology. Let us now turn to a more realistic and complex example and illustrate how the time-adjusted techniques can be applied to judge the desirability of the project. For the purpose we shall employ first a typical replacement problem and second a generalized example with more aspects added. Before we go on to calculating the more sophisticated measures, it will be useful to refine the components of economic analysis somewhat. One cannot overstress the need to understand fully the reasoning behind net investment, operating cash flows, and economic life. The application of the appropriate techniques of measurement then becomes almost automatic.

For purposes of illustration we shall use a more complex investment problem, which involves the replacement of an existing machine tool with a more automatic and faster model. Let us assume that this is the only alternative feasible under the circumstances. We further assume that five years remain before the old machine becomes unusable, and that the new machine will be serviceable for ten years before it must be scrapped. The old machine cost $25,000 five years ago and has a current book value of $12,500 (depreciated straightline at $2,500 per year). It can be sold for $15,000 cash. The new machine will cost $40,000, will be depreciated over ten years, and will likely be worth at least its book value if it should be sold before the end of its physical life. The product made on the machine is expected to continue in the market for at least ten years without any serious threat to its existence. The company can even expect to sell at least 25 percent more than its current volume, using additional selling and promotional effort.

The new machine, if run at full speed, will turn out 125,000 units per year as compared to 100,000 units on the old equipment, and it will do so at lower costs for both labor and materials. In fact, the machine will use slightly less labor in total than the old machine because of fewer setups. It will require the same two operators but release some of the skilled setup men's time to be used productively elsewhere in the plant. It will also use material more efficiently. The extra 25,000 units which can be turned out by the new machine are expected to be sold with some incremental selling and promotional expenses, and will provide an additional contribution before taxes of $5,000.

Conditions as described here are quite common in practice. We shall now discuss the economic analysis of these complications in detail.

Net Investment Refined

We are looking for the *net change* in funds committed to the project, as stated in our earlier definition. Two events are to be considered. First, there is the outlay of $40,000 for the new machine (no investment tax credit assumed[1]), which is a

---

[1] Any applicable investment tax credit is simply a reduction in the cost of the machine, since federal income taxes for the period are reduced by the amount of the credit allowed.

straightforward cash commitment. Second, there is a recovery of cash from the sale of the old machine, which is attributable to our decision to replace and therefore is relevant. The amount of cash retained is somewhat less than the $15,000 cash value of the machine, however, since for tax purposes a gain on the sale must be recognized. We recall that the book value was $12,500, and therefore the company will be taxed on the difference of $2,500. For simplicity we assume this to be at the normal corporate tax rate of 46 percent. The tax due on the transaction thus is $1,150.

We now have all the components of the initial net investment figure relevant in this example:

Cost of new machine	$40,000
Cash from sale of old machine ...	(15,000)
Tax due on capital gain	1,150
Net investment	$26,150

We must observe that the economic analysis does not recognize *for other than tax purposes* the fact that a book value remained on the old machine. What was spent in the past is irrelevant and represents a *sunk cost*. We are interested only in the changes that take place *now;* therefore, the tax due on the transaction is a current expense caused by the decision. Had the old machine been unsalable in spite of its book value of $12,500, the only relevant element would have been the tax savings from the capital loss incurred under those conditions, but *not* the past investment represented by the book value. Nevertheless, inclusion of the latter is a very common mistake which confuses accounting and economics.

The net investment thus represents a balance of *cash* movements, in and out, *caused* by the investment decision. Additional investments or capital recoveries in later periods are relevant also, but so far we have not described the techniques of handling these. This will be done shortly.

Operating Cash Flows Refined

As discussed before, the operating cash flows are the aftertax cash changes brought about by an investment proposal. In the present case, we must carefully sort out the comparable conditions to develop *differential* revenues and costs. We must distinguish between the operating savings achieved through greater efficiency for the current volume of operations and the contribution provided through profitable sale of the additional output. The analysis appears in Table 4–5.

The calculations in Table 4–5 are carried out in three stages. First, the *operating savings* for the current volume of output (100,000 units) are determined by comparing the annual costs of operating the old machine and the new machine. Labor and materials provide some savings each, while overhead, though different, is not relevant from an economic standpoint. The fact that the cost accounting system, for valid reasons, allocates

Table 4– 5
DIFFERENTIAL COST AND REVENUE ANALYSIS

	Old Machine	New Machine	Relevant Annual Differences
1. Operating savings from current volume of 100,000 units:			
Labor (2 operators plus setup)	31,000	$ 30,000	$1,000
Material	38,000	36,000	2,000
Overhead (120% of direct labor)	37,200	36,000	—*
	$106,200	$102,000	3,000
2. Contribution from additional volume of 25,000 units:			
25,000 units sold at $1.50 per unit		$ 37,500	
Less:			
Labor (no additional operators)		—	
Material cost at 36¢/unit		(9,000)	
Additional selling expense		(10,500)	
Additional promotional expense		(13,000)	5,000
Total savings and additional contribution			8,000
3. Differential depreciation (additional expense; for tax purposes only)	$ 2,500	4,000	(1,500)
Taxable operating improvements			6,500
Tax at 46%			2,990
Aftertax profit improvement			3,510
Add back depreciation			1,500
Aftertax operating cash flow			$5,010

* Not relevant, since it represents an allocation only.

overhead at 120 percent of direct labor does not alter the reality that our decision has not introduced any change in spending for overhead. What has changed is the *basis* of allocation, which in this case happens to be direct labor, but not the total amount of overhead. The plant manager and his office staff still receive the same salaries, and other overhead costs are unchanged. Only if the replacement decision had in fact brought a change in spending, such as higher property taxes and insurance fees or additional maintenance or technical support, would such a change have to be recognized in the calculation. We would then estimate the annual amount of expenditure and develop the differential cost. As a general rule it should be observed that it is better to deal with *annual totals* of cost and revenue elements than with *unit cost* values, since the latter increase the risk of being trapped into the use of accounting allocations, which are appropriate for costing purposes (cost of goods sold, inventory values, etc.) but are generally irrelevant for economic analysis.

Second, we make the calculation of the *additional contribution* from the higher volume of the new machine. This calculation represents incremental profit, since the output increase was not possible to achieve with the old equipment. The relevant elements involved are the sales revenue ($37,500) less those costs which are affected by the additional output. Since no additional operators are required to operate the machine at its top speed, no additional labor cost is incurred. Additional materials, however, are used up and these are charged at the usage rate of the new machine (36 cents per unit). Selling and promotional expenses required to move the additional volume are estimated at $10,500 and $13,000 per year, respectively.

Third, the *differential depreciation* is calculated. As we discussed in detail in Chapter 1, depreciation has no relevance as an economic funds flow, and in our analysis it has merit only as a tax-deductible expense. The ability to charge depreciation against federal income taxes normally reduces the tax payment of the business, and in that sense the depreciation write-off serves as a "tax shield." If an investment alternative results in higher or lower depreciation charges, the change must be analyzed with regard to the impact on federal income tax. This was done in the present case, where the differential depreciation for the next five years of operations will be $1,500, an increase in write-off due to the higher cost of the new machine. After the tax calculation, the depreciation differential is added back to the aftertax profit improvement of $3,510 to arrive at the operating cash flow of $5,010. In this way the depreciation charge correctly caused a tax reduction but was not left in the final result to distort the economic impact of the investment. The same result can, of course, be obtained by doing the analysis in two stages: (a) determining the tax on the operating improvement before depreciation and (b) determining the tax shield effect of the differential depreciation. In our example the picture would be as follows, with exactly the same result:

Taxable operating improvement	$8,000
Tax at 46%	3,680
Aftertax operating improvement	4,320
Tax shield at 46%* of depreciation of $1,500 ...	690
Aftertax operating cash flow	$5,010

* Note that each dollar of depreciation provides a tax shield of $1 times the tax rate applicable.

The applicable tax rate will normally be the rate a company would be paying on any incremental profit.

Economic Life Refined

A complication has been introduced because of the assumed difference in lives between the old and the new machines. Since the old machine is expected to expire in five years while the new one will last for ten, the period of comparability is only the next five years. After that period, the original alternative no longer exists, and something would have to be done at that point in any case. We can picture the situation as in Figure 4–3.

Figure 4–3
OVERLAPPING ECONOMIC LIFE SPANS

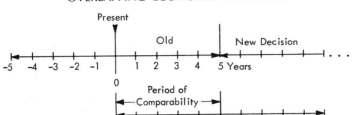

Differential revenues and costs exist only as long as both alternatives exist *together*, and after five years the old machine will be gone. Consequently, we *cannot* analyze the situation beyond five years without making some assumptions about the life remaining in the new machine. While the economic life of the new machine is likely to be ten years, as we have no doubts about selling the output for that length of time, the economic comparison can be made only over five years. There are two ways of handling this problem. First, we can cut off the analysis at year 5, by determining the economic value of the new machine at this point and counting this "capital recovery" as a benefit. This is done quite commonly in practice. Second, we can alternatively assume that a new machine would take the place of the old one at year 5, with a life of ten years, and a similar replacement would be made at year 10 when our current new machine expires. This approach involves a great deal of guessing about replacement conditions five and ten years hence, and it will be difficult under any circumstances to arrive at a fully comparable life span. Both approaches require the more flexible present value techniques.

From the preceding discussion it has become clear that rules of thumb and rough analyses can serve only limited purposes, especially if the additional considerations are complex and the timing of cash inflows and outflows varies significantly. For this purpose we now return to the use of the time-adjusted techniques which are generally able to provide us with reasonable economic answers to our investment problems.

Application of Present Value Analysis

We recall that the replacement involved a current net investment of $26,150 and operating cash flows of $5,010 per year for the five-year period of comparison. 'It was also indicated that the analysis would have to consider the fact that after five years a new decision had to be made in any case, and that the most straightforward way of handling the problem of uneven lives was to cut off the analysis at the fifth year and to recognize the economic value of the new machine at that time. We shall assume that the economic value of the new machine will be equal to its book value of $20,000 ($40,000 less five years' depreciation at $4,000 per year) with no taxable gain or loss expected. This judgment would, of course, have to be modified if the circumstances indicated a different value (higher or lower) to be expected due to technological change or other conditions. Book value is often used because it is simple to do (no need to recognize taxable gains or losses) and also since the power of discounting tends to minimize judgmental errors on such elements of analysis which are placed further out in time.

With these data at hand, we can now lay out the problem for present value analysis, assuming a 10 percent return standard, as shown in the time pattern of Table 4–6. The result of the calculation is a sizable net present value of better than $5,200 which indicates that the replacement is desirable. Note that the analysis recognizes the recovery of the book value of the machine at the end of year 5 as an *inflow* even though there may be no intention of selling the machine in fact. This is recognition of an economic value not chargeable to the current decision covering the five-year period ahead. The net investment in present value terms thus becomes a smaller figure, $13,730, representing the actual commitment of economic value to the proposition.

Table 4–6
PRESENT VALUE ANALYSIS OF REPLACEMENT

Time Period	Investment	Operating Cash Inflows	P.V. Factors at 10 Percent*	P.V. of Net Investment	P.V. of Operating Inflows
0	−$26,150	—	1.000	−$26,150	—
1	—	+$ 5,010	0.909	—	+$ 4,554
2	—	+ 5,010	0.826	—	+ 4,138
3	—	+ 5,010	0.751	—	+ 3,763
4	—	+ 5,010	0.683	—	+ 3,422
5	—	+ 5,010	0.621	—	+ 3,111
5 (end) ...	+ 20,000	—	0.621	+ 12,420	—
	−$ 6,150	+$25,050		−$13,730	+$18,988
				Net present value = +$ 5,258	

* For years 1 to 5, we could use 3,791 from Table 4–11.

The *present value index* of the project is $18,988 ÷ $13,730 = 1.38, again an indication of a quite favorable project, given validity of the estimates. Some analysts prefer to express the present value index by relating the present value of *all* inflows, including capital investment recoveries, to the original net investment at point zero. The result in this case would be $31,408 ÷ $26,150 = 1.20, again a favorable showing. While there are arguments for and against both methods, a consistent application of either will be satisfactory.

The *present value payback* (minimum life) must be found by cumulating the present values of the operating inflows until they approximate the net investment of $13,730. A quick addition shows that this will happen after about 3⅓ years, leaving a cushion of 1⅔ years against uncertainty. Now the question arises whether the recovery assumed at the end of year 5 should be considered at an earlier point for a more correct answer. To do this, however, would involve a process of *iteration,* since not only would the present value of the recovery rise but so would the economic value itself in earlier years. Normally such a refinement is not called for, but it can certainly be handled, especially if a company employs a computer program for present value analysis.

The *annualized net present value* in this case is $5,258 ÷ 3.791, or approximately $1,400 per year. All other elements being equal, the project would still be acceptable if the annual operating cash inflows over the five years were only $3,623, a possible error of almost 30 percent!

Another way of looking at the net present value cushion would be, of course, to ask how much of a reduction in expected capital recovery would be tolerable. This can easily be found by reconstituting a dollar amount at the end of year 5 which has a present value of $5,258. We simply divide this present value by the 10 percent factor for period 5 in Table 4–10 of 0.621 and find that the expected recovery of $20,000 could be reduced by about $8,500 and still leave the project acceptable.

The *yield* of the project has to be found by trial and error, since the cash flow pattern is complicated by the capital recovery at the end of year 5. The problem can be handled as shown in Table 4–7. A trial at 15 percent indicates that the net present value is still a positive $584, which is reversed to a negative $227 at 16 percent. Thus the yield must be slightly less than 16 percent.

A more general *complex cash flow pattern* is represented by the next illustration, as displayed in Table 4–8, which assumes

Table 4–7
PRESENT VALUE ANALYSIS TO FIND YIELD

Time Period	Cash Flows	P.V. Factors at 15 Percent	Present Values	P. V. Factors at 16 Percent	Present Values
0	−$26,150	1.000	−$26,150	1.000	−$26,150
1 ⎫					
2 ⎪					
3 ⎬	+ 5,010/yr.	3.352*	+ 16,794	3.274	+ 16,403
4 ⎪					
5 ⎭					
5 (end) ...	+ 20,000	0.497	+ 9,940	0.476	+ 9,520
	+$18,900		+$ 584		−$ 227

* From Table 4–11.

Table 4–8
PRESENT VALUE ANALYSIS OF COMPLEX PROJECT

Time Period	Investments	Operating Cash Inflows	P.V. Factors at 12 Percent	Present Value of Investments	P.V. of Operating Inflows
0	−$130,000 (facilities)		1.000	−$130,000	—
1	− 25,000 (working capital)	+$ 20,000	0.893*	− 22,325	+$ 17,860
2	− 20,000 (working capital)	+ 40,000	0.797*	− 15,940	—
3	—	+ 40,000	2.144†	—	+ 85,760
4	—	+ 40,000		—	—
4 (end)	− 15,000 (additional equipment)‡		0.636*	− 9,540	—
5	—	+ 50,000	1.075†	—	+ 53,750
6	—	+ 50,000		—	—
6 (end)	− 10,000 (equipment overhaul)‡	—	0.507*	− 5,070	—
7	—	+ 20,000	0.452*	—	+ 9,040
8	—	+ 10,000	0.404*	—	+ 4,040
8 (end)	+ 25,000 (equipment recovery)‡	—	0.404*	+ 24,240	—
8 (end)	+ 35,000 (working capital recovery)‖	—		—	—
	−$140,000	+$270,000 (all tax adjustments made)		−$158,635	+$170,450

Net present value = +$ 11,815

* From Table 4–10
† From Table 4–11, representing the difference between the annuity factors applicable: 3.037−.893, and 4.112−3.037, respectively.
‡ Additional depreciation has been reflected in cash inflows.
‖ Assume loss in liquidation of $10,000.

not only an initial capital outlay for facilities and a terminal recovery but also the commitment of *working capital* in the first two years of the project, and additional *equipment outlays* with recoveries assumed at the end of eight years. Furthermore, the operating cash flows *vary considerably* over the years. Nothing new in methodology is required to handle these situations. Working capital (additional inventories and receivables less trade obligations) represents a commitment of capital just as definite as is the case with buildings and equipment, except that no depreciation is incurred. We can assume that commitments are made *during* a given time period instead of at the end, since the requirements for working capital build up or decline gradually in response to volume changes. If all inventories and receivables (less payables) can be expected to be liquidated at the end of the economic life, the capital will be fully recovered and can be shown as an inflow. If some losses are expected, a lower figure must be used.

Additional facilities expenditures during the life of the project are simply recognized as cash outflows when incurred, and care must be taken to reflect their depreciation patterns as additional tax shields in future operating periods. Uneven operating cash flows present no further problems. If partial annuities are encountered, the additive nature of Table 4–11 can be exploited to reduce the chore of analysis somewhat in stages, as illustrated.

All of these elements are combined in our general example and would appear as shown in Table 4–8. The result is a positive net present value of about $12,000, which leaves little margin for error, since on an annualized basis the operating cash inflows can be off by only $11,815 ÷ 4.968, or approximately $2,400 per year. The minimum life is a little more than six years, and the yield about 13 percent. (The reader is invited to check the yield by reworking the analysis at 14 percent.) The present value index is approximately 1.07 if we relate the present values of the investments and the operating inflows. If we use the concept of relating only the present value of the outflows to the present value of all inflows, including recoveries, the present value index drops slightly to about 1.06.

Accelerated depreciation commonly used for tax purposes causes additional complications. Since the various methods of fast depreciation write-offs invariably result in uneven declining amounts per year, the calculation of the tax shield effect year by year becomes tedious. Moreover, economic and depreciation lives often differ, adding to the complexity. Many users of present value analysis have found it useful to develop sets of tables for this particular need which provide factors to find the present value of all depreciation write-offs over the economic life in one lump, from which the total tax shield can be determined. A sample page of such tables (Table 4–12) is found at the end of the chapter, and the references contain publications with such tables. The use of computer models eases the calculation problems, of course. At this writing, legislative proposals to speed up tax depreciation write-offs further as an incentive to business investment were being actively reviewed.

Uneven lives among alternatives are often a problem. It is critical that alternatives be analyzed over a comparable time span. In our example, on page 159, the approach of cutting off the analysis was taken. Another way of handling such problems is to annualize the relevant cash flows. In the case of replacement analysis, one can determine the annualized cost of going on as is and compare this amount with the annualized cost over the economic life of a new piece of equipment, including the net investment amortization. These methods raise additional detailed conceptual questions which are best dealt with in more specialized texts, such as are listed in the references.

Mutually exclusive alternatives (with equal lives) for handling a given investment proposal are often best handled through incremental analysis. For example, if three types of machines are available to handle the production of a new product, and each not only requires a different capital outlay but also provides different operating cash flows over the same time span, incremental analysis will be quite helpful. It becomes relevant and least strenuous to analyze first the alternative requiring the *least* capital outlay. If the investment passes the test, the next lowest capital outlay should be compared to the first based on the *additional* (incremental) capital required and the *additional* (incremental) operating cash flow generated. If it turns out that this incremental outlay is justified by the incremental cash flow, then the second alternative appears to be the proper choice. The third (and any other) even costlier alternative can be handled in the same way. The advantage of this approach is that normally the first analysis will establish the desirability of the investment move per se, and further analysis is made dependent on this decision. Also, one can avoid the trap of choosing a costlier alternative which still passes the criteria, when in fact a less costly one would have been a more efficient use of capital, freeing the incremental funds for better uses elsewhere. Again, however, a final decision cannot be made without reference to the total capital budgeting process.

Leasing has found increasing popularity as a means to obtain the use of a wide variety of capital assets. This has led to the need for a consistent framework of analysis. Leasing is a form of financing which should be considered *after* the basic investment has been established as acceptable under the methods we have discussed in this chapter. The charges levied against the lessee contain elements of interest, risk, obsolescence, maintenance charges, and profit to the owner, all depending on the nature of the lease written, which can vary widely. Since we have viewed capital investment analysis as an economic cash flow trade-off independent of the financing needed to acquire the asset in question, lease analysis must—for consistency—be carried out in a way which eliminates the financing aspect of the arrangement for the cash flow calculations. The most common of the several techniques (available also on computer time-share systems) strips the leasing cash flows of imputed financing charges. Because of the complexity of the analysis required to deal with leasing, and because of its specialized nature, the reader is referred to the literature at the end of this chapter.

Inflationary effects on investment analysis are often raised as an issue. If projections are made in constant dollars, that is, only reflecting cost/price changes beyond general inflation— "real" changes—the discount rate applied will not have to be adjusted. If a more normal projection method is used, with increases in prices and costs spelled out, it may be useful to raise the discount standard to compensate for the loss in purchasing power. Care must be taken in the projections, however, to reflect proper price trends of the individual elements, instead of assuming the same level of inflation for each. At the same time, the discount standard must reflect an overall inflation adjustment. The many issues connected with this problem go beyond the scope of our discussion, and the reader is invited to check the references at the end of the chapter.

The *accuracy* implied in the precise mathematical nature of the present value process and the tables of factors calls for a final word of caution. As pointed out before, the character of the cash flows analyzed is that of estimates, projections, forecasts, and sometimes guesses. It would therefore be spurious indeed to carry the analysis to the final precision possible. In our examples we have provided the analysis at greater levels of accuracy than probably is necessary, with the mere intention that the reader could check the data for complete understanding. In practice, liberal rounding of the various calculations, particularly of the final results, is desirable, to keep the process from overwhelming the realistic judgments required. This was at times implied in this chapter by our use of approximate results in the discussion. The need for perspective is even greater when we realize that the power of discounting, particularly in more distant periods, is such that through the reduction to present value, even widely varying estimates will often not greatly affect the end result. A glance at the present value tables, which show the shrinkage of the factors in later periods and at higher discount rates, should drive this point home.

RISK ANALYSIS

As we discussed the various present value tools for analysis, an informal methodology for risk adjustment emerged. The determination of minimum life and the annualization of the net present value are *in effect* risk analyses, which serve to establish parameters within which the project remains acceptable. More formal methods are called for, however, to assess risk and the effect of uncertainty surrounding key variables on the final results. We have referred before to "sensitivity analysis," which is a way of systematically working through the impact of assumed changes in revenues, operating savings, costs, size of outlays and recoveries, and so on, on the final result. Often major projects are analyzed at three levels of assumptions— expected, optimistic, and pessimistic—to see if the project is acceptable under most conditions likely to be encountered.

An even more formal approach is found in the use of assigned probability weights to a variety of conditions and key variables, to determine the weighted average outcome as a measure of the project's attractiveness. The calculation of this "expectation," based on careful judgments by those in a company best qualified to make them, might take the form shown in Table 4–9. The calculated expectation, on average, will not necessarily come true as the *specific* result of the project, since the most likely estimated occurrence is $40,000 (25 percent probability). The weighted average, however, can often be a useful and consistent input to present value analysis as the basis of comparison for various projects whose results have been similarly calculated. Much more theoretical and conceptual background is necessary to develop these ideas further, and references for additional study are provided at the end.

The most recent practical applications of risk analysis go beyond the mere probabilistic assessment of a calculated result, such as annual operating cash flows. The development of fairly sophisticated computer models has made it possible for decision makers to estimate, for each of a dozen or more key variables of major projects, ranges of possible outcomes and

Table 4–9
RANGE OF LIKELY RESULTS
AND THEIR PROBABILITIES

Possible Levels of Annual Operating Cash Inflows	Probability (weights)	Adjusted Results
$20,000	0.05	$ 1,000
25,000	0.10	2,500
30,000	0.15	4,500
40,000	0.25	10,000
50,000	0.15	7,500
55,000	0.10	5,500
60,000	0.10	6,000
65,000	0.10	6,500
	1.00	$43,500
		(expectation)

the probability distributions for these ranges. Such "distributions" may be placed around unit volume, prices, key cost elements, cost of facilities, recoveries at the end of the project life, and so on. The computer model will then simulate, based on the specified probabilities and within a present value framework, a series of outcomes of the project and summarize the results. This "Monte Carlo technique" is an application of probability theory receiving much attention in industry, since it is possible to simulate on paper hundreds and even thousands of trials of the proposition. The output of the computer model allows the following type of statement to be made: "There is a probability of 60 percent that the net present value of the project will be at least $0.5 million or better"; or, "Chances are 9 out of 10 that the project will meet the minimum standard of 10 percent." A "risk profile" can be drawn in the form of a cumulative probability distribution for competing projects which graphically displays the probability of reaching or exceeding any specified level of such measures as net present value, yield, or years of present value payback. A display such as Figure 4–4 provides management with a tool to match the riskiness of the project against its own risk preferences.

Table 4-10

PRESENT VALUE OF SINGLE SUM OF $1 RECEIVED OR PAID AT END OF PERIOD

Period of Receipt or Payment	1%	2%	4%	5%	6%	8%	10%	12%	14%	15%	16%	18%	20%	22%	24%	25%	26%	28%	30%	35%	40%	45%	50%
1	0.990	0.980	0.962	0.952	0.943	0.926	0.909	0.893	0.877	0.870	0.862	0.847	0.833	0.820	0.806	0.800	0.794	0.781	0.769	0.741	0.714	0.690	0.667
2	0.980	0.961	0.925	0.907	0.890	0.857	0.826	0.797	0.769	0.756	0.743	0.718	0.694	0.672	0.650	0.640	0.630	0.610	0.592	0.549	0.510	0.476	0.444
3	0.971	0.942	0.889	0.863	0.840	0.794	0.751	0.712	0.675	0.658	0.641	0.609	0.579	0.551	0.524	0.512	0.500	0.477	0.455	0.406	0.364	0.328	0.296
4	0.961	0.924	0.855	0.823	0.792	0.735	0.683	0.636	0.592	0.572	0.552	0.516	0.482	0.451	0.423	0.410	0.397	0.373	0.350	0.301	0.260	0.226	0.198
5	0.951	0.906	0.822	0.784	0.747	0.681	0.621	0.567	0.519	0.497	0.476	0.437	0.402	0.370	0.341	0.328	0.315	0.291	0.269	0.223	0.186	0.156	0.132
6	0.942	0.888	0.790	0.746	0.705	0.630	0.564	0.507	0.456	0.432	0.410	0.370	0.335	0.303	0.275	0.262	0.250	0.227	0.207	0.165	0.133	0.108	0.088
7	0.933	0.871	0.760	0.711	0.665	0.583	0.513	0.452	0.400	0.376	0.354	0.314	0.279	0.249	0.222	0.210	0.198	0.178	0.159	0.122	0.095	0.074	0.059
8	0.923	0.853	0.731	0.677	0.627	0.540	0.467	0.404	0.351	0.327	0.305	0.266	0.233	0.204	0.179	0.168	0.157	0.139	0.123	0.091	0.068	0.051	0.039
9	0.914	0.837	0.703	0.645	0.592	0.500	0.424	0.361	0.308	0.284	0.263	0.225	0.194	0.167	0.144	0.134	0.125	0.108	0.094	0.067	0.048	0.035	0.026
10	0.905	0.820	0.676	0.614	0.558	0.463	0.386	0.322	0.270	0.247	0.227	0.191	0.162	0.137	0.116	0.107	0.099	0.085	0.073	0.050	0.035	0.024	0.017
11	0.896	0.804	0.650	0.585	0.527	0.429	0.350	0.287	0.237	0.215	0.195	0.162	0.135	0.112	0.094	0.086	0.079	0.066	0.056	0.037	0.025	0.017	0.012
12	0.887	0.788	0.625	0.557	0.497	0.397	0.319	0.257	0.208	0.187	0.168	0.137	0.112	0.092	0.076	0.069	0.062	0.052	0.043	0.027	0.018	0.012	0.008
13	0.879	0.773	0.601	0.530	0.469	0.368	0.290	0.229	0.182	0.163	0.145	0.116	0.093	0.075	0.061	0.055	0.050	0.040	0.033	0.020	0.013	0.008	0.005
14	0.870	0.758	0.577	0.505	0.442	0.340	0.263	0.205	0.160	0.141	0.125	0.099	0.078	0.062	0.049	0.044	0.039	0.032	0.025	0.015	0.009	0.006	0.003
15	0.861	0.743	0.555	0.481	0.417	0.315	0.239	0.183	0.140	0.123	0.108	0.084	0.065	0.051	0.040	0.035	0.031	0.025	0.020	0.011	0.006	0.004	0.002
16	0.853	0.728	0.534	0.458	0.394	0.292	0.218	0.163	0.123	0.107	0.093	0.071	0.054	0.042	0.032	0.028	0.025	0.019	0.015	0.008	0.005	0.003	0.002
17	0.844	0.714	0.513	0.436	0.371	0.270	0.198	0.146	0.108	0.093	0.080	0.060	0.045	0.034	0.026	0.023	0.020	0.015	0.012	0.006	0.003	0.002	0.001
18	0.836	0.700	0.494	0.416	0.350	0.250	0.180	0.130	0.095	0.081	0.069	0.051	0.038	0.028	0.021	0.018	0.016	0.012	0.009	0.005	0.002	0.001	0.001
19	0.828	0.686	0.475	0.396	0.331	0.232	0.164	0.116	0.083	0.070	0.060	0.043	0.031	0.023	0.017	0.014	0.012	0.009	0.007	0.003	0.002	0.001	
20	0.820	0.673	0.456	0.377	0.312	0.215	0.149	0.104	0.073	0.061	0.051	0.037	0.026	0.019	0.014	0.012	0.010	0.007	0.005	0.002	0.001		
21	0.811	0.660	0.439	0.359	0.294	0.199	0.135	0.093	0.064	0.053	0.044	0.031	0.022	0.015	0.011	0.009	0.008	0.006	0.004	0.002	0.001		
22	0.803	0.647	0.422	0.342	0.278	0.184	0.123	0.083	0.056	0.046	0.038	0.026	0.018	0.013	0.009	0.007	0.006	0.004	0.003	0.001	0.001		
23	0.795	0.634	0.406	0.326	0.262	0.170	0.112	0.074	0.049	0.040	0.033	0.022	0.015	0.010	0.007	0.006	0.005	0.003	0.002	0.001			
24	0.788	0.622	0.390	0.310	0.247	0.158	0.102	0.066	0.043	0.035	0.028	0.019	0.013	0.008	0.006	0.005	0.004	0.003	0.002	0.001			
25	0.780	0.610	0.375	0.295	0.233	0.146	0.092	0.059	0.038	0.030	0.024	0.016	0.010	0.007	0.005	0.004	0.003	0.002	0.001	0.001			
26	0.772	0.598	0.361	0.281	0.220	0.135	0.084	0.053	0.033	0.026	0.021	0.014	0.009	0.006	0.004	0.003	0.002	0.002	0.001				
27	0.764	0.586	0.347	0.268	0.207	0.125	0.076	0.047	0.029	0.023	0.018	0.011	0.007	0.005	0.003	0.002	0.002	0.001	0.001				
28	0.757	0.574	0.333	0.255	0.196	0.116	0.069	0.042	0.026	0.020	0.016	0.010	0.006	0.004	0.002	0.002	0.002	0.001	0.001				
29	0.749	0.563	0.321	0.243	0.185	0.107	0.063	0.037	0.022	0.017	0.014	0.008	0.005	0.003	0.002	0.002	0.001	0.001	0.001				
30	0.742	0.552	0.308	0.231	0.174	0.099	0.057	0.033	0.020	0.015	0.012	0.007	0.004	0.003	0.002	0.001	0.001	0.001	0.001				
35	0.706	0.500	0.253	0.181	0.130	0.066	0.036	0.019	0.010	0.008	0.006	0.003	0.002	0.001									
40	0.672	0.453	0.208	0.142	0.097	0.046	0.022	0.011	0.005	0.004	0.003	0.001	0.001										
45	0.639	0.410	0.171	0.111	0.073	0.031	0.014	0.006	0.003	0.002	0.001	0.001											
50	0.608	0.372	0.141	0.087	0.054	0.021	0.009	0.003	0.001	0.001	0.001												
60	0.550	0.305	0.095	0.054	0.030	0.010	0.002	0.001															

1. To find P.V. of future amount:
   P.V. = Factor × Amount
2. To find future amount representing given P.V.:
   Amount = P.V./Factor
3. To find period given future amount, P.V. and yield:
   Factor = P.V./Amount; locate in column
4. To find yield given future amount, P.V. and period:
   Factor = P.V./Amount; locate in row

Table 4–11

PRESENT VALUE OF $1 PER PERIOD RECEIVED OR PAID AT END OF EACH PERIOD

Number of Periods	1%	2%	4%	5%	6%	8%	10%	12%	14%	15%	16%	18%	20%	22%	24%	25%	26%	28%	30%	35%	40%	45%	50%
1	0.990	0.980	0.962	0.952	0.943	0.926	0.909	0.893	0.877	0.870	0.862	0.847	0.833	0.820	0.806	0.800	0.794	0.781	0.769	0.741	0.714	0.690	0.667
2	1.970	1.942	1.886	1.859	1.833	1.783	1.736	1.690	1.647	1.626	1.605	1.566	1.528	1.492	1.457	1.440	1.424	1.392	1.361	1.289	1.224	1.165	1.111
3	2.941	2.884	2.775	2.722	2.673	2.577	2.487	2.402	2.322	2.283	2.246	2.174	2.106	2.042	1.981	1.952	1.923	1.868	1.816	1.696	1.589	1.493	1.407
4	3.902	3.808	3.630	3.545	3.465	3.312	3.170	3.037	2.914	2.855	2.798	2.690	2.589	2.494	2.404	2.362	2.320	2.241	2.166	1.997	1.849	1.720	1.605
5	4.853	4.713	4.452	4.329	4.212	3.993	3.791	3.605	3.433	3.352	3.274	3.127	2.991	2.864	2.745	2.689	2.635	2.532	2.436	2.220	2.035	1.876	1.737
6	5.795	5.601	5.242	5.075	4.917	4.623	4.355	4.111	3.889	3.784	3.685	3.498	3.326	3.167	3.020	2.951	2.885	2.759	2.643	2.385	2.168	1.983	1.824
7	6.728	6.472	6.002	5.786	5.582	5.206	4.868	4.564	4.288	4.160	4.039	3.812	3.605	3.416	3.242	3.161	3.083	2.937	2.802	2.508	2.263	2.057	1.883
8	7.652	7.325	6.733	6.463	6.210	5.747	5.335	4.968	4.639	4.487	4.344	4.078	3.837	3.619	3.421	3.329	3.241	3.076	2.925	2.598	2.331	2.108	1.922
9	8.566	8.162	7.435	7.108	6.802	6.247	5.759	5.328	4.946	4.772	4.607	4.303	4.031	3.786	3.566	3.463	3.366	3.184	3.019	2.665	2.379	2.144	1.948
10	9.471	8.983	8.111	7.722	7.360	6.710	6.145	5.650	5.216	5.019	4.833	4.494	4.192	3.923	3.682	3.571	3.465	3.269	3.092	2.715	2.414	2.168	1.965
11	10.368	9.787	8.760	8.307	7.887	7.139	6.495	5.938	5.453	5.234	5.029	4.656	4.327	4.035	3.776	3.656	3.544	3.335	3.147	2.752	2.438	2.185	1.977
12	11.255	10.575	9.385	8.863	8.384	7.536	6.814	6.194	5.660	5.421	5.197	4.793	4.439	4.127	3.851	3.725	3.606	3.387	3.190	2.779	2.456	2.196	1.985
13	12.134	11.343	9.986	9.393	8.853	7.904	7.103	6.424	5.842	5.583	5.342	4.910	4.533	4.203	3.912	3.780	3.656	3.427	3.223	2.799	2.468	2.204	1.990
14	13.004	12.106	10.563	9.898	9.295	8.244	7.367	6.628	6.002	5.724	5.468	5.008	4.611	4.265	3.962	3.824	3.695	3.459	3.249	2.814	2.477	2.210	1.993
15	13.865	12.849	11.118	10.379	9.712	8.559	7.606	6.811	6.142	5.847	5.575	5.092	4.675	4.315	4.001	3.859	3.726	3.483	3.268	2.825	2.484	2.214	1.995
16	14.718	13.578	11.652	10.838	10.106	8.851	7.824	6.974	6.265	5.954	5.669	5.162	4.730	4.357	4.033	3.887	3.751	3.503	3.283	2.834	2.489	2.216	1.997
17	15.562	14.292	12.116	11.274	10.477	9.122	8.022	7.120	6.373	6.047	5.749	5.222	4.775	4.391	4.059	3.910	3.771	3.518	3.295	2.840	2.492	2.218	1.998
18	16.398	14.992	12.659	11.690	10.828	9.372	8.201	7.250	6.467	6.128	5.818	5.273	4.812	4.419	4.080	3.928	3.786	3.529	3.304	2.844	2.494	2.219	1.999
19	17.226	15.678	13.134	12.086	11.158	9.604	8.365	7.366	6.550	6.198	5.877	5.316	4.844	4.442	4.097	3.942	3.799	3.539	3.311	2.848	2.496	2.220	1.999
20	18.046	16.351	13.590	12.463	11.470	9.818	8.514	7.469	6.623	6.259	5.929	5.353	4.870	4.460	4.110	3.954	3.808	3.546	3.316	2.850	2.497	2.221	1.999
21	18.857	17.011	14.029	12.821	11.764	10.017	8.649	7.562	6.687	6.312	5.973	5.384	4.891	4.476	4.121	3.963	3.816	3.551	3.320	2.852	2.498	2.221	2.000
22	19.660	17.658	14.451	13.163	12.042	10.201	8.772	7.645	6.743	6.359	6.011	5.410	4.909	4.488	4.130	3.970	3.822	3.556	3.323	2.853	2.498	2.222	2.000
23	20.456	18.292	14.857	13.489	12.303	10.371	8.883	7.718	6.792	6.399	6.044	5.432	4.925	4.499	4.137	3.976	3.827	3.559	3.325	2.854	2.499	2.222	2.000
24	21.243	18.914	15.247	13.799	12.550	10.529	8.985	7.784	6.835	6.434	6.073	5.451	4.937	4.507	4.143	3.981	3.831	3.562	3.327	2.855	2.499	2.222	2.000
25	22.023	19.523	15.622	14.094	12.783	10.675	9.077	7.843	6.873	6.464	6.097	5.467	4.948	4.514	4.147	3.985	3.834	3.564	3.329	2.856	2.499	2.222	2.000
26	22.795	20.121	15.983	14.375	13.003	10.810	9.161	7.896	6.906	6.491	6.118	5.480	4.956	4.520	4.151	3.988	3.837	3.566	3.330	2.856	2.500	2.222	2.000
27	23.560	20.707	16.330	14.643	13.211	10.935	9.237	7.943	6.935	6.514	6.136	5.492	4.964	4.524	4.154	3.990	3.839	3.567	3.331	2.856	2.500	2.222	2.000
28	24.316	21.281	16.663	14.898	13.406	11.051	9.307	7.984	6.961	6.534	6.152	5.502	4.970	4.528	4.157	3.992	3.840	3.568	3.331	2.857	2.500	2.222	2.000
29	25.066	21.844	16.984	15.141	13.591	11.158	9.370	8.022	6.983	6.551	6.166	5.510	4.975	4.531	4.159	3.994	3.841	3.569	3.332	2.857	2.500	2.222	2.000
30	25.808	22.396	17.292	15.372	13.765	11.258	9.427	8.055	7.003	6.566	6.177	5.517	4.979	4.534	4.160	3.995	3.842	3.569	3.332	2.857	2.500	2.222	2.000
35	29.408	24.999	18.665	16.374	14.498	11.654	9.644	8.175	7.070	6.617	6.215	5.539	4.992	4.541	4.164	3.998	3.845	3.571	3.333	2.857	2.500	2.222	2.000
40	32.835	27.355	19.793	17.159	15.046	11.925	9.779	8.244	7.105	6.642	6.234	5.548	4.997	4.544	4.166	3.999	3.846	3.571	3.333	2.857	2.500	2.222	2.000
45	36.094	29.490	20.720	17.774	15.456	12.108	9.863	8.282	7.123	6.654	6.242	5.552	4.999	4.545	4.166	4.000	3.846	3.571	3.333	2.857	2.500	2.222	2.000
50	39.196	31.424	21.482	18.256	15.762	12.234	9.915	8.304	7.133	6.661	6.246	5.554	4.999	4.545	4.167	4.000	3.846	3.571	3.333	2.857	2.500	2.222	2.000
60	44.955	34.761	22.623	18.929	16.161	12.376	9.967	8.324	7.140	6.665	6.249	5.555	5.000	4.545	4.167	4.000	3.846	3.571	3.333	2.857	2.500	2.222	2.000

1. To find P.V. of series of equal receipts or payments:
   P.V. = Factor × Annuity

2. To find annuity representing given P.V.:
   Annuity = P.V./Factor

3. To find number of periods to recover investment:
   Factor = Investment/Annuity; locate in column

4. To find yield of annuity given investment:
   Factor = Investment/Annuity; locate in row

Table 4-12

SAMPLE PRESENT VALUE TABLE FOR ACCELERATED DEPRECIATION

Present Value of Depreciation Write-Off Using
Double-Declining Balance Method with Switch
to Straight-Line Method*

Opportunity Rate	Asset Tax Life	Analysis Life in Years							
		4	5	6	8	10	12	15	20
6%	3	0.890	0.890	0.890	0.890	0.890	0.890	0.890	0.890
	4	0.823	0.869	0.869	0.869	0.869	0.869	0.869	0.869
	6	0.655	0.728	0.797	0.830	0.830	0.830	0.830	0.830
	10	0.465	0.533	0.584	0.688	0.742	0.759	0.759	0.759
	12	0.404	0.469	0.521	0.596	0.659	0.715	0.728	0.728
	16	0.319	0.377	0.425	0.497	0.548	0.591	0.646	0.671
	20	0.263	0.315	0.358	0.426	0.475	0.511	0.556	0.616
	45	0.125	0.153	0.179	0.222	0.257	0.285	0.318	0.354
8%	3	0.857	0.857	0.857	0.857	0.857	0.857	0.857	0.857
	4	0.789	0.830	0.830	0.830	0.830	0.830	0.830	0.830
	6	0.626	0.692	0.753	0.781	0.781	0.781	0.781	0.781
	10	0.443	0.504	0.550	0.622	0.683	0.697	0.697	0.697
	12	0.384	0.444	0.489	0.554	0.606	0.650	0.660	0.660
	16	0.303	0.356	0.398	0.461	0.502	0.537	0.579	0.596
	20	0.250	0.297	0.335	0.394	0.434	0.463	0.497	0.539
	45	0.119	0.144	0.167	0.204	0.233	0.256	0.280	0.306

10%								
3	0.825	0.825	0.825	0.825	0.825	0.825	0.825	0.825
4	0.756	0.794	0.794	0.794	0.794	0.794	0.794	0.794
6	0.598	0.658	0.712	0.737	0.737	0.737	0.737	0.737
10	0.422	0.478	0.518	0.580	0.631	0.642	0.642	0.642
12	0.366	0.420	0.460	0.516	0.559	0.594	0.602	0.602
16	0.289	0.336	0.374	0.427	0.462	0.489	0.521	0.534
20	0.238	0.280	0.314	0.365	0.398	0.421	0.447	0.476
45	0.113	0.136	0.156	0.188	0.212	0.230	0.249	0.266
12%								
3	0.794	0.794	0.794	0.794	0.794	0.794	0.794	0.794
4	0.725	0.759	0.759	0.759	0.759	0.759	0.759	0.759
6	0.572	0.626	0.674	0.696	0.696	0.696	0.696	0.696
10	0.402	0.453	0.488	0.542	0.584	0.593	0.593	0.593
12	0.349	0.397	0.433	0.481	0.517	0.545	0.551	0.551
16	0.275	0.318	0.351	0.397	0.426	0.447	0.472	0.481
20	0.226	0.264	0.295	0.338	0.366	0.384	0.404	0.424
45	0.107	0.128	0.146	0.173	0.193	0.208	0.222	0.234

Example 1

To find the present value of all depreciation over a 10-year analysis life for a $10,000 asset with a tax life of 16 years, when the opportunity rate is 10%:

$$P.V. = f \times S = 0.462 \times \$10,000 = \$4,620$$

Example 2

To find the present value of the depreciation tax shield of the asset in Example 1 over an eight-year analysis life, when the opportunity rate is 12% and the income tax rate is 46%:

$$P.V. = f \times S \times Tx = 0.397 \times \$10,000 \times 0.46 = \$1,826$$

* The continuous method of discounting employed here differs slightly from that of Tables 4–10 and 4–11. Thus, these factors lead to values lower than if the process of Tables 4–10 and 4–11 had been employed.

Figure 4—4

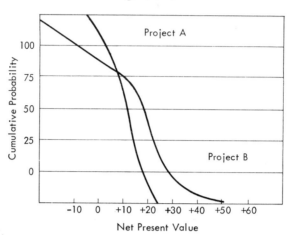

The use of such models is most attractive for major commitments with sizable uncertainties, such as new ventures, rather than for fairly well understood routine requests for funds. Again, the required background for this type of analysis must be sought in literature beyond the scope of this book.

SUMMARY

In this chapter we have provided the highlights of the analytical framework for investment analysis in capital budgeting. The buildup of techniques reached from crude yardsticks to advanced present value concepts. *Critical* to the whole process, however, is the analysis *preceding* the application of the techniques. Here we refer to the statement of the problem, the development and selection of alternatives, and the careful preparation of relevant investment, revenue, and cost data. Once these inputs are satisfactorily developed, the application of the techniques for evaluation becomes *relatively easy*. Conceptual problems still surround the exact interpretation of the measures of economic desirability, but increasingly net present value, accompanied by several other related measures and at times supported by probabilistic analysis, has become accepted in practice. The results of these analyses then become an input to the broader strategic planning task of management known as capital budgeting—the matching of long-range investment commitments with appropriate funds sources, in light of corporate objectives and goals.

SELECTED REFERENCES

Analytical Process

Anthony, Robert N., and Reece, James S. *Accounting: Text and Cases.* 6th ed. Homewood, Ill.: Richard D. Irwin, 1979.

Grant, Eugene. *Principles of Engineering Analysis.* 3d ed. New York: Ronald Press, 1950.

Henry, William R., and Haynes, Warren W. *Managerial Economics.* 4th ed. Dallas, Texas: Business Publications, 1978.

Horngren, Charles T. *Cost Accounting, a Managerial Emphasis.* 4th ed. Englewood Cliffs, N.J.: Prentice-Hall, 1977.

Moore, Carl, and Jaedicke, Robert K. *Managerial Accounting.* 5th ed. Cincinnati, Ohio: South-Western Publishing, 1980.

Pappas, James L., and Brigham, Eugene F. *Managerial Economics.* 3d ed. Hinsdale, Ill.: Dryden Press, 1979.

Weston, J. Fred, and Brigham, Eugene F. *Essentials of Managerial Finance.* 4th ed. Hinsdale, Ill.: Dryden Press, 1977.

Wright, Maurice Gordon. *Discounted Cash Flow.* 2d ed. London, New York: McGraw-Hill, 1973.

Broader Framework of Capital Budgeting

Bierman, Harold Jr., and Smidt, Seymour. *The Capital Budgeting Decision.* 5th ed. New York: Macmillan, 1980.

Christenson, Charles J.; Vancil, Richard F.; and Marshall, Paul W. *Managerial Economics: Text and Cases.* Rev. ed. Homewood, Ill.: Richard D. Irwin, 1973.

Hunt, Pearson; Williams, Charles M.; and Donaldson, Gordon. *Basic Business Finance: Text.* Part IV. Homewood, Ill.: Richard D. Irwin, 1974.

Johnson, Robert W. *Capital Budgeting.* Dubuque, Iowa: Kendall/Hunt Publishing, 1977.

Palda, Kvishan S., ed. *Readings in Managerial Economics*. Englewood Cliffs, N.J.: Prentice-Hall, 1973.

Porterfield, James T.S. *Investment Decisions and Capital Costs*. Englewood Cliffs, N.J.: Prentice-Hall, 1965.

Sharpe, William F. *Portfolio Theory and Capital Markets*. New York, N.Y.: McGraw-Hill, 1970.

Van Horne, James C. *Financial Management and Policy*. 5th ed. Englewood Cliffs, N.J.: Prentice-Hall, 1980.

Specialized Areas

Present Value Tables

Gushee, Charles II., ed. *Financial Compound Interest and Annuity Tables*. 6th ed. Boston: Financial Publishing, 1980.

Thorndike, David. *The Thorndike Encyelopedia of Banking and Financial Tables, 1980 Yearbook*. Boston: Warren, Gorham & Lamset.

Rosen, Lawrence R. *Dow Jones–Irwin Guide to Interest: What You Should Know about the Time Value of Money*. Homewood, Ill.: Dow Jones–Irwin, 1974.

MAPI Method

Terborgh, George. *Business Investment Management*. Washington, D.C.: Machinery and Allied Products Institute, 1967.

Probability Analysis

Hertz, David B. *New Power for Management, Computer Systems and Management Science*. New York: McGraw-Hill, 1969.

Levy, Haim; and Sarna, Marshall. *Capital Investment and Financial Decisions*. Englewood Cliffs, N.J.: Prentice-Hall, 1978.

Schlaifer, Robert O. *Probability and Statistics for Business Decisions*. New York: McGraw-Hill, 1959.

Leasing

Hunt, Pearson; Williams, Charles M.; and Donaldson, Gordon. *Basic Business Finance: Text*. Case 33, pp. 824–32. Homewood, Ill.: Richard D. Irwin, 1974.

Pritchard, Robert E., and Hindelang, Thomas J. *The Lease/Buy Decision*. New York: Amacom, 1980.

Vancil, Richard F., ed. *Financial Executive's Handbook*. Chap. 20. Homewood, Ill.: Dow Jones–Irwin, 1970.

EXERCISES AND PROBLEMS

1. An investment proposition costing $60,000 is expected to result in aftertax cash flows over seven years (received continuously) in the following pattern:

Year	
1	$10,000
2	15,000
3	15,000
4	20,000
5	15,000
6	10,000
7	5,000

  a. Calculate the net present value at 10 percent and at 16 percent.
  b. Determine the yield of the proposition.
  c. If the annual cash flows were an even $13,000 per year for seven years, what would be the net present value at 10 percent?
  d. What level annual cash flows would be required to yield 16 percent?
  e. How would the results of (a) and (b) change if there were a capital recovery of $10,000 at the end of year 7?
  f. How would the result of (d) change if there were a capital recovery of $10,000 at the end of year 7?

2. After having spent and written off against expenses of past periods an estimated $1,150,000 of research and development funds on a new product, the ABC Company is faced with the decision to invest a total of $1,500,000 in a large-scale initial promotional and advertising campaign to bring the product to market. The campaign will be conducted over a six-month period, and all costs will be charged off as expenses in the current year. The effect of the campaign is an estimated average incremental profit of $400,000 per year for at least the next five years, before taxes and without the initial promotional costs. The likely pattern of profits is estimated to be $200,000 in the first year, $300,000 in the second, $600,000 in the third, $500,000 in the fourth, and $400,000 in the fifth year.

Assume that income taxes on incremental profits are paid at the rate of 46 percent and that the company normally has the opportunity to earn 12 percent after taxes. Calculate the various measures of investment desirability, first on the average profit and then on the annual pattern expected. Determine the simple payback and return on investment, average return, net present value, present value index, present value payback, annualized net present value, and yield. What is the effect of the research and development expenditures on these results? Discuss your findings.

3. After careful analysis of a number of possible investments, a trustee of a major estate is weighing the choice between two $100,000 investments he considers to be of equal risk. The first (A) will provide a series of 8 year-end payments to the estate of $16,500 each, while the second (B) will provide a single lump sum of $233,000 at the end of 11 years. Which proposition provides the higher yield? If the normal return experienced by the estate for investments of this risk category is 6 percent, which investment is preferable? Should the pattern of cash flows be a consideration here, and how would this affect the choice? Ignore taxes and discuss your findings.

4. In an effort to replace a manual operation with a more efficient and reliable automatic process, the DEF Company is considering the purchase of a machine which will cost $52,800 installed and has an expected economic life of eight years. It will be depreciated over this period on a straight-line basis for both book and tax purposes, with no salvage value foreseen. The main benefit expected is a true reduction in labor costs due to the elimination of two operator positions and less materials spoilage. There will be some additional costs such as power, supplies, and repairs. The net annual savings are estimated to be $12,100, and the machine will be scrapped at the end of its life.

   Assume that income taxes on incremental profits are paid at the rate of 46 percent and that normal opportunities return 10 percent after taxes. Calculate the simple payback and return on investment, average return, net present value, present value index, present value payback, annualized net present value, and yield. Discuss your findings.

5. The strategy of the XYZ Corporation includes the periodic introduction of a new product line, which involves investments in research and development, promotion, plant, equipment, and working capital. Now the company has readied a new product after an expenditure of $3.75 million on research and development during the past 12 months. The decision to be made is whether to invest $6.3 million for the production of the new line. The economic life of the product is estimated at 12 years, while straight-line depreciation will be taken over 15 years. At the end of 12 years, the book value of the equipment is expected to be recovered through sale of the machinery. Working capital of $1.5 million will have to be committed to the project during the first year, and $1.25 million of this amount is expected to be recovered at the end of

the 12 years. An expenditure of $1 million for promotion will have to be made and expensed in the first year as well.

The best estimate of profits before depreciation, promotion expenses, and income taxes is $1.9 million per year for the first three years, $2.2 million per year for the fourth through eighth years, and $1.3 million per year for years 9 through 12. Assume that income taxes on incremental profits are paid at the rate of 46 percent and that the company normally earns 10 percent after taxes on its investments. Calculate the various measures of investment desirability. Which of these indicates best the attractiveness of the project? Should the company plan to develop similar opportunities by spending research and development funds? How much margin for error exists in this project? Discuss your findings.

6. The ZYX Company has found that after only two years of using a new machine for a semiautomatic production process, a more advanced and faster model has arrived on the market which not only will turn out the current volume of products more efficiently but will allow an increased output of the item. The original machine had cost $32,000 and was being depreciated straight-line over a ten-year period, at the end of which it would be scrapped. The market value of this machine currently is $15,000, and a buyer is interested in acquiring it.

The advanced model now available costs $55,500 installed, and because of its more complex mechanism is expected to last eight years. A scrap value of $1,500 is considered reasonable.

The current level of output of the old machine, now running at capacity, is 200,000 units per year, which the new machine would boost by 15 percent. There is no question in the minds of the sales management that this additional output could be sold. The current machine produces the product at a unit cost of 12 cents for labor, 48 cents for materials, and 24 cents for allocated overhead (at the rate of 200 percent of direct labor). At the higher level of output, the new machine would turn out the product at a unit cost of 8 cents for labor (because of one less operator), 46 cents for materials (because of less spoilage), and 16 cents for allocated overhead. Differences in other operating costs, such as power, repairs, and supplies, are negligible at both volume levels.

If the new machine were run at the old 200,000-unit level, the operators would be freed for a proportionate period of time for reassignment in other operations of the company.

The additional output is expected to be sold at the normal price of $0.95 per unit, but additional selling and promotional costs are expected to amount to $5,500 per year.

Assume that income taxes are paid at the rate of 46 percent and that the company normally earns 15 percent after taxes on its investments. Calculate the various measures of investment desirability and select those most meaningful for this analysis. What major considerations should be taken into account in this decision? Discuss your findings.

7. The UVW Company, a small but growing oil company, was about to invest $275,000 in drilling development wells on a lease near a major oil field with proven reserves. Since other companies were also drilling in the vicinity, the volume of the flow of oil expected could not be predicted except within wide limits. Nevertheless, some oil would be obtained for a period of 12 years, in the best judgment of the geologists. After careful evaluation of the market and distribution aspects, the company management decided that the major uncertainty lay in the physical yield, with lesser risk in the other areas. Consequently, an assessment was made of the range of aftertax cash flows (after considering depletion, depreciation, etc.) at various levels of production and the likelihood of occurrence of these levels was estimated. There was believed to be a 5 percent chance that the cash flow would be $15,000 yearly over the life of the project, a 15 percent chance that it would be $35,000 yearly, a 40 percent chance that it would be $45,000 yearly, a 25 percent chance that it would be $50,000, and a 15 percent chance that it would be $60,000 per year. It was expected that oil would flow at any given level for the full life of the project, although there was the risk that the wells could run dry sooner. Would this be a worthwhile project if the company normally earned 10 percent after taxes? What considerations are critical? Discuss your findings.

5　ANALYSIS OF FINANCIAL FUNDS SOURCES

After our discussion of operational analysis and projection and the key elements of capital investment decisions, it is now time to turn to the third area of management decisions—the analysis of and choice among financial funds sources, which are the fuel of business activity. The development and maintenance of a company's capital structure, long-term and short-term, result from many strategic considerations and choices, which rest on quantitative as well as qualitative processes.

This chapter will deal with the main considerations in reviewing the financing options open to management, but with different degrees of thoroughness. After a brief review of the major questions involved in *choosing among alternative financing* sources, the discussion will focus on three key analytical areas: (1) the *cost* of different funds sources from the point of view of management; (2) the *cost of capital* as a composite, from the point of view of the enterprise as a whole; and (3) the *value* of different financing devices to the provider of the funds, the investor. It is necessary to distinguish clearly between these viewpoints in looking at funds sources, as the techniques to be applied will differ. In keeping with the purpose of this book, the main emphasis will be on the viewpoint of the management of the business. Only a few of the concepts of valuation will be given from the investor's standpoint, enough to provide a flavor of the concern and desires of the funds providers. Also, we shall only briefly discuss the more complex issues and concepts of investor preferences for different types of securities in the context of portfolio analysis. Much advanced work has been done over the past ten years to quantify both investor preferences and the larger context of risk/performance trade-offs in the marketplace. The references at the end of this chapter contain extended discussions of these concepts.

Throughout the existence of a business, management makes financing decisions which result in changes in the funds sources employed, and quite often in changes in the capital structure itself. In each case, specific *costs* are incurred or changed as part of the tangible impact of such changes. The choice of appropriate financing sources over time is part of the planning task of management, and is closely linked with the nature of the operations, the projected conditions, the industry, and the style of management. As we already expressed in the earlier chapters, this planning task involves an economic matching of appropriate funds sources to the current and expected future operations and investments, and we shall take up the techniques of measuring the specific cost implications of the choices as a major topic.

The concept of *cost of capital* has been paid increasing attention in recent years, especially as its use affects the proper economic choices among investment opportunities. There has also been considerable discussion on the proper measurement of the cost of capital itself, and how the circumstances around such an analysis affect the methods chosen. Cost of capital, as a composite, is frequently used as a cutoff criterion in capital budgeting. If a satisfactory expression of the long-term expectations about a company's capital structure policies and the cost of its components can be developed, it can serve as the minimum return standard against which capital investments can be compared. The concept, though deceptively simple, is laden with theoretical and practical issues which have yet to be fully resolved. The interested reader will find references for further study at the end of the chapter.

The question of *valuation* of debt and equity instruments is likewise a vast area of learned discourse. We shall briefly take the point of view of the investor on the basis of a few commonly encountered examples, to demonstrate key valuation techniques. We shall discuss the concepts of income yield, risk, and value considerations. As will become clear, many of the techniques to be discussed tie directly to our past chapters on ratio analysis and financial projection—as we would expect, since they are part of the total operating picture. But again, to obtain a more exhaustive treatment of these questions, the references at the end of the chapter should be reviewed.

Before we turn to the discussion of the framework for choosing among funds sources, it will be useful to stipulate two assumptions. The first relates to the analytical process presented in Chapter 4, which focused on the proper selection of investment opportunities. We shall now assume, as we analyze the funds sources required, that management has planned and fully thought out the intended use of the funds. In other words, we shall only concern ourselves with the problem of obtaining the funds and discuss the costs and obligations incurred in the choices to be made.

The second assumption relates to the nature of the company for which the analysis is made. We shall not cover the special circumstances of new enterprises, which face a more limited choice of funds, but rather concentrate on a going concern in our discussion. Moreover, the stress will be on *incremental* financing, although the consideration of existing funds sources is part of the total picture and will be covered when necessary.

Finally, our discussion of techniques of funds source analysis will be built around a common example of the major options, without going into detail on the many institutional, legal, and organizational concepts. These represent a vast body of knowledge and practice and are best found in works on corporate finance and investment management.

THE CHOICE AMONG THE ALTERNATIVES

Sources of funds for a going enterprise are numerous and varied, and the types of contracts, understandings, and arrangements can be suited in a tailor-made fashion to almost any conceivable set of circumstances. This variety is introduced, however, largely through modifications of two basic choices: *debt,* on the one hand, and *equity,* on the other; with a third choice, *preferred equity,* representing a middle ground. Debt, of course, is created through a contract which calls for eventual repayment of value provided, usually at interest; while equity is an ownership commitment, generally without termination and carrying all the risks of ownership. Preferred equity has elements of both, even though it basically is an ownership involvement. Normally, there exists a wide choice which is open to management. Many points must be considered in judging the alternative options, and only some of these are supported by quantitative techniques.

We shall make selected comments on the major issues to be weighed by management in making the choices, grouped into five major areas: *risk exposure, specific cost, flexibility, timeing,* and *control.* The techniques to be explored in this chapter will address largely the first two areas.

First, the alternative funds sources available to management involve varying degrees of *risk exposure,* since the proportion of debt and equity (see Chapter 2) to a large extent determines the ability of a company to fulfill its obligations in periods of high and low earnings. Management, responsible to the stockholders for a fair return on their investments, must therefore spend much thought and care to determine the right mix of debt and equity in a company's capital structure—enough low-cost debt to boost the owner's return by applying debt to projects earning more than the cost of borrowing the necessary funds, and not so much debt as to endanger the stockholders' return and even the company's solvency in low earning periods. The latter point relates to the fact that fixed debt obligations must be met regardless of circumstances. One aspect of risk exposure, of course, is the degree to which earnings and cash flow fluctuate in a given business. The introduction of fixed obligation securities, such as debt or preferred stock, will tend to magnify such fluctuations through the principle of *leverage*, which will be discussed in this chapter and the following one.

Next is the question of the *specific cost* of the various alternative funds sources. As we shall see, the range of costs normally incurred can be quite sizable. This has implications both for the type of investment opportunity to be financed and for the impact on the earnings pattern, particularly if fluctuations can be expected. Clearly, the decision maker will wish to minimize the cost he has to pay for funds in the interest of enhancing the stockholders' earnings.

The third area is the question of *flexibility*, which refers to the future options for management. As an increment of capital is raised, the choice among the alternatives may be more limited on the next round. The current choice may have imposed fixed obligations, restrictive covenants, and other constraints. This problem is important in considering future capital needs, and the deliberations must include long-range plans and corporate policies with regard to expansion and diversification. The flexibility question arises also with the problem of the funds flows required to service each alternative. Again, long-range planning is required to forecast the impact of these burdens on the corporate treasury.

The fourth element in the decision is *timing* in relation to the movements of prices in the securities markets. There is a direct relationship to relative specific cost, since price and cost are inseparable. The timing aspect will therefore influence the cost spread between the alternatives and at times preclude or favor particular alternatives. For instance, in times of depressed stock prices, bonds may prove to be the most suitable alternative from both a cost and a demand standpoint. Since the proceeds from an issue depend on the success of the placement—public or private—of the securities involved, the market conditions at the time can seriously affect the choice.

Finally, there is the element of *control*, that is, the relative dilution of ownership and control of the enterprise suffered by the existing stockholders. This issue is most important in the case of the common stock alternative, since dilution of these current stockholders' earnings and proportion of ownership can come from issuing additional shares. In the other alternatives, the control of existing stockholders may indirectly be endangered by restrictive provisions and covenants necessary to obtain bond financing, or by the prior and more senior rights of preferred stockholders. The degree of dilution of ownership will be a very important problem in closely held corporations, as it may affect the immediate control certain majority stockholders exercise over the company. The dilution of earnings and the possible retardation of earnings growth connected with dilution of ownership is, of course, a generally applicable phenomenon.

It is clear from this brief résumé of considerations that the decision among the alternative sources of incremental capital is one that cannot simply be made on cost alone, even though cost is a most important early consideration. There are no hard-and-fast rules as to precisely how such decisions can be made, since they depend so much on the circumstances, points of view, and negotiating skills of the decision makers. The techniques to be presented now can assist in specifically calculating quantifiable results, which then must be entered in the broader decision process.

THE COST OF DIFFERENT FUNDS

As management makes financing decisions, each increment of change involves an increment or decrement of cost, as well as impacting the cost of the total capital structure. For the time being, let us concentrate on the incremental effects involved when a corporation incurs additional debt or raises funds through issuing additional preferred or common stock. We shall return to the cost of capital as a composite later.

The Cost of Debt

In the course of its operations, a business commonly employs many forms of debt, which range from trade obligations (accounts payable) to long-term mortgage loans or debenture (bond) issues, and which include simple notes payable to banks or individuals, tax payments owed to various governmental agencies, wages due, payments due on installment purchases, and even lease obligations. For all types of debt, which include many others not mentioned, the *specific cost* involved for the company can be derived relatively easily. Normally, debt arrangements carry specified interest provisions payable either during the debt period, at its end, or deducted in advance from principal (called discounting). In those cases the cost of debt is simply the cost of this interest commitment.

Before we take up specific examples of debt and the analysis of the cost of these forms of debt, it should be remembered that interest is *tax deductible* for corporations and that, therefore, the cost to a corporation (at least those with sufficient profits to pay taxes or able to apply tax-averaging provisions) will be the annual interest payment multiplied by a factor f of one minus the applicable tax rate. For example, if a corporation pays 9 percent per year on the principal of a note and its effective tax rate t for incremental revenue or cost is 46 percent, the net annual effective interest cost i of this note will be:

$$f = 1 - t$$
$$f = 1 - 0.46 = 0.54$$
$$i = 9\% \times 0.54 = 4.86\% \text{ (after taxes)}$$

The effect of tax deductibility is a reduction of the cost of debt to corporations (and to individuals under many circumstances) to a net amount after applying the prevailing tax rate if the company is in a tax position where income changes affect taxes due. This is in contrast to situations involving other forms of capital, as will be shown later.

Operating Debt. First, a few comments should be made about operating debt, which is defined as short-term or re-volving obligations incurred in the ordinary everyday opera-tions of most businesses. Some of these debt funds are in fact provided *free* of any explicit cost, under trade terms generally accepted in the type of industry in which the company oper-ates. Foremost in this category are accounts payable, which are incurred under terms such as 2/10, n/30; or 3/15, n/45; or many variations thereof. Up to 10 or 15 days, therefore, or even as long as 45 days, the company being billed for goods or services can hold off payment and, without cost, can make use of the funds received on credit. We recall from Chapter 1 that trade credit is in fact a significant funds source.

In most cases of trade credit, when payment is made within a specified period it is possible to earn a discount of, for example, 2 percent if paid within 10 days (2/10), or 3 percent if paid within 15 days (3/15) from the date of the invoice. This practice allows the customer effectively to reduce the cost of the goods or services by the specified amount. The purpose of this inducement is to help the vendor collect his funds faster and thus to reduce the level of his own funds tied up in accounts receivable. If the discount period is missed, however, the net amount comes due by the end of the credit period specified (n/30, n/45, etc.). If the debtor company makes use of this option, a very definite cost has been incurred for pro-longing the time during which it can make use of the funds. This is an *opportunity cost* in the form of cash discounts lost. For instance, if the credit terms are 2/10, n/30, the cost of using the funds for the extra 20 days amounts to 2 percent in cash discount lost, or an annual rate of:

$$\frac{360 \text{ days}}{20 \text{ days}} \times 2\% = 36\% \text{ (before taxes)}$$

The company loses as taxable income the cash discount it would have otherwise earned, and the specific net cost must be reduced by the taxes saved. If taxes are assumed to be 46 percent of income, the net cost for the extra 20 days' use of the creditor's funds amounts to:

$$1 - 0.46 = 0.54$$
$$2\% \times 0.54 = 1.08\% \text{ (after taxes)}$$

This cost remains a fairly sizable figure on a *annual* basis when compared to the prime interest rate under normal conditions generally charged large corporations of impeccable credit rating:

$$\frac{360 \text{ days}}{20 \text{ days}} \times 1.08\% = 19.44\% \text{ (after taxes)}$$

Some companies, especially small and rapidly growing enterprises, make it a practice to use accounts payable as a convenient source of credit, often unilaterally *exceeding* the outside limits of credit terms by sizable periods. The longer the funds are kept, of course, the lower becomes the specific cost of accounts payable, since normally no interest charges are levied by the trade creditor. In extreme cases, unpaid accounts may be converted to notes payable, with or without interest, upon the request of the trade creditor who wishes to establish a somewhat stronger claim. From the standpoint of creditworthiness and company reputation, it is clearly a poor practice to go beyond the stipulated credit period, since other prospective creditors will take such tardy performance into account when they evaluate further credit extension. This aspect is part of the *implicit* cost of credit and other forms of capital, which will be discussed later.

Another form of operating debt is the short-term note and the installment contract, in which interest is either charged ahead of time or is added to the amount of principal stated in the contract. For example, a $1,000 note which carries 9 percent interest will provide the debtor with only $910 if the time period is one year and the note is discounted by deducting the interest in advance. The effective cost before taxes now becomes higher than the stated interest, since the company is paying $90 for the privilege of borrowing $910 for one year:

$$\frac{\$90}{\$910} = 9.89\% \text{ (before taxes)}$$

The adjustment for income taxes is made exactly as shown previously. In the case of an installment contract for, say, $1,000 payable in four quarterly installments, with interest of 10 percent on the original balance, the effective cost of interest is much higher than stated, since over the term of the contract decreasing amounts of principal are outstanding and used by the borrowing company.

In this case, a quick method of calculating the approximate effective cost uses the argument that over the term of the contract the principal amount dropped from $1,000 to zero, with the average amount outstanding being roughly half of the principal, or $500. The contractual interest was 10 percent on $1,000, or $100, which became part of each of the four payments. When the interest paid is related to the average amount of capital in the hands of the borrowing company over the period of the loan, the following doubling of cost is the result:

$$\frac{\$100}{\$500} = 20\% \text{ (before taxes)}$$

Again, the adjustment for income taxes is the same as before. If the contract runs over more than one year, care must be taken to *annualize* the interest cost, that is, to relate the interest amount to the specific time period involved in order to arrive at a true cost *per year*, which is the normal period of comparison.

If more precision is required, we can refine the approximate results achieved with the calculations presented above through the use of present value techniques (time discounting) described in Chapter 4. Such an approach is useful where exactness is important and where the incidence of the funds flows covers considerable time periods and a variety of patterns. Banks and other lending institutions use tables based on present value techniques to calculate with precision the charges and payments connected with contracts of this sort. It should be added, however, that the simple averaging technique is useful in many circumstances, including personal finance, to obtain for decision purposes a fair approximation of the true (effective), or specific cost of contracts of this type.

The preceding discussion dealt with ways to ascertain the cost of common operational debt obligations, whose specific cost may range from zero to quite substantial rates of interest. This specific cost is not the only aspect of debt, however. As already mentioned, principal repayment schedules have to be met with *cash flow*. While there is no specific cost connected with the repayment of principal, the obligation to do so in a timely fashion forces the financial manager to forecast and plan *cash* receipts and disbursements with care. Chapter 2 has shown the basic techniques of such cash projection. Another element of the debt burden, as already mentioned, is the implicit impact of various forms of debt obligations on the credit-worthiness of a company contemplating future capital needs. In other words, the balance between debt and equity may become precarious and forestall further borrowing for some time, until the company has worked itself from under its debt obligations. Having "closed off the top," as debt-heavy operations are often characterized, can be a costly endeavor, both in terms of the risk of not meeting obligations as they fall due and in having to turn to much costlier sources of credit or equity funds as additional needs arise.

Debt in the Long-Term Capital Structure.   So far we have concentrated on operating debt and its cost, represented by essentially short-term obligations. More important for a company in the long run, however, is the cost and proportion of debt in its more permanent form—debt as part of the long-term capital structure of the corporation. Here management must make well-planned decisions which involve the cost and amount of debt relative to investments in expanded or diversified activities. Commitments made here are by their very nature bound to have a much more lasting impact than short-term working capital decisions. At times refinancing or even recapitalization may be involved, with significant and far-reaching changes in a company's capital structure. As we turn our attention to the cost of debt in the long-term capital structure, we shall focus our discussion on incremental amounts of debt added to an existing situation.

The basic objective and obligation of management normally is to provide adequate and growing earnings to the stockholders, and to at least maintain and hopefully enhance the value of their investment. We shall incorporate these characteristics in the analysis of a hypothetical company, the ABC Corporation, whose balance sheet (abbreviated) appears as shown in Figure 5–1. The corporation has one million shares of common stock outstanding, with a par value of $10 per share. Most recently, ABC Corporation has earned $11 million before taxes on sales of $115 million. Income taxes paid amounted to $5.1 million. We begin our appraisal of the current position of ABC Corporation and its stockholders by calculating the earnings per share of common stock (EPS), using a format which will be applied throughout this chapter. The format is based on a step-by-step development of the earnings impact of obligations in order of their normal priority.

We first state the earnings before interest and taxes (EBIT) and subtract from that figure a variety of charges applicable to different obligations. The first of these is *interest* charges on

Figure 5–1
ABC CORPORATION
Balance Sheet
($ millions)

Assets		*Liabilities and Net Worth*	
Current assets	$15	Current liabilities	$ 7
Fixed assets (net)	29	Common stock	10
Other assets	1	Retained earnings	28
Total assets ...	$45	Total liabilities and net worth ...	$45

long-term debt; normally we ignore short-term interest unless it is a significant amount. The assumption is that because of the temporary nature of such obligations, as part of normal operations, these charges have been deducted properly in arriving at the EBIT figure quoted. The data will be arranged as in Figure 5–2.

Figure 5–2
ABC CORPORATION
Earnings per Share Calculation
($000, except per share)

Earnings before interest and taxes (EBIT)	$11,000
Less: Interest charges on long-term debt . . .	–0–
Earnings before income taxes	11,000
Less: Federal income taxes at 46%	5,060
Earnings after income taxes	5,940
Less: Preferred dividends	–0–
Earnings available for common stock	$ 5,940
Common shares outstanding (number)	1 million
Earnings per share (EPS):	$ 5.94
Less: Common dividends per share	2.50
Retained earnings per share	3.44
Retained earnings in total	3,440

The analysis format has made provision for interest and preferred dividends, but no amounts are shown since our hypothetical ABC Corporation has at this point neither long-term debt nor preferred stock outstanding. The result of the calculations in Figure 5–2 shows a residual earnings available to common stockholders of $5.94 per share, from which a dividend of $2.50 per share has been voted as a cash distribution by the board of directors. We assume that this dividend payout (between 50 and 60 percent of earnings) has been maintained for many years, and that earnings have steadily grown by about 6 percent over the years. Let us further assume that the stock is widely held and traded, and that it commands a price of about $50 to $60 in the stock market, roughly ten times current earnings. Such is the present condition of ABC Corporation.

The introduction of debt to this capital structure and the earnings position of the company will again demonstrate the concept of specific cost discussed earlier in this chapter. Let us assume that the corporation is planning to borrow $10 million in order to exploit a new product it has developed. There is the possibility of issuing bonds, which are not secured by assets of the company but are based on the general corporate credit standing. Such debenture bonds will carry an interest rate of 9 percent, will become due 20 years from date of issue, and will carry a sinking fund provision of $400,000 per year beginning with the fifth year. The balance outstanding at the end of 20 years will become payable as a "balloon" payment of $4 million. After the new product has been introduced, the company hopes for incremental earnings of at least $2.0 million before taxes, and expects little risk of obsolescence or competitive inroads for the next 10 to 15 years.

We can now trace the impact of debt on the current corporate situation, both in terms of earnings and dividends, and in terms of the specific cost of the newly created debt. Two conditions will be analyzed: first, the immediate impact of the debt without any offsetting benefits of profitable investment; and, second, the picture presented once the investment has become operative and the incremental earnings from the new product have been brought about.

The results of the calculations are shown in Figure 5–3. The effect of adding debt is a reduction of the stockholders' earnings, an immediate dilution caused by the interest cost entering the earnings pattern of ABC Corporation. Earnings after interest and taxes dropped $486,000, which is, of course, 54 percent $(1 - 0.46)$ of the pretax interest cost of $900,000. Earnings per share dropped about 49 cents, a reduction of 8.2 percent from the prior level, purely because of the additional interest burden, which on a per share basis amounts to the same 49 cents ($486,000 ÷ 1 million shares).

The specific cost of the incremental funds is therefore 54 percent of 9 percent, or 4.86 percent per year, given a tax rate of 46 percent. Another way of figuring this cost is, of course,

Figure 5–3
ABC CORPORATION
Earnings per Share with New Bond Issue
($000, except per share)

	Current	With New Product
Earnings before interest and taxes (EBIT)	$11,000	$13,000
Less: Interest charges on long-term debt . . .	900	900
Earnings before income taxes	10,100	12,100
Less: Federal income taxes at 46%	4,646	5,566
Earnings after income taxes	5,454	6,534
Less: Preferred dividends	–0–	–0–
Earnings available for common stock	$ 5,454	$ 6,534
Common shares outstanding (number)	1 million	1 million
Earnings per share (EPS)	$ 5.45	$ 6.53
Less: Common dividends per share	2.50	2.50
Retained earnings per share	2.95	4.03
Retained earnings in total	2,954	4,034
Original EPS (Figure 5–2)	5.94	5.94
Change in EPS	–0.49	+0.59
Percent change in EPS	–8.2%	+9.9%

the relationship of the annual aftertax interest cost to the amount provided, which is $486,000 for $10 million, or 4.86 percent. Finally, we can also argue that the specific cost is the specific change in earnings to the stockholders, as pointed out before. If earnings are not disturbed by any other factor, as we have assumed, the earnings drop represents the specific cost. If earnings on the new investment are sufficient just to offset the earnings drop from interest, leaving earnings unchanged, the investment would earn (yield) precisely the specific cost of the capital required.

This thinking is reflected in the second column of Figure 5–3, where we observe that as soon as the new product has been successfully brought out the additional earnings generated have more than offset the specific cost of the debentures. The aftertax earnings jumped to $6,534,000, a net increase of $594,000 over the original $5,940,000. As a consequence, earnings per share rose 59 cents above the original amount of $5.94, an increase of about 10 percent. The successful investment of the funds provided by the debentures has more than offset their specific cost, and thereby boosted common earnings. Incremental earnings exceed incremental cost, and the investment—if our earnings assumption proves true—has made possible a true increment of value.

This condition raises the following questions: Would it not have been sufficient for the investment to earn only $486,000 after taxes, since this would leave the stockholders as well off as before? By earning more, ABC Corporation has used financial leverage (Chapter 6) and given the equity owners a "free ride"—or has it? At first glance, it might be reasonable to believe so. But a number of points must be raised here to be developed more fully later. First of all, no mention has been made so far of the *sinking fund obligations* which will begin five years hence and which call for a cash outlay of $400,000 per year. Even though this amount is not tax deductible and must be paid out of the cash flows generated by the company, are we justified in ascribing no "cost" to this obligation? In fact, this debt service amounts to 40 cents per share per year in cash, which is no longer available for dividends or other corporate purposes, since it is committed to the repayment of principal. If the investment were just to earn the interest cost on the debt, how would we repay this principal? Chapter 4 has dealt with the concept of how to calculate properly the payout of such an investment.

Another question addresses the *implicit cost of risk:* What if the earnings of the investment turned out to be much worse than expected? Should such a risk be expressed as part of the cost considerations? Is the payment obligation pattern of interest and principal an appropriate concern to current and future creditors, stockholders, and other interested parties? Finally, should the *specific aftertax cost* of 4.86 percent per year be used as a criterion for judging the return or yield of the investment, or is a broader, more overall *cost of capital* applicable here? Will there always be an opportunity to borrow at this cost, and will it not be necessary to raise funds in some form other than debt next time? Could the investment project stand up under such conditions? In other words, is it possible to look at capital costs in small increments, depending on the type of capital raised?

These significant questions and many more lead toward the economic framework of capital budgeting, which properly views incremental decisions in the total context of long-term spending plans, desired capital structure, and economic decision criteria. For the moment, however, it is clear that the debt service burden implicitly costs the company some of its flexibility. The risk of earnings fluctuations impairing the fulfillment of the contract for fixed debt service payments is real, and must be carefully appraised. Some of the ratios discussed in Chapter 2 are helpful here, and clues as to the reasonableness of "earnings coverage" of the obligations can be gained. The investment must be judged in broader terms; incremental debt cost is *not* a sufficient criterion, as we saw in Chapter 4. In short, we are only at the beginning of the full analysis of the funds source decision and are limited by the scope of this book from considering all aspects. Yet we have established the need to relate the cost and other effects of different types of capital sources to operational and investment strategy, and we shall return to this broader subject in later sections of this chapter as well as in Chapter 6.

The Cost of Preferred Stock

When considering the cost of adding preferred stock to a capital structure, we must consider that this type of equity holds the middle ground between debt and common stock. Subordinated to the various creditors of the corporation, the preferred stockholder has a prior claim to corporate earnings up to the amount of the preferred dividend. In liquidation, his claims are satisfied prior to the residual claims of the common stockholders. Because of the near-equity nature of preferred stock, preferred dividends are not considered tax deductible by the Internal Revenue Service. Such dividends therefore represent an outflow of aftertax funds from the corporation. For instance, a share of 10 percent preferred stock, par value

$100, costs the issuing corporation $10 in aftertax earnings. For each dollar of dividends to be provided, the corporation must therefore earn $1.85 before taxes. Where the 9 percent bond discussed before had an aftertax cost of 4.86 percent, the 10 percent preferred has an aftertax cost of 10 percent. Thus, the stated dividend rate on a preferred stock is directly comparable to the *tax-adjusted* interest rate on a bond.

All along we have assumed, of course, that in the examples shown the bonds or preferreds were issued at such prices as to yield proceeds exactly equal to the par or face value—in other words, that the corporation receives $100 for a share of $100 preferred after expenses of issuing the shares. Where there is a difference—where proceeds are either greater or smaller than the par value of a bond or preferred, as often happens because of market conditions—it is necessary first to calculate an *effective* interest or dividend rate based on the proceeds, and then to develop the tax adjustments to arrive at comparable figures.

To illustrate further the effect of introducing preferred stock to a corporate capital structure, we return to the example of the ABC Corporation. This time the $10 million in capital to be added is raised via 10 percent preferred stock (100,000 shares) at $100 per share net proceeds to the corporation after legal and issuing expenses.

The results of the calculations in Figure 5–4 reflect a sizable drop in the earnings from those of the initial condition—a much more serious effect than in the case of the 9 percent bonds. A small increase in earnings is achieved after the investment becomes operative, which again is much different from the bond alternative. The cause for this is the stated 10 percent dividend rate, which, while only slightly higher than the bond interest, has a much costlier effect because it is not tax deductible. This time the annual cost is shown as a deduction from aftertax earnings, and the immediate dilution amounts to $1.00 per share, or 16.8 percent. With the new earnings, the eventual earnings increase is only 8 cents per share or 1.3 percent. The corporation is committed to a total of $1,000,000 of aftertax funds, which leaves very little room for a

Figure 5–4
ABC CORPORATION
Earnings per Share with New Preferred Issue
($000, except per share)

	Current	With New Product
Earnings before interest and taxes (EBIT)	$11,000	$13,000
Less: Interest charges on long-term debt ...	–0–	–0–
Earnings before income taxes	11,000	13,000
Less: Federal income taxes at 46%	5,060	5,980
Earnings after income taxes	5,940	7,020
Less: Preferred dividends	1,000	1,000
Earnings available for common stock	$ 4,940	$ 6,020
Common shares outstanding (number)	1 million	1 million
Earnings per share (EPS)	$ 4.94	$ 6.02
Less: Common dividends per share	2.50	2.50
Retained earnings per share	2.44	3.52
Retained earnings in total	2,440	3,520
Original EPS (Figure 5–2)	5.94	5.94
Change in EPS...........................	– 1.00	+0.08
Percent change in EPS	–16.8%	+1.3%

net gain from the earnings generated by the investment, which are $2.0 million before taxes and $1,080,000 after taxes.

In this situation the assumed conditions provide very limited financial leverage. Only a little more than a 1 percent rise in common earnings over prior levels is achieved, since the fixed costs imposed have risen to $1,000,000. Were the investment in the new product to earn precisely

$$\frac{\$1,000,000}{0.54} = \$1,851,852$$

before taxes, we would observe no change in earnings per share—incremental cost would offset incremental earnings, for a break-even situation. Note that this sizable earnings requirement compares with only $900,000 required by the bonds.

Questions similar to those of the first case arise: What about the repayment of the principal? Even though preferred stock is generally a very long-term proposition, many preferreds contain a call provision, and a sinking fund may be established to retire the stock eventually. Such potential actions, even though not necessarily contractual obligations, can cause future funds drains. There is also the risk of defaulting on the dividend, which would block payment of the common dividends. Again, such risks must be evaluated in terms of the likely range of earnings to be encountered and the uncertainties in the corporate and industry picture. While the specific cost of the preferred was established as the effective dividend rate, what impact is there of preferred stock on future financing? Is it fair to assess the merits of the investment proposal against this specific cost only? Only a broader analysis can answer these and other questions.

The Cost of Common Stock

Generally, management is obligated to provide a mixture of three types of benefits to its common stockholders: first, the *earnings* performance of the company; second, the payment of *dividends* to pass part of the earnings on to the stockholder; and third, the *appreciation* of the value of the shares of stock in the market in response to growing earnings or dividends or both. As discussed earlier, it is generally desirable to demonstrate consistency and a fairly stable long-term growth trend in any or all of these aspects, even though the relative emphasis on any one area will depend on the nature of the company and its industry. Any action, especially in the form of a long-term commitment, which jeopardizes or materially changes the stockholder's expectations about these benefits in a particular company should be deemed harmful or at least worthy of serious reappraisal. More will be said on these points later in the chapter.

How are these considerations related to calculating a cost of common stock? In the case of common stock we do not have a directly measurable element as was the case with interest for bonds and dividends for preferred. Common dividends are declared at the discretion of the corporate board of directors, and while many companies strive for a stable and consistent policy (e.g., American Telephone and Telegraph Company), others pay very erratic dividends or none at all. In fact, many small "growth situations" of the space age variety or many large capital gains-oriented conglomerates would not even consider paying a cash dividend, since stockholders of this type of company prefer to see earnings reinvested to achieve maximum acceleration of growth and hopefully a corresponding rise of market value. Yet one cannot argue that in a situation where payment of dividends is not expected new common stock has *no* cost to the issuing company and the existing stockholders!

In the previous examples, we calculated earnings per share as a measure and discussed the effect of the cost of incremental capital in terms of the immediate dilution of earnings. We shall now use the same approach for common stock. ABC Corporation, we assume, will issue $10 million worth of new common stock at a net price of $45.45 per share to the corporation after underwriters' fees and legal expenses. Such a discount from the current market price of $55 should ensure the success of the issue. Under these conditions, a total of 220,000 shares have to be issued, an increase of 22 percent in the number of shares outstanding. A calculation of the earnings picture is shown in Figure 5–5.

We observe that the initial dilution under current conditions is a full $1.07 per share, a drop of 18 percent, which is the most severe among the three examples analyzed. Common stock, when viewed in this light, must surely be the costliest type of capital, since it causes the greatest dilution in the stockholders' position. Moreover, an annual funds drain of at least $550,000 in aftertax earnings is imposed in the form of dividends, assuming that the corporation will continue its policy of paying regular cash dividends at $2.50 per share at least. The funds drain amounts to a pretax earnings requirement of:

$$\$2.50 \times 220{,}000 \text{ shares} = \$550{,}000 \text{ (after taxes)}$$

$$\frac{\$550{,}000}{0.54} = \$1{,}018{,}518 \text{ (before taxes)}$$

Figure 5–5

ABC CORPORATION

Earnings per Share with New Common Stock Issue

($000, except per share)

	Current	With New Product
Earnings before interest and taxes (EBIT)	$11,000	$13,000
Less: Interest charges on long-term debt . . .	–0–	–0–
Earnings before income taxes	11,000	13,000
Less: Federal income taxes at 46%	5,060	5,980
Earnings after income taxes	5,940	7,020
Less: Preferred dividends	–0–	–0–
Earnings available for common stock	$ 5,940	$ 7,020
Common shares outstanding (number)	1.22 million	1.22 million
Earnings per share (EPS)	$ 4.87	$ 5.75
Less: Common dividends per share	2.50	2.50
Retained earnings per share	2.37	3.25
Retained earnings in total	2,890	3,970
Original EPS (Figure 5–2)	5.94	5.94
Change in EPS	– 1.07	–0.19
Percent change in EPS	–18.0%	–3.2%

We can directly compare this requirement of about $1 million to $900,000 for the bonds and $1,351,852 for the preferred.

Not only is there the effect of immediate dilution, but dilution will *continue,* since (in contrast to the other two types of capital, which had fixed interest and dividend provisions) the new shares we have created are on an equal footing with the old shares in participating in any increase (or decrease) in corporate earnings. Growth in earnings per share will thus tend to be retarded because of the additional new shares outstanding.

When we turn to the second column of Figure 5–5 to study the effect of the increased earnings from the new product, it is quite apparent that a net dilution of earnings per share of 19 cents or 3.2 percent will remain. The contribution from the new investment was not sufficient to offset the earnings claims of the new stockholders and at the same time to maintain the old per-share earnings level. The specific cost of the stock is thus greater than the earnings from the capital raised. As a rule, the specific cost of the common stock can be calculated by relating the earnings required to maintain the old EPS level to the amount of funds provided by the stock. This is done most easily on a per-share basis, where the earnings required for each new share are precisely $5.94 (the old level). The proceeds to the company were assumed to be $45.45, and the result of the calculation can be shown as follows:

$$\frac{\$5.94}{\$45.45} = 13.07\% \text{ (after taxes)}$$

It should be noted that this result can be compared with the 4.86 percent for the bonds and 10 percent for the preferred. We can arrive at the same answer by making the analysis on a *total* basis. The $10 million provided is represented by 220,000 shares, for each of which earnings of $5.94 must be provided to leave the old stockholders' earnings position unchanged. A total of $1,306,800 in earnings after taxes ($2,420,000 before taxes) must therefore be achieved by the investment to maintain the break-even situation. This works out to 13.1 percent after taxes, or a full 24 percent before taxes. One look at the investment proposition shows that projected earnings are not sufficient to provide this offsetting effect. Were the expected earnings from the new product higher than $2.4 million before taxes, the investment would, of course, boost the earnings per share of *both* old and new stockholders.

Our discussion of specific cost has so far not touched a key expectation of stockholders, namely, growth in the market value of their shares. This growth is related, although not exclusively, to the performance of corporate earnings over the long run, and the static picture shown so far is not flexible enough to deal with this aspect. We also recall that earlier, with two of the alternatives, some questions were raised regarding earnings fluctuations and their effect upon the fixed obligations incurred by the corporation. Since it would be quite laborious to calculate earnings per share and other data for a great number of earnings levels and assumptions, we can exploit the linear relationships between the factors analyzed and use a graphic approach to compare the alternate sources of financing and to gauge the relative impact of fluctuations in EBIT as part of the measurement of cost and relative desirability. Such a model is quite a helpful device, as we shall now demonstrate.

Graphic Analysis

First, Figure 5–6 will be used to recap the data developed up to this point, for the original situation as well as for the three alternatives of financing the new product. The EPS data will be recorded as points on a graph, often called an EBIT chart, on which we show earnings per share in dollars on the vertical axis and EBIT levels on the horizontal axis. Straight lines can be drawn once two points have been determined for each alternative.

It is common to use as one of these points the intersection of each line with the horizontal axis, at the EBIT level where EPS are zero. These points can easily be found by working our framework of analysis *backward*, that is, starting with EPS of zero and building up to an EBIT which just provides for this

Figure 5–6
ABC CORPORATION
Recap of EPS Analyses
($000, except per share)

	Original	*Debt*	*Preferred*	*Common*
EBIT	$11,000	$13,000	$13,000	$13,000
Less: Interest	–0–	900	–0–	–0–
Earnings before taxes	11,000	12,100	13,000	13,000
Less: Taxes at 46%	5,060	5,566	5,980	5,980
Earnings after taxes	5,940	6,534	7,020	7,020
Less: Preferred dividends	–0–	–0–	1,000	–0–
Earnings to common	$ 5,940	$ 6,534	$ 6,020	$ 7,020
Common shares	1 million	1 million	1 million	1.22 million
EPS	$ 5.94	$ 6.53	$ 6.02	$ 5.75
Less: Common dividends	2.50	2.50	2.50	2.50
Retained earnings	3.44	4.03	3.52	3.25
Total retained	3,440	4,034	3,520	3,970
Original dilution	–0–	–8.2%	–16.8%	–18.0%
Final EPS change	–0–	+9.9	+ 1.3	– 3.2
Specific cost	–0–	4.86	10.0	13.07

condition. This calculation, for each of the alternatives and the original situation, is shown in Figure 5–7.

Figure 5–7
ABC CORPORATION
Zero EPS Calculation
($000)

	Original	Debt	Preferred	Common
EPS	–0–	–0–	–0–	–0–
Common shares	1 million	1 million	1 million	1.22 million
Earnings to common	–0–	–0–	–0–	–0–
Preferred dividends	–0–	–0–	$1,000	–0–
Earnings after taxes	–0–	–0–	1,000	–0–
Taxes at 46%	–0–	–0–	852	–0–
Earnings before taxes ...	–0–	–0–	1,852	–0–
Interest	–0–	$900	–0–	–0–
EBIT for zero EPS	–0–	900	1,852	–0–

The calculations in the two tables give us sufficient data to draw the linear functions of EPS and EBIT for the various situations, as shown in Figure 5–8. We can quickly observe visually that the conclusions drawn from the two previously analyzed EBIT levels, $11,000 and $13,000, hold true over the fairly wide range of earnings presented. There is one difference, however, and that is the behavior of EPS under the common stock alternative, which has a slope different from all others and in fact intersects the debt and preferred EPS lines. The latter two are parallel lines which are also parallel to the line representing the original situation. This phenomenon is easily explained, since the shift to the right of the original line is caused by the imposition of fixed interest or dividend charges on the earnings available to the common stockholders, whose number of shares does *not* change over the whole range of EBIT studied. The use of common stock, on the other hand, represents a proportional dilution of earnings for the common stockholders at *all* levels, and the introduction of additional shares causes earnings per share for everyone to rise less rapidly with EBIT. The lesser slope of the common stock line is the result.

Figure 5–8
ABC CORPORATION
Range of EBIT and EPS Chart

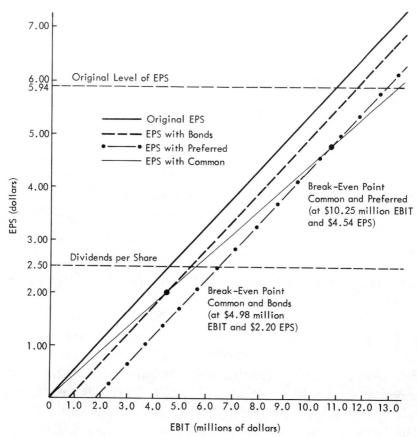

EBIT (millions of dollars)

The significance of the intersection should now become clear: it is not possible to speak of the cost of capital for incremental common stock without defining the "normal" earnings level which the existing stockholders have come to expect—if we accept the framework of analysis used here. In fact, there are EBIT levels in the lower ranges where the imposition of additional common stock can have a lesser effect upon EPS than one of the other alternatives or both, which results in a different cost of common stock.

These conditions bear upon the analysis of the choice to be made, in a dynamic sense, since it is impossible to tell the effects on EPS should EBIT fluctuate rapidly in the future. If future EBIT levels are expected to move fairly well *within* the range bounded by the two break-even points, common stock looks more attractive than preferred stock from the standpoint of diluting EPS. If EBIT can be expected to grow and move fairly well to the *right* of the second break-even point, the issuance of common stock is the least desirable alternative in terms of EPS dilution. All these considerations are based, of course, on unchanging assumptions about the terms under which the three forms of capital could be issued. If any terms, such as the issue price of common stock, can be expected to change significantly, a new chart must be drawn up, or a discontinuity reflected for the extreme EBIT ranges.

We can quite easily calculate the intersections between the EPS lines, which represent the *break-even* points among the alternatives. For this purpose we express the assumptions about any pair of lines in the form of simple equations. EPS are then considered equal for the pair, and we solve the equations for EBIT. To illustrate, let us use the following definitions:

E = EBIT level for break-even among alternatives.
i = Annual interest on bonds, in dollars (before taxes).
t = Tax rate applicable.
p = Annual preferred dividends, in dollars.
n = Number of common shares outstanding.

The equation for any particular line can be found by substituting known facts in the following expression:

$$EPS = \frac{(E - i)(1 - t) - p}{n}$$

We can now find the EBIT break-even levels for bonds and common stock at the point of EPS equality. For this purpose, we write the two expressions and consider them as equal:

$$\underset{Bonds}{\frac{(E - \$900{,}000)0.54 - 0}{1{,}000{,}000}} = \underset{Common}{\frac{(E - 0)0.54 - 0}{1{,}220{,}000}}$$

Solving for E, we obtain the following result:

$$0.54E - \$486,000 = \frac{0.54E}{1.22}$$
$$0.659E - \$592,920 = 0.54E$$
$$E = \$4,982,521$$

This result can easily be verified on the EBIT chart in Figure 5–8. When the same approach is applied to the preferred and common stock alternatives, the following result emerges:

$$\underset{\text{Preferred}}{\frac{(E - 0)0.54 - \$1,000,000}{1,000,000}} = \underset{\text{Common}}{\frac{(E - 0)0.54 - 0}{1,220,000}}$$

$$0.54E - \$1,000,000 = \frac{0.54E}{1.22}$$
$$0.659E - \$1,220,000 = 0.54E$$
$$E = \$10,252,101$$

Again, the chart can be used for verification of this result.

It is also possible to use the EBIT chart to display the impacts on the three alternatives of any dividend requirement for common stock. The horizontal line at EPS of $2.50 in the chart represents the current annual dividend, and where this line intersects any alternative EPS line we can read off the minimum level of EBIT required to supply this dividend. Similarly, it is possible to reflect on the chart the burden of sinking funds or other regular repayment provisions, by carrying the calculations one step further and arriving at "uncommitted earnings per share" (UEPS) for each alternative. This is done by simply subtracting the aftertax cost of such repayments on a per share basis from the EPS of those alternatives where they apply, and redrawing lines on the chart, which will fall to the right of the previous EPS lines. For example, a sinking fund requirement in the bond alternative of $500,000 per year would represent 50 cents per share, and the line would thus be shifted to the right by this amount over the whole range. Zero UEPS would move from the zero EPS of $900,000 EBIT to $1,825,926, since the sinking fund of

$500,000 represents an additional pretax earnings requirement of $500,000 ÷ 0.54, or $925,926. In fact, the UEPS line for bonds would closely correspond to the EPS line for preferred stock in Figure 5–8.

By now the usefulness of this framework for the analysis of the various alternatives should be clear, and the reader is invited to think through the implications of the variety of tests that can be applied. It is possible, for instance, to check the EBIT level under each alternative which would endanger the $2.50 per share dividend, assuming a variety of payout ratios, such as 50 percent. In this case, a line could be drawn at the $5 EPS level extending horizontally, and the intersections would represent the minimum EBIT levels required to support a $2.50 dividend under a 50 percent payout assumption. The decision maker would have to assess the likelihood of the EBIT reaching this level and the risk this represents to the stockholders. Again it must be emphasized, however, that the chart works only under the *fixed assumptions* about proceeds received and unchanging interest and preferred dividend rates. If one can reasonably assume that these will change, the positions of the EPS lines on the graph must be changed.

An additional word about the significance of changes in the issuing conditions: as the spread between the alternatives increases, that is, as the differences among the specific costs of the alternatives widen, the distance between the parallel lines will increase. This is simply a reflection of the depressant effect on EPS which the imposition of fixed obligations brings about. A similar effect is achieved by increasing the relative size of the incremental capital issue, since the slope of the line is governed by the degree of leverage in the existing capital structure. In other words, if there had already been debt or preferred stock in the original capital structure, the original EPS would have risen and fallen much more sharply, and with them the EPS of the fixed-cost alternatives. The slope of the EPS line for the common stock alternative is, of course, governed by the relative number of shares issued, which in turn is related to the specific cost of common stock as we have defined it—normal EPS compared to the issue proceeds. As we have mentioned in earlier chapters, a computerized analysis with the help of a financial planning model can be quite revealing, since it is possible to make changes in a greater number of variables and to calculate the effect of these on the earnings pattern.

COST OF CAPITAL IN COMPOSITES

At the beginning of this chapter we stated that our emphasis would be on incremental reasoning. We have done this and wound up with an overall framework of analysis. In order to have a better perspective of cost of capital, it is necessary to cover briefly the most difficult area in this economic analysis—the problem of an overall *composite* cost of capital in an *existing* capital structure as one guide in judging the desirability of existing and new investment projects. Here a variety of problems converge: the reliability and meaning of *recorded values* carried on the balance sheet, the reliability and meaning of *earnings* in the measurement process, and the reliability and meaning of *market values* for stock involved, to name just the most important ones.

To keep the discussion manageable within the framework of this book, we shall assume from the start that a *weighted* cost of capital is a reasonable concept to use and that common equity consists of two parts, stated stock values and retained earnings. Furthermore, we shall not deal with the problem of funds flow from depreciation and its cost, since some aspects of this were covered in Chapters 1 and 4. The interested reader is referred to the bibliography at the end of this chapter for further materials on these aspects, as well as on the ones briefly covered here.

From the outset we have stipulated that any source of funds to a corporation has a cost, either specific or implicit. At times this may be in the form of an opportunity cost. The composite of funds which corporate management can employ contains many types, the relative importance of which usually is determined by corporate policy, but whose amounts may fluctuate from time to time as conditions change. Therefore, no *one* particular funds source can be used as a cost standard to gauge the desirability of investments; rather, over the long run it is the *mixture* of funds sources that will determine the economic cutoff point for investment propositions.

A common attempt to arrive at such a measure, namely, the minimum acceptable return from an investment in the interest of the stockholders, is the *weighted cost of the capital structure*. In order to calculate one example, we return to our ABC Corporation, which we now assume has undergone a few changes over the years, and presently has a capital structure which in the view of its management closely represents relationships they would like to see perpetuated. An abbreviated balance sheet is shown in Figure 5–9.

Figure 5–9
ABC CORPORATION
Condensed Balance Sheet
($000)

Assets		Liabilities and Net Worth	
Current assets	$27,500	Current liabilities	$ 9,500
Fixed assets (net)	35,000	Bonds (9%)	12,000
Other assets	1,500	Preferred stock ($10)	6,000
		Common stock	10,000
Total assets	$64,000	Retained earnings	26,500
		Total liabilities and net worth	$64,000

We further assume that the market price of the common stock currently fluctuates between $70 and $75, and that most recent EPS were $7.95. Overall company prospects are assumed to be satisfactory, with a normal growth in earnings per share forecasted by financial analysts. Management is faced with the problem of having to decide among a variety of capital investments, both of a replacement and minor expansion nature, and wishes to set a minimum floor in the form of a weighted cost of capital below which the yield of future investments should not fall.

The first step will be to determine the proportions of the types of capital in the long-term capital structure; the second will be to attach a relevant specific cost to each; and finally the weighted cost will be calculated. In the first step we take each of the long-term forms of capital and make a judgment about its relative value. The obvious initial reaction will be to take the book value of each as recorded on the balance sheet. Upon some reflection, however, doubts arise. For instance, the bonds of the corporation, if traded publicly, may currently be quoted above or below par and thus represent a value quite different from the balance sheet figure. Similarly, preferred stock may be traded at market values different from what is recorded on the books. The most critical difference of this sort is likely to exist in the case of common stock, whose value in the market rarely corresponds to the recorded owner's equity: stated value plus retained earnings and any unspecified surplus reserves. We observe that in the case of ABC Corporation there is such a differential; while the one million shares on the books of the corporation are represented by a book value of $36.50 per share, the current market is trading these shares between $70 and $75—about twice the stated value.

Those arguing for taking the book value of each type of capital will say that the assets recorded on the other side of the balance sheet are represented in the same terms (original cost), and that this would preserve consistency of approach. Others argue, however, that the increase in the market value of the stock in fact represents an increase in the economic value of the corporation's assets, or the forces of inflation. It represents a market judgment about the earning power of these assets in the framework of the company and its industry. In this view, the balance sheet is no longer an indicator of economic facts, and must be adjusted to reflect the realities of valuation with which the common stockholder is faced. The present efforts to require the disclosure on published statements of the effect of current replacement value accounting are a recognition of this problem. (Some valuation concepts will be discussed later in this chapter.) A counterargument is that the vagaries of the marketplace are not a reliable judgment of value, as witnessed, for instance, by the great slides in the stock market in 1969–70 and 1974–75, when within a few months the stock market averages dropped by more than one third from the record highs achieved.

Without going into the many fine points, it should be obvious that a satisfactory answer to the first step will lie neither in the precise book value proportions (although many financial analysts will start from here) nor in current market value proportions, but somewhere between these values. In some cases, neither measure may provide any satisfaction, and a judgmental valuation must be used. In keeping with the basic nature of the book, we shall present two of the approaches mentioned while cautioning that many more considerations call for utmost care in the application of the results.

The *book value* approach will result in the following proportions of capital sources:

Bonds	$12,000	22.02%
Preferred	6,000	11.01
Common stock ...	36,500	66.97
Totals	$54,500	100.00%

The *market value* approach will bring the following results if we assume that common stock has a fair market value of $72.50 per share and that preferred stock is traded at $110 per share, with bonds at par:

Bonds	$12,000	13.18%
Preferred	6,600	7.24
Common stock ...	72,500	79.58
Totals	$91,100	100.00%

The second step is to determine the cost of the individual components. The simplest of these is the cost of the bonds, whose specific cost based on the interest charges is 4.86 percent after taxes, as calculated earlier. The next item, preferred stock, can differ depending on whether we take the book value or the market value into our calculations. In the first instance, the aftertax cost is simply the $10 dividend rate, or 10 percent; while in the other, we must adjust for the premium at which the stock is trading in the market by relating the $10 dividend to the $110 market price per share. This works out to an effective cost of $10 ÷ $110, or 9.09 percent. Finally, the specific cost of the common stock was established earlier as the normal earnings per share related to the normal market value. In the case of ABC Corporation, this works out to current EPS of $7.95 related to a price of $72.50, or 10.96 percent. An argument for consistency could be made to require, under the book value basis, that the cost of common stock be based on earnings related to book value. This is not done in practice, however. The completed calculations will now appear as shown in Table 5–1.

Table 5–1

	Book Value Approach			Market Value Approach		
	Cost	Weight	Composite	Cost	Weight	Composite
Bonds	4.86%	0.220	1.0692%	4.86%	0.132	0.6415%
Preferred	10.00	0.110	1.1000	9.09	0.072	0.6545
Common stock ...	10.96	0.670	7.3432	10.96	0.796	8.7242
Totals		1.000	9.5124%		1.000	10.0202%

The results under the two approaches do not differ materially here, yet under other circumstances there could be sizable differences in the two cost-of-capital figures. These could be due to varying spreads among the types of capital provided; the relative proportions of capital in the company's structure; and, in the case of common stock, the size, stability, and nature of earnings and their valuation in the marketplace. The reader is invited to make sample calculations to observe the differences under varying assumptions. One example would be to calculate the results for the ABC Corporation in the earlier sections of this chapter, by assuming acceptance of the different incremental capital proposals.

There are a number of other approaches to calculating cost of capital beyond the examples shown here. Some of these use theoretical refinements which, given the nature of the estimates used in the practical applications to which cost of capital is introduced, do not often warrant the extra effort for the extra precision achieved. The practitioner must always balance the trade-off between effort expended for a refined concept and the benefits likely to be obtained in the economic results which, after all, are the justification for the series of decisions underlying them.

This brief discussion of cost of capital has served to demonstrate the complexity of the problem and the need to analyze carefully the many economic issues involved. The concept of cost of capital cannot be separated from the particular application intended; otherwise the results are meaningless. As stated before, the point of view of any analysis must be carefully spelled out. Yet, as applications and points of view differ, so do the results of the calculations, and assumptions even within a specified framework for analysis can become tenuous. One way to help minimize the problem of uncertainty about the results is to determine the range within which variables can be reasonably expected to fluctuate, and then to establish the limits or extremes for the results as the basis for deliberation. Such an approach to sensitivity analysis is sound under most problem-solving conditions, and cost of capital considerations are no exception.

THE VALUE OF DIFFERENT FUNDS TO THE INVESTOR

So far we have taken the point of view of the user of the funds, the business enterprise, in discussing the impact of funds selection decisions. While these questions are of critical importance, corporate management must not overlook the point of view of the provider of the funds. Moreover, the concepts of evaluating the economic and other values of the key legal instruments by which funds sources are opened to business enterprise are by themselves a vast subject of considerable complexity. We shall discuss only the highlights and the key techniques, to provide the full perspective of funds source analysis.

As we mentioned before, a more recent development in the theoretical framework of financial management and analysis is an expanded and quantified approach to *portfolio theory*. This set of concepts, often linked in a structural concept called "capital asset pricing model," quantifies the relative attractiveness of corporate securities, particularly equity issues, to the investor. It takes into account both the types of risk encountered in the movements of the securities markets in general, and the more specific risks encountered with the particular company's conditions. Furthermore, it allows one to view a security in the context of the investor's portfolio of holdings, the nature of which has an impact on his judgments regarding an individual security. While this broader approach to risk and value is gaining increasing use in securities analysis, the nature of the assumptions, the theoretical construct, and the development of the specific framework go beyond the scope of this book. We shall concentrate on basic concepts as the foundation of analytical insights, and continue to provide references for further study.

The provider of funds, ranging from the holder of long-term notes and bonds to the preferred stockholder and common stockholder (subject to myriad variations in terms), looks upon his investment in two main ways. First, he is interested in the *value* of his stake, which depends on the operational performance and conditions of the company in which he has invested as well as on the value of the assets backing up the various claims. Of interest to him will also be the movement of value, in the securities markets, if the issue is traded. Second, he is interested in the *compensation* he receives for the risk undertaken in providing funds to the enterprise. The two aspects are, of course, interwoven, and their priorities will shift, depending on the interests of the investor and the type of security he holds.

We shall discuss valuation from the point of view of the holder of each of the three types of securities we used earlier in the chapter to demonstrate the cost of different funds sources to the company—namely, straight bonds, preferred stock, and common stock, with some comments on convertible stocks and stock rights. All calculations will be made on a *pretax* basis, in contrast to our earlier analyses, since the tax considerations of individual investors vary so widely that assumptions about them would be tenuous at best. It should also be pointed out that in the course of this discussion we shall deal with several *types of value,* which must be recognized as part of a whole series of concepts, the most important of which are briefly defined as follows:

Market value is the value placed at any one time on a security traded in a stock exchange or over the counter, or even between private parties in an unencumbered transaction without duress. There is nothing absolute in the market value, since it represents a momentary consensus of two or more parties to a trading proposition, and this value is therefore subject to the whims of the individuals involved, the psychology of the stock market in general, economic conditions, industry developments, political conditions, and so forth. Moreover, the degree of trading taking place in any one security will influence the value at any one time. Still, market value is generally a more valid concept than *book value,* which is the stated value of a debt or equity security based on the accounting concepts of recorded value as reflected in the balance sheet. This concept is subject to all the limitations of historical accounting, which is not designed to reflect economic values at any one time. *Economic value* has been used before in the earlier chapters, and we refer to the value of an asset or claim as reflected by its current and future earnings power plus any potential recovery of all or part of the investment. Other value concepts include *liquidation value,* which expresses the cash value to be received from disposal of all assets of an operation being dissolved (normally relatively low values, since liquidation takes place under stress). *Reproduction value* is the replacement cost of an asset which had been acquired in the past, while *collateral value* is the amount of value ascribed to an asset when pledged as a security. *Assessed value* is, of course, the value ascribed to property as the basis of taxation, while *appraised value* refers to the value ascribed to assets by an impartial expert in the absence of clearly defined market values. Finally, *going-concern value* represents the economic value of an operation as a cohesive, functioning unit, which may exceed the individual values of the parts.

Bond Values

The bondholder's contract with the issuing company normally presents a fairly straightforward valuation problem. The corporate bond, without complicating aspects such as convertibility, participation, and so on, is a simple debt instrument which generally provides for semiannual interest payments based on a stated par (nominal) value, usually $1,000 per bond, and which promises repayment at a specific maturity date a number of years hence. In this sense the bond is representative of most normal debt arrangements.

We recall that from a company's point of view we recognized a specific cost and a future repayment obligation when analyzing the impact of bond financing. The bondholder in turn looks to a specific promise for interest income and the eventual return of the face value (principal) at a fixed date. One can choose to keep the bond until maturity or trade the contract to others at any one time. The value of the bond contract to the investor must therefore be based on his own assessment of the attractiveness of this stream of future receipts and the quality of the promise for eventual return of the principal at maturity. Risk and uncertainty play a role here, since the investor must judge the quality of the enterprise and its future ability to generate sufficient cash to pay interest and principal. We recognize also that this proposition is an exact analogy to the investment problems we dealt with in Chapter 4. The valuation of bonds is readily achievable through present value analysis, using the types of tables presented at the end of Chapter 4.

To determine the value of a bond at any one time, therefore, we must find the present value of the interest payments to maturity and the present value of the final principal payment. A discount rate to be applied will, just as in the previous investment analysis, be the opportunity rate which represents the investor's own standard of alternative earnings possibilities, with the type of risks and rewards attractive to him. For example, an investor with an 8 percent annual return standard (4 percent per six-month period) will value a 6 percent bond as shown in Table 5–2. The value derived in this fashion is $832.89, which is the maximum amount our investor should be willing to pay (or the minimum price for which he should be willing to sell) if he normally expects a return (yield) of 8 percent from this type of investment. He would thus acquire the bond only at a considerable discount from par, if it were offered to him. Note that the stated interest rate on the bond is relevant only in determining the semiannual cash receipts in absolute terms; it is the investor's own opportunity rate which is used as the valuation yardstick. This very same principle applies to the market quotation for publicly traded

Table 5–2

Date of analysis:	July 1, 1982
Face value (par) of bond:	$1,000
Maturity date:	July 1, 1996
Bond interest (coupon rate):	6% per year
Interest receipts:	$30 semiannually

	Total Cash Flow	Present Value Factors, 4 Percent*	Present Value
28 receipts of $30 over 14 years (28 periods)	$ 840	16.663 (× $30)	$499.89
Receipt of principal 14 years hence (28 periods)	1,000	0.333	333.00
Totals	$1,840		$832.89

* From Tables 4–11 and 4–10, respectively.

Table 5–3

	Total Cash Flow	Present Value Factors, 2 Percent*	Present Value
28 receipts of $30 over 14 years (28 periods)	$ 840	21.281 (× $30)	$ 638.43
Receipt of principal 14 years hence (28 periods)	1,000	0.574	574.00
Totals	$1,840		$1,212.43

* From Tables 4–11 and 4–10, respectively.

bonds—the price (value) quoted is a function of the desired return of the parties to the transaction.

If our investor was for some reason satisfied with a low annual yield of only 4 percent on the same bond (2 percent per six-month period), the value to him would rise considerably above par, as shown in Table 5–3. Under these conditions he should be willing to pay up to a $212.43 premium for the bond, since his own return standard is lower than the stated interest rate. If his own standard and the stated interest rate coincided precisely, the value of the bond would, of course, be exactly $1,000. In fact, the market price of a bond will approach $1,000 as it reaches maturity, since the only remaining value will be the imminent principal repayment—assuming the company is able to pay.

Bond Yields

A more common problem for the investor is to determine the yields represented by the *quoted prices* for various bonds in the securities markets. The relationship of value and yield discussed above is the key to this analysis, which again uses present value concepts. Just as we were able to find the yield of an investment project in Chapter 4, we can use a trial-and-error approach on a bond cash flow pattern to find the exact discount rate at which the present value of the interest and principal receipts will equal the quoted price. Quite clearly, the tables provided in Chapter 4 are not of sufficient detail to handle the precision of analysis required. Not only must we deal with semiannual periods, but bond prices are quoted in a very specific manner as a percentage of par (for example, a bond quoted at 103⅜ has a price of $1,033.75). Also, yields are calculated rather precisely, normally two places beyond the decimal point (for instance, 6.95 percent). To ease this task, therefore, "yield tables" are in use (see reference at end of this chapter) which provide the fine gradation required to answer the problems with sufficient accuracy. The principle of the tables is exactly the same as that of the tables in Chapter 4; only the details and format differ. A small section of such a table is shown as Table 5–4; it relates the stated interest rate, the yield to maturity, and the time period remaining to the current price. Note that the answer to our example of the 6 percent bond in the previous section can be found quickly on the 4 percent line and in the 28-period column.

Should yield tables be unavailable, it is possible to use a quick shortcut to derive an approximate yield from a price quotation. If we assume that our 6 percent bond was quoted at $832.89 on July 1, 1982 (the result of our earlier calculation), we note that the discount from par is $167.11. The investor

Table 5–4
SAMPLE OF BOND TABLE
6 Percent Bond

Maturity Yield	13 Years (26 periods)	13½ Years (27 periods)	14 Years (28 periods)	14½ Years (29 periods)	15 Years (30 periods)	15½ Years (31 periods)
3.80% ...	1.224 043	1.230 661	1.237 155	1.243 528	1.249 782	1.255 919
3.85	1.218 284	1.224 709	1.231 012	1.237 196	1.243 263	1.249 215
3.90	1.212 559	1.218 793	1.224 907	1.230 904	1.236 787	1.242 557
3.95	1.206 868	1.212 913	1.218 841	1.224 654	1.230 354	1.235 944
4.00	1.201 210	1.207 068	1.212 812*	1.218 443	1.223 964	1.229 377
4.05	1.195 585	1.201 260	1.206 821	1.212 273	1.217 616	1.222 853
4.10	1.189 993	1.195 486	1.200 868	1.206 142	1.211 310	1.216 375
4.15	1.184 434	1.189 747	1.194 952	1.200 051	1.205 046	1.209 940
4.20	1.178 908	1.184 043	1.189 073	1.193 999	1.198 823	1.203 549
4.25	1.173 414	1.178 374	1.183 230	1.187 985	1.192 642	1.197 201

* Example used in previous section (slight difference due to rounding of present value factors).

will thus not only receive interest of $30 for 28 periods each, but will also earn the $167.11 if he holds the bond to maturity and receives the $1,000 par value. The shortcut method involves an amortization of the $167.11 discount over the 28 interest periods (which is commonly done for accounting purposes), which results in a periodic value increment of $5.97 ($167.11 divided by 28 periods). This increment is added to the periodic interest of $30, resulting in a six-month earnings pattern of $35.97.

The next step is to relate the periodic earnings to the average investment outstanding over the 28 periods. The current quote is $832.89, while the value at maturity is $1,000, an average of $916.45. The periodic yield then is:

$$\frac{\$35.97}{\$916.45} = 3.925\%, \text{ or } 7.85\% \text{ per year}$$

This result is slightly below the precise yield of 8 percent per year on which the original calculation was built. As yield rates and time periods increase, larger errors result; yet, the rough calculation provides satisfactory initial results for most purposes.

If a premium had been involved, the shortcut calculation would call for a reduction of the periodic interest amount by the amortization of the premium. The second example in the previous section involved such a condition, and the results would be as follows, again a close approximation of the 4 percent solution:

$$\frac{\$22.41}{\$1,106.22} = 2.026\%, \text{ or } 4.05\% \text{ per year}$$

The reader is invited to check the details of this calculation.

Bond Complications

The simple value relationships discussed earlier are affected by specific conditions surrounding the company and its industry, and by additional elements in the character of the bond instrument itself. The quality of the promise to pay must be assessed through careful analysis of the earnings pattern and projections of the company. Techniques of Chapters 2, 3, and 4 are helpful in this process. The ability to pay is a function of projected cash flows and the coverage by these cash flows of debt service, both interest and principal. Sensitivity analysis based on high and low estimates in performance may be useful here.

Variations in the bond instrument will affect value and yield. *Mortgage bonds* are secured by the specific assets acquired with their proceeds, and they provide a cushion against the risk of default on the principal. *Income bonds* are on the other extreme of the risk scale, since they are unsecured and will pay interest only if earned. The attractiveness of participating in the future appreciation of the market value of common stock is built into the increasingly popular device of *convertible bonds*, which can be converted into a specified number of common shares during a stipulated time span. Normally, the conversion price of common stock will be above the current market value of common, to build in an expectation for future growth. With convertibility, the bond acquires some aspects of ownership in its original form, and the bond can be turned into full ownership at the investor's option. This potential has an effect on value and yield, since the value will no longer be determined purely on the future cash flows of the contract. In fact, convertible bonds quotations are increasingly affected by the market values of the common shares they represent, especially if these common shares trade near or above the conversion price.

The variation in bond provisions calls for careful judgments beyond the simple analysis tools displayed earlier, since these tools are only the starting point of analysis. No hard-and-fast techniques and rules exist to weigh all aspects of the problem mechanically. In the final analysis, adjustments in value and yield must be made within the individual's scheme of economic and risk preferences and the specific objectives of ownership of debt instruments. The reader is referred to literature which covers these aspects in more detail.

Preferred Stock Values

Preferred stock, by its nature, is a middle ground between debt and outright common stock ownership. The investor looks to a series of dividend payments as compensation, but has normally no specific contract for these or for the repayment of the par value of the stock. While he enjoys a preferential position regarding dividends and proceeds in case of liquidation of the enterprise, he is an owner to the extent that he may have to forgo dividends if performance is poor and may suffer impairment of his capital. Dividends are declared at the discretion of the board of directors and may not be made up if missed, unless there are specific legal provisions to the contrary.

The valuation problem thus is less definite than in the case of bonds, since the only reasonably certain element is the stipulated dividend based on a percentage of par value. For example, an 8 percent preferred stock usually refers to a $100 share of stock which pays a dividend of $8 per year. The investor is faced with the valuation of this stream of prospective dividends. If he paid $100 for the stock and intended to hold it indefinitely, the yield on this stock would be 8 percent, assuming that the company is likely to be able to pay the dividend regularly. If he paid more or less than the $100, the yield could be found by relating the amount of the dividend to the actual investment per share, based on this formula:

$$\text{Preferred yield} = \frac{\text{Dividend per share}}{\text{Price paid per share}}$$

If the investor could expect to sell the stock at $110 five years hence, one could determine the precise yield through the present value techniques or the shortcut methods discussed earlier. The problem of determining value at a future time is one of speculation, however, unless the issuing company had a mandatory call provision at a specific price.

If we look at preferred stock values from the point of view of the investor's own return (yield) standards, we can use the following simple rule to arrive at the maximum price the investor should be willing to pay or the minimum price at which he should be willing to sell. We must relate the stipulated dividend rate to the required opportunity rate of our investor to arrive at this answer. If our investor had a 9 percent standard against which to analyze the 8 percent preferred, he would arrive at a value as follows (stated dividend rate based on $100 par):

$$\text{Value per share} = \frac{\text{Stated dividend rate}}{\text{Required return}} = \frac{0.08}{0.09} = \$88.89$$

If he were satisfied to achieve only a 7 percent return, the value would be:

$$\text{Value per share} = \frac{0.08}{0.07} = \$114.28$$

The main judgments remaining would be, of course, the uncertainty of the dividend pattern and any material change in the future value of the stock, either through changing market conditions or through a call provision at a usually higher-than-par price.

Preferred Stock Complications

As in the case of bonds, preferred stock can have many modifications. An added attraction is at times provided through a *participation* feature, which enables the preferred holder to share (in the form of higher dividends) in earnings above a set level. This feature can favorably affect the yield, and a judgment must be made as to the likelihood of such an improvement taking place. A more common feature is *convertibility*, which adds the attraction of changing the preferred position into full ownership if favorable operating and stock market conditions come about. The value of this feature cannot be calculated precisely, as was true in the case of bonds. Again, convertible preferred stock will tend to reflect the market value of the equivalent number of shares of common as the common reaches and exceeds the conversion price, while it will be valued largely as a regular preferred in advance of this situation. Normally, convertibility is accompanied by a *call provision*, at a price somewhat above par, to enable the company to bring about conversion when conditions are right.

The challenge of preferred stock valuation thus lies in the judgments beyond the simple techniques shown, and in a careful assessment of the relative attractiveness of the features of the specific issue.

Common Stock Values

As we already observed, the most complex problem of valuation is found in the case of common stock, since the full ownership aspects of this type of security remove all relative certainty about earnings potential and principal recovery. Common stock investment is a sharing of the risks and rewards of the performance of the enterprise, and measurement techniques can be applied only to highly judgmental variables. Moreover, the rewards of successful common stock ownership are severalfold: there may be cash dividends or additional stock distributions, and there may be a sharing of growing earnings which are partly reinvested by management. Finally, there is a potential appreciation of the market price of the stock, if the issue is traded with reasonable volume and frequency. The subject of stock values contains so many theoretical and practical issues that we must limit ourselves here to only a few selected highlights. The basic problem is to develop some approximation of share value, and also to find an expression for the yield an investor is deriving from an investment.

Earnings Approaches to Common Stock Value

The most obvious way to arrive at a value for a share of common stock is to make a judgment about the likely future level of earnings and to capitalize these earnings at an appropriate rate which represents the relative desirability of the earnings stream—the investor's opportunity rate or a rate applicable to the industry in question. The approach will appear as follows:

$$\text{Value per share} = \frac{\text{Earnings per share (projected)}}{\text{Rate of capitalization}}$$

While the concept is attractive, the serious practical problem remains one of finding both an appropriate earnings level to be expected for the future and the proper rate of capitalization. Estimating earnings is made more difficult by the need to project total performance of the enterprise, its industry, and the economy, and by all the problems of accounting and reporting. Some of these have been encountered in earlier chapters. Determining the proper rate of capitalization is to a large extent a question of individual preference. There is a relationship between required earnings and the relative uncertainty and risk surrounding the enterprise. The greater the uncertainty, the greater will be the required rate of earnings, which will decrease the value of the stock. One should also note that the approach implicitly assumes no major change in capital structure, which could seriously affect earnings per share as we saw earlier.

A similar concept can be employed to find the yield of a share of stock. Here we can employ the current market price or the original investment and relate them to the projected earnings per share:

$$\text{Earnings yield} = \frac{\text{Earnings per share (projected)}}{\text{Market price per share}}$$

or:

$$\text{Earnings yield} = \frac{\text{Earnings per share (projected)}}{\text{Original price paid}}$$

The inverse of the above formulations is, of course, the familiar price-earnings ratio, which is used quite frequently in securities analysis. Reference was made to this ratio in Chapter 3, but for purposes of completeness we shall restate it here:

$$\text{Price-earnings ratio} = \frac{\text{Market price per share}}{\text{Earnings per share (projected or current)}}$$

This measure reflects the estimate of value the marketplace is willing to assign to per share earnings. The market price is normally a reflection of the projected earnings, although the concept can be applied to past and current earnings as well. The earnings multiple typical for the company or its industry can be applied to projected earnings levels to derive estimated future market values. It is frequently used as a quick way to derive approximate value.

Upon closer examination, however, these simple measures of value and yield are not sufficiently precise to allow for two important aspects of normal common stock ownership. First, no allowance is made for the fact that many stockholders look to cash *dividends* as a way of participating in the success of the business. The size, regularity, and trend in dividend payout to the stockholders can be quite important in affecting the value of a share of stock, depending on the stockholders' objectives. There is some uncertainty surrounding dividends, not only with regard to the ability of the company to pay but also due to the fact that dividends are declared at the option of the corporate board of directors. No general rule is followed by companies; dividend policies can range from no or only token dividends to regular payment of 75 percent or more of current earnings. The only rule one can apply with some degree of confidence is that many boards of directors see value in the consistency with which dividends are paid, and major changes in payout, up or down, are made only with extreme reluctance. Regardless of the policies of an individual company, one can certainly not be indifferent to the impact of various levels of dividend payments on common stock values.

The second critical aspect ignored so far is the relative rate of *earnings growth* achieved by a company. The use of a single projected earnings figure as part of the formula represents a static viewpoint which may not do justice to a company's prospects to grow in earnings at 5, 10, or even 15 percent per year or more. There certainly must be economic attractiveness in such performance, particularly when backed up by an historic record of growth, or when contrasted with static or even declining earnings.

As a result of dividends paid and earnings growth, appreciation of market value per share can occur, which is at times built into techniques of calculating the investor's return on common stock. Thus it is not uncommon to find yield developed from the sum of annual dividends and annual growth in market value:

$$\text{Yield} = \frac{\text{Dividend} + \text{Growth in market value}}{\text{Price paid}}$$

Without going into the many ramifications of theory and practice, we shall present briefly some approaches which attempt to take into account either dividends alone or dividends and earnings growth together. So far no universal and generally applicable rule or method of analysis is available, although much advanced research has gone into the problem. A simplistic way of looking at dividends would be to capitalize the estimated dividend stream at an appropriate discount rate, quite like the approach used for earnings earlier. The only difference would be the focus on dividends as a cash flow received by the stockholder, in contrast to the economic claim held against earnings, part or all of which are reinvested for the stockholder by company management. Problems arise, of course, when a company does not pay cash dividends at all, which complicates valuation and forces the analyst to rely on earnings approaches.

A promising approach for valuing common stock is the following growth model, which is one of many concepts which can be employed here. The formula relates dividends per share to a net capitalization rate, which is composed of the difference between the investor's own opportunity rate and the rate of earnings growth of the company. The argument here is that the company growth is a stimulant which has a proportional effect on value. Also, the higher dividend per share, the greater should be the value:

$$\text{Value per share} = \frac{\text{Dividend per share}}{\substack{\text{Investor's opportunity rate } minus \\ \text{company growth rate}}}$$

An alternative calculation is the attempt to find the price-earnings ratio from a relationship of the percentage payout of dividends to the difference between the opportunity rate and the growth rate. The result can then be used to derive a per-share value from earnings estimates for future years:

$$\text{Price-earnings ratio} = \frac{\text{Percent dividend payout}}{\text{Investor's opportunity rate } minus \text{ company growth rate}}$$

While these formulas represent an intriguing attempt to relate dividends, growth, and stockholder expectations, there are some obvious problems in their use. Theoretically, the company growth rate might exceed the investor's opportunity rate, which would result in a negative value and would be obviously nonfunctional, unless one interpreted this result to mean simply that the investor's expectations do not match the characteristics of the company. One could, of course, argue that investment in a very fast-growing company would also call for high return expectations. In the second formula, a high payout of dividends is likely to be coupled with a low growth rate and vice versa, although this is not necessarily so. We shall discuss more aspects of this in the next chapter. For perspective, we should observe that several studies of the performance of the stock market have indicated that the long-run (20 years or more) return to common stockholders has been around 8–10 percent per year in dividends and capital gains from growth in market value.

While not conclusive, the approaches shown nevertheless illustrate the type of analysis which is possible. There are many more sophisticated ways of dealing with the valuation problem for which we do not have sufficient space. The references at the end of the chapter will be helpful for further reading.

Other Common Stock Values

One value often quoted for common stock is *book value* per share. This value represents the residual recorded claims on the balance sheet and does not take into account earnings or dividends. Only under unusual conditions will book value per share be reasonably representative of anything approximating the economic value of a share of common stock. If a company has just started or is about to be liquidated, the book value may be close to an economic value. Under normal conditions, however, book value per share becomes increasingly remote from current values, since changes in economic values of existing assets and the going-concern values of the various parts of an organization are rarely, if ever, reflected in an adjustment of the books of account. In a stagnant company it is possible to find that book value exceeds market value, which is one signal used by acquisition-minded conglomerates to find potential candidates for acquisition.

The question of *market values* for common stocks is being treated very lightly in this chapter. It is the subject of much learned analysis and speculation, and this book of techniques is not the place in which to go into detail. Suffice it to say that several attributes will make the market value of the share of common stock reasonably representative of economic value. First, a stock should be *traded frequently* and in fairly sizable volume to ensure that transactions take place between parties at arm's length. Second, the share ownership ideally should be fairly *widespread*, to avoid the movement of blocks of stock between narrowly concerned parties. Third, stock should be traded on one or more *exchanges*, or be part of the increasingly important *over-the-counter* market. Even under all of these conditions, however, the market value of a share of stock at any one point in time could still be subject to a great many psychological, economic, and other pressures and thus not necessarily reflect the potential of the corporation. Normally it is best to analyze the range within which market values have moved, preferably over at least one full year, and to chart the movement of prices and weekly or monthly ranges relative to the movement of the stock market as a whole. It is against this complex background, however, that corporate management must often make the decision to issue additional shares of equity, as we discussed earlier in the chapter.

One valuation issue of occasional importance is the question of *rights values*. Rights represent the privilege of purchasing additional securities, based on the number of shares currently held by existing stockholders of the corporation. There is usually a time limit on this right, which allows the purchase of new shares at a price below the current market. Such rights protect the current stockholders' proportionate share in the total earnings of the corporation, since the exercise of the right will prevent any dilution in ownership on their part. Normally detachable and salable separately, rights assume a value and are traded as they represent a potential discount in buying new shares.

The value of such a right (R), prior to its expiration, depends on the current market price (M) of a share of common stock, the number of old shares (N) required to acquire one new share, and the subscription price (S) at which the new share can be acquired. The formula relates these magnitudes to each other to determine the value of an individual right as follows:

$$R = \frac{M - S}{N + 1}$$

We can illustrate the value of rights by using the following example. If a stock with rights attached (cum rights) were trading at $95, the issue price were $80, and 15 rights were required to buy a new share, the theoretical value of the right derived through our formula would be as follows:

$$R = \frac{\$95 - \$80}{15 + 1} = \frac{\$15}{16} = \$0.94$$

The value per right of slightly under $1 in effect represents the proportionate discount from market value provided by the ability to buy a new share advantageously. We can demonstrate the calculation in a different way:

Investment in old shares (cum rights), 15 × $95 ... $1,425
Additional investment to acquire 1 share 80
Total investment (16 shares) $1,505

The 16 shares now owned represent an investment of $1,505, or $94.06 per share, which is a drop in value per share of $0.94. This must be the value of the right to protect the existing holder from this dilution. In fact, the actual drop in quoted market value per share encountered from the cum rights to the ex-rights position (after rights are traded separately from the old stock), is normally very close to that range.

SUMMARY

This chapter has presented the major basic techniques of analyzing the implications to corporate management of choosing among major sources of funds, and the major considerations the holders of various forms of securities have in investing their funds. Many aspects of this analysis are judgmental beyond the specific tools of analysis, since the complexities of the marketplace and the difficulty of dealing with future projections subject many of the variables to considerable uncertainty. Moreover, the theoretical questions behind some of these concepts are knotty and not fully resolved. Nevertheless, the development of the appropriate funds sources and the formation of an appropriate balance between debt, preferred, and equity is one of the critical planning tasks of management. It is part of the complex problem of capital budgeting which attempts to optimize the expected pattern of investments and the supporting capital structure. It must be undertaken with full knowledge of the implications to the enterprise as a whole and the types of obligations undertaken vis-à-vis current and potential investors and their objectives.

SELECTED REFERENCES

Bonbright, J. C. *The Valuation of Property.* 2 vols. New York: McGraw-Hill, 1937.

Donaldson, Gordon. *Corporate Debt Capacity.* Boston: Division of Research, Graduate School of Business Administration, Harvard University, 1961.

Graham, B.; Dodd, D. L.; and Cottle, S. *Security Analysis.* Part 4. 4th ed., Englewood Cliffs, N.J.: Prentice-Hall, 1962.

Helfert, Erich A. *Valuation: Concepts and Practice.* Belmont, Calif.: Wadsworth Publishing, 1966.

Hunt, Pearson; Williams, Charles M.; and Donaldson, Gordon. *Basic Business Finance: Text.* Homewood, Ill.: Richard D. Irwin, 1974.

Levine, Sumner N., ed. *Financial Analyst's Handbook: Portfolio Management.* Part 2. Homewood, Ill.: Dow Jones–Irwin, 1975.

Van Horne, James C. *Financial Management and Policy.* 5th ed. Englewood Cliffs, N.J.: Prentice-Hall, 1980.

Walsh, Francis J. *Planning Corporate Capital Structures.* New York: The Conference Board, 1972.

Weston, J. Fred, and Brigham, Eugene F. *Essentials of Managerial Finance.* 4th ed. Hinsdale, Ill.: Dryden Press, 1977.

EXERCISES AND PROBLEMS

1. The ABC Corporation is planning the financing of a major expansion program for late 1981. Common stock has been chosen as the vehicle, and the 50,000 shares to be issued in addition to the 300,000 shares outstanding are to bring estimated proceeds of $5 million. The new program is expected to raise current operating profits of $14.5 million by 20 percent. The company's capital structure contains long-term debt of $10 million, with an annual sinking fund provision of $900,000 and interest charges of 8 percent. The most recent estimated operating statement of the company, which includes the additional profit, appears as follows:

ABC CORPORATION
Pro Forma Operating Statement
For the Year Ended December 31, 1978
($000)

Net sales	$69,000
Cost of goods sold*	42,300
Gross profit	26,700
Selling and administrative expenses	9,300
Operating profit	17,400
Interest on debt	800
Profit before taxes	16,600
Federal income tax (46%)	7,600
Net income	$ 9,000

* Includes depreciation of $2,250.

a. Develop an analysis of earnings per share, uncommitted earnings per share, and cash flow per share, and show the effects of dilution in earnings.

b. Develop the same analysis for an alternative issue of $5 million of 10 percent preferred stock, and an alternative issue of $5 million of 9 percent debentures due in full after 15 years.

c. Develop the specific comparative cost of capital for all three alternatives and discuss your findings.

2. XYZ Corporation is planning to raise an additional $30 million in capital, either via 240,000 shares of common at $125 per share net proceeds, or via 300,000 shares of 9 percent preferred stock. Current earnings are $12.50 per share on one million shares outstanding, $2.5 million in interest is paid annually on existing long-term debt, and dividends on existing preferred stock amount to $1.5 million per year.

a. Develop the specific cost of capital for each alternative and show calculations (long form). Assume income taxes at 46 percent.

b. Develop the point of earnings per share equivalence between the common and preferred alternatives. Assuming a common dividend of $8 per share, develop the EPS/DPS break-even point for the common stock alternative, by calculation. Discuss.

c. Assuming EBIT levels of $10 million, $15 million, $22.5 million, and $33.75 million, demonstrate the effect of leverage with the preferred stock alternative, by graph and calculation. Discuss your findings.

3. The DEF Company was weighing the choice among three financing options for a diversification program which would require $50 million and provide greater stability in sales and profits. The options were as follows:

a. One million common shares at $50 net to the company.

b. 500,000 shares of 9.5 percent preferred stock.

c. $50 million of 8.5 percent sinking fund debentures (sinking fund of $2 million per year).

The current capital structure contained debt on which $1 million per year was paid into a sinking fund and on which interest of $1.2 million was currently paid. Preferred stock obligations were dividends of $1.8 million per year. Common shares outstanding were two million, on which $2 per share was paid in dividends. EBIT levels had fluctuated between $22 million and $57 million, and earnings before interest and taxes from diversification were expected to be about $8 million. The most recent EBIT level of the company had been $34 million.

Assume that proceeds to the company after expenses would equal the par value of the securities in the second and third alternatives; also, disregard the obvious exaggerations in the relationships which were made for better contrast. Income taxes are 46 percent.

Develop a graphic analysis of the data given and establish by calculation the earnings per share, uncommitted earnings per share, dilution, explicit costs of capital, break-even points, dividend coverage, and zero earnings per share. Discuss your findings.

4. Using the present value tables at the end of Chapter 4, develop the value (price) of bonds having the following characteristics:

   a. A bond with a face value of $1,000 carries interest at 8 percent per year, paid semiannually. It will be redeemed for $1,075 at the end of 14 years. What price would yield a prospective investor a return of 6 percent? What price would yield 10 percent?

   b. A bond with a face value of $1,000 carries interest at 8.5 percent per year, paid semiannually. It is callable at 110 percent of face value beginning October 1, 1994, and will be redeemed (unless called) on October 1, 2004. What price on October 1, 1982, would yield a prospective investor a return of 6 percent? What price would yield 9 percent? (Use interpolation.)

5. Develop the approximate yield (return) of bonds having the following characteristics:

   a. A bond with a face value of $1,000 carries interest at 7 percent per year, paid semiannually on January 15 and July 15. It will be redeemed at 110 on July 15, 1996. The market quotation on July 15, 1982, is 124⅛. What is the approximate yield to an investor who purchases the bond on this date? What is the exact yield given in an appropriate bond table?

   b. The same bond is quoted at 122½ on September 1, 1982. (Accrued interest is paid by the purchaser in addition to the market price if trades take place between interest dates.) What is the exact yield given in an appropriate bond table?

   c. A bond with a face value of $500 carries interest at 8 percent per year, paid annually. It will be redeemed at par on March 1, 2006. The bond was purchased on August 20, 1982, for $487.50, including accrued interest. What is the approximate yield? What is the exact yield given in an appropriate bond table?

6. The MNO Company's stock was closely held, and the volume of stock traded over the counter represented only a small fraction of the total shares outstanding. You have been asked to develop as many valuation approaches as possible in preparation for the disposition of a 25 percent block of common stock held by the estate of one of the founders. The executor of the estate will be interested in the possible viewpoints to be taken in arriving at a fair value. The following data have been made available for the purpose:

MNO COMPANY
Balance Sheet, December 31, 1981
($000)

Assets

Current assets:

Cash	$ 230	(working balance, $150)
Marketable securities	415	(held for payment of taxes and investment in equipment)
Accounts receivable	525	(94% collectible, net of expenses)
Inventories	815	(quick disposal value ⅔ of book, normal sale 95%)
Total current assets	1,985	
Fixed assets	1,715	(quick sale value $225, replacement value $2,500)
Less: Accumulated depreciation	820	
Net fixed assets	895	
Prepaid expenses	40	(insurance, licenses, etc.)
Goodwill	175	(based on previous acquisitions)
Organization expense	20	(legal fees, taxes)
Total assets	$3,115	

Liabilities and Net Worth

Current liabilities:

Accounts payable	$ 370	($350 current, $20 overdue)
Notes payable	125	(due 60 days' hence)
Accrued liabilities	290	(wages, interest, etc.)
Accrued taxes	150	(income taxes, withholding)
Total current liabilities	935	
Mortgage payable	175	(80% of fixed assets as security)
Bonds, net of sinking fund	520	(unsecured)
Deferred income taxes	55	
Reserve for self insurance	110	(contingency surplus reserve)
Preferred stock	300	(7% preferred, 3,000 shares)
Common stock	525	(52,500 shares, $10 par)
Capital surplus	110	(excess paid in for common)
Earned surplus	385	(accumulated earnings)
Total liabilities and net worth . . .	$3,115	

MNO COMPANY
Operating History

	1977	1978	1979	1980	1981	3–31–82*
Profit after taxes (000)	$92	$110	$126	$139	$118	$34
Earnings per share	1.75	2.10	2.40	2.65	2.25	0.65
Dividends per share	1.20	1.60	1.60	1.80	1.80	0.45
Market price, high	31⅜	33¼	39⅞	34⅛	29¾	30⅞
Market price, low	13⅞	19¾	23⅝	22⅛	19¼	19⅜
Market price, average	22⅝	26½	31¾	28⅛	24½	25⅛
Industry price-earnings ratio . . .	14×	15×	16×	12×	11×	—

* Quarter.

Develop valuation approaches based on book values, market values, past trends, and projections (no significant changes are expected in the operations of the company and the industry), taking into account redundant assets and limited trading of the stock. Stipulate your assumptions and list additional information you would consider necessary for a recommendation. Discuss your findings.

7. Develop and discuss the theoretical value (cum rights) of individual rights to subscribe to shares of stock under the circumstances of (a) and (b), and calculate the subscription price in (c):

a. A company is offering its common stockholders the right to subscribe to one share of common at $65 for each 12 shares held. At the time of the offering the common is trading at $89. What is the likely market value of the common going to be after the offering period (ex-rights)?

b. A company is offering its common stockholders the right to purchase one share of 7 percent convertible preferred at 82 for each six shares of common stock held. A reasonable expectation is that the preferred will be trading at 105, once issued. What would the rights value be if the offer were made for each four shares of common held?

c. If the theoretical value of a right is expected to be $2, and the theoretical market price is expected to be $123 after exercise of the rights, what is the subscription price under a subscription ratio of 11:1?

6

BUSINESS AS
A DYNAMIC SYSTEM

In the previous five chapters we mentioned frequently the need to view business as a *system* of interconnected conditions, objectives, and policies. It was necessary, however, to discuss key aspects of financial analysis *separately* in order to highlight and explain the concepts involved. This was done under the several headings of the earlier chapters. In this final chapter on techniques we shall provide an overview, not so much of all of the detailed and specialized aspects of financial analysis, but of the use of selected approaches toward broad financial and operational planning. We have continually distinguished between decisions about investment, operations, and financing, and now the ensuing pages will provide a format by which to test these key decisions *as they affect each other*. The overview provided will be that of a *dynamic* closed system, rather than a *static* look at any one set of conditions.

Among the specific dynamic elements of the system to be discussed will be a closer analysis of the concepts of operating and financial *leverage* which were mentioned in Chapters 2, 3, and 5. Furthermore, a deeper insight will be provided into the effect of the *disposition of profits* on financial plans, and into the *capability to make investments* as affected by retained earnings and the debt-equity balance. In addition, we shall test the *constraints* under which specific financial objectives, such as growth in equity or earnings, must be planned. The thrust of the discussion will be that of *financial planning,* and the analytical framework will display the effect of financial objectives and goals as constrained by specific policies decided upon by management.

THE BUSINESS SYSTEM: AN OVERVIEW

It will be useful to visualize the concept of a closed business system with the help of a diagram on which to display the ideas and measures discussed earlier in the book. Figure 6–1 represents such a business model, which is separated into four areas of management attention and strategy: (1) the conduct of operations, (2) the disposition of profits, (3) financing strategy, and (4) investment strategy. Note that disposition of profits has been added to our previous three areas. It merits special attention because of the impact profit disposition has on the future growth of the business.

The key strategies for the *conduct of operations* involve the appropriate *deployment of assets* to serve selected markets, and the use of appropriate price and service strategies to do so effectively. At the same time, care must be taken to *operate efficiently,* which will depend to a large extent both on the level and proportion of fixed (period) costs incurred which are not changed by volume fluctuations, and on the level of variable costs expended on manufacturing, service, or trading operations. It is this interplay of forces which brings about the operating profit for the period: the effect of market selection and position on pricing, the price-volume trade-off in the competitive environment, and the operating efficiency based on cost-effective management and leverage conditions. The de-

Figure 6–1

THE BUSINESS SYSTEM: AN OVERVIEW

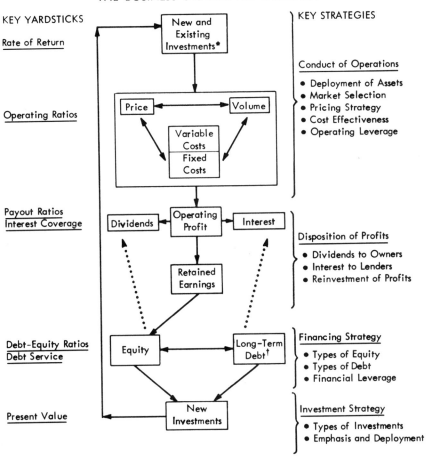

KEY YARDSTICKS

Rate of Return

Operating Ratios

Payout Ratios
Interest Coverage

Debt-Equity Ratios
Debt Service

Present Value

KEY STRATEGIES

Conduct of Operations

- Deployment of Assets
- Market Selection
- Pricing Strategy
- Cost Effectiveness
- Operating Leverage

Disposition of Profits

- Dividends to Owners
- Interest to Lenders
- Reinvestment of Profits

Financing Strategy

- Types of Equity
- Types of Debt
- Financial Leverage

Investment Strategy

- Types of Investments
- Emphasis and Deployment

New and Existing Investments*

Price ← → Volume

Variable Costs / Fixed Costs

Dividends — Operating Profit — Interest

Retained Earnings

Equity ← → Long-Term Debt†

New Investments

* Assumes an amount *equal* to depreciation continuously reinvested here, to maintain existing investments in good order.

† Assumes continuous rollover, with no reduction through repayments.

ployment of existing and new investments—whether they be plant and machinery, various physical resources, manpower development, working capital, or promotional investments—is the action trigger for almost any kind of business, and it causes the other operating decisions to take place.

The key measures in this area, of course, include the rate of return on net assets (capitalization) before interest, as an overall judgment of the effectiveness of capital deployment. Furthermore, we encounter the now familiar variety of operating ratios, ranging from gross margins to specific expense and profit ratios, as discussed in Chapter 2. We shall return shortly to the impact of operating leverage on these results.

The *disposition of profits* amounts essentially to a three-way split, each part of which is subject to current or prior management decisions and policies. The payment of *dividends* to owners, as observed before, is a matter of discretion by the board of directors. The rate of payout, however, affects the possible use of profit dollars for reinvestment and growth. The payment of *interest* is a matter of contractual obligation, but the relative amount incurred is a function of the management policies regarding the use of debt—the higher the debt proportion of the capital structure, the greater the demand on profit dollars for use as interest payments, given a normal return on assets. Furthermore, high debt proportions will generally require higher interest rates to compensate for potential risk to the holders. Finally, retained earnings will be the residual amount of profit available to fuel additional investment and growth, together with new capital provided by investors and lenders. Payout ratios and coverage of interest are key measures in this area.

Financial strategy represents the selection and balancing of the relative proportions of *ownership* and *debt* funds to bring about an acceptable level of profitability with due regard to business risks and the obligations of debt service. The types of equity which can be employed are numerous, as we already observed in Chapter 5, and the same is true of the choice of debt instruments. Here the key concept is the impact of *financial leverage,* to be taken up in more detail later. This refers to the prudent use of fixed-cost debt obligations and the investment of such funds in opportunities with potential earnings higher than the interest obligation itself. Key measures include the ratio of debt to equity, debt service coverage, and return on equity.

Investment strategy covers the whole area of *capital budgeting*, that is, the selection of investments to match not only the operational characteristics and objectives of the business but also the financial policies management deems acceptable. Various types of capital outlays must be analyzed and matched with plans; market selection and emphasis will govern the deployment of these investments. Economic analysis tools, including present value techniques as described in Chapter 4, are applicable here.

Our simplified model of the business system contains two key assumptions worth spelling out. First, *depreciation* is not recognized as such, since it is assumed that an amount equal to depreciation each year will have to be *reinvested* to maintain the productive capacity of the business without providing any incremental profits. Consequently, we show operating profit instead of cash flow as one of the bases for new investment. Second, the amount of *long-term debt* outstanding is assumed to be *unchanged* by any repayments, since only a continuous rollover of expiring debt through new borrowing can provide a steady debt-equity ratio. As the equity balance grows, management will likely want to match this increase with an appropriate incremental amount of debt, unless a change in policy is desired. As we shall see, these assumptions permit us to develop meaningful financial plans without simulating complex details. A more specific approach can, of course, be built on this base.

It should by now be obvious that this concept of a business system forces us to recognize interrelationships. For example, it would be ineffective for a company to have the conduct of operations governed by a set of venturesome objectives unrelated to conservative financing and investment strategies. Similarly, high payout of profit in the form of dividends together with a very restrictive policy on the use of debt would not match, for example, an objective of fast growth, since adequate funds for new investments could simply not be made available under these constraints. A *consistent* set of objectives, goals, and strategies must therefore be the basis for proper financial analysis and planning. Our systems approach shows a way to recognize these interconnections and to test decisions accordingly.

We shall now turn to a more detailed analysis of the importance of operating and financial *leverage*, and then combine all concepts into a simplified version of a financial long-term plan. Leverage, as mentioned before, refers to the often favorable condition of having a stable element of cost support a wide range of profit levels. Leverage appears in the *operating* environment of a business when part of the costs of operations are fixed over a broad range of operating volume. Profits are boosted or depressed more than in proportion to the relative change in volume when leverage is present. Similarly, leverage appears in the *financing* conditions of a business when fixed interest obligations are introduced to the capital structure. As profit levels vary, the earnings accruing to the owners of the business will again tend to be boosted or depressed more than proportionately by the presence of the fixed interest cost. In principle the concepts of operating and financial leverage are one and the same. The differences lie in the elements of the process and in the methods of calculation. Both operating and financial leverage can be present in a business, and their impacts can reinforce each other. The significance of these forces and the potential distortions they may cause will become apparent as we take up each one in turn.

OPERATING LEVERAGE

The concept of separating fixed and variable costs, that is, costs that vary with time and costs that vary with the level of activity, is an old idea and the basis of *break-even point* analysis. We are particularly interested in this approach, not only for an improved understanding of the operational aspects of a business and for better financial projections and planning but also, in a broader sense, for an awareness of the distorting effect significant operating leverage can have on the ratios, comparisons, and other tools employed in financial analysis.

The introduction of fixed or period costs to the operations of a business tends to magnify the profitability of the higher levels of operations, as each unit of additional output contributes a sizable margin of profit based on strictly variable costs only. Once all fixed (period) costs have been recovered by a minimum level of operations, profits rise proportionately faster than the rate of increase in volume itself. Unfortunately a similar condition holds for declining operations, with acceleration of losses out of proportion to the rate of volume reduction.

The formal way of describing these conditions is quite simple. We are interested in the effect on profit I of changes in volume V. The elements which bear on this are unit price P, unit variable costs C, and fixed costs F. The relationship is as follows:

$$I = VP - (VC + F)$$

This formula can be rewritten as:

$$I = V(P - C) - F$$

which illustrates that profit depends on the number of goods or services sold times the difference between unit price and unit variable cost—which is the contribution to the constant element, fixed costs. As unit volume changes, the unit contribution $(P - C)$ times the change in volume will be equal to the total change in profit. The constant fixed costs F will remain just that, under normal conditions. The relative changes in profit for a given change in volume will, of course, be magnified as long as the fixed element remains. Another way of stating the leverage relationships is to use profit as a percent of sales s, one of our familiar ratios. Using the previous notation,

$$s = \frac{I}{VP}$$

and if we define I in terms of its components, the formula becomes:

$$s = \frac{V(P - C) - F}{VP}$$

and slightly rewritten:

$$s = \left(1 - \frac{C}{P}\right) - \frac{F}{VP}$$

This indicates that the profit-to-sales ratio depends on the percent contribution per unit of sales, less fixed costs as a percent of sales revenue. We observe that to the extent fixed costs are present in a business, they cause a reduction in profit ratio. The larger F, the larger the reduction. As volume, price, or unit cost change, however, they will tend to have a dispro-portionate impact on s because of the constant nature of F. We shall demonstrate this shortly in graphic form.

Let us now examine how the process works on the basis of some examples. Figure 6–2 is a representation of a simple business with relatively high fixed costs of $200,000 in relation to volume of output and variable costs per unit. The company has a maximum level of production of 1,000 units, and for simplicity we assume that there is no lag between production and sales. Units sell for $750 each, and variable costs of mate-rials, labor, and supplies amount to $250 per unit. As a conse-quence, each unit provides a contribution of $500 toward fixed costs and profit.

The *break-even chart* is a simple representation of the condi-tions just outlined. At zero volume, fixed costs amount to $200,000 and these remain level as volume is increased until full capacity has been reached. Variable costs, on the other hand, accumulate at $250 per unit as volume is increased until a level of $250,000 has been reached at capacity, for a total cost of $450,000. Revenue rises from zero, in increments of $750, until the total revenue has reached $750,000 at capacity.

Where the revenue and variable cost lines cross (at 400 units of output), *a break-even condition* of no profit and no loss has

Figure 6–2
ABC CORPORATION
Simple Operating Break-Even Chart No. 1
Basic Conditions

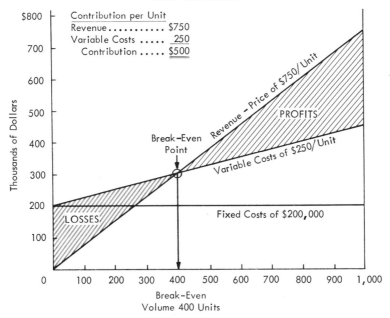

Profits and Losses as a Function of Volume

Volume	Increase	Profits	Increase
400	—	–0–	—
500	25%	$ 50,000	Infinite
625	25	112,500	125%
781	25	190,500	69
976	25	288,000	51

Volume	Decrease	Losses	Increase
400	—	–0–	—
300	25%	$ 50,000	Infinite
225	25	87,500	75%
169	25	115,500	32
127	25	136,500	18

been reached, since the total cumulative revenue of $300,000 at that point is just sufficient to offset the fixed costs of $200,000 and the total variable costs of 400 units at $250 each ($100,000). If operations increase beyond this point, profits begin to appear; while at volumes less than 400 units, losses are incurred. The break-even point can be found numerically, of course, by simply dividing the total fixed costs of $200,000 by the unit contribution of $500, which results in 400 units, as we expected:

$$\text{Break-even point } (I = 0): \frac{F}{P - C} = V$$

$$\text{Zero profit} = \frac{\$200,000}{\$500} = 400 \text{ units}$$

The most interesting aspect of the break-even chart, however, is the clear demonstration of *proportionality* which we discussed above in our formulas. A series of 25 percent increases in volume above the break-even point will result in much larger percentage jumps in profit growth. The results applicable to our example are displayed in the table under the chart, and show a gradual decline in the profit growth rate from infinite to 51 percent. Similarly, as volume decreases below the break-even point in 25 percent decrements, the growth rate of losses declines from infinite to a modest 18 percent, as volume approaches zero. Thus changes in operations close to the break-even point, whether up or down, are likely to produce sizable swings in earnings. Changes in operations well above or below the break-even point will cause lesser fluctuations.

We must be careful in interpreting these changes, however, as in any percentage analysis the specific results depend on the starting point and the relative magnitudes. Nevertheless, the concept should be clear—the closer a firm is to its break-even point, the more dramatic will be the profit impact of volume changes. This can be serious and must not be overlooked in operational or financial analysis, since financial projections should reasonably represent the expected operating characteristics of the business.

Furthermore, the greater the relative level of fixed costs, the more powerful leverage becomes and with it the need to understand this operating condition. Capital-intensive industries, such as steel, mining, forest products, and heavy manufacturing are all subject to highly leveraged operations. Most of the costs of production, including some of the labor costs, will be fixed for a wide range of volumes, and this condition will tend to accentuate profit swings as such companies move away from break-even operations. Another example is the airline industry, which from time to time has added sizable increments of capacity to its flight equipment. These have caused most major airlines to suffer sharp drops in profit. As business and private travel rose to approach the new levels of capacity, many airlines in turn experienced dramatic profit improvements. In contrast, service industries, such as professional advisers, can usually influence their major cost—manpower—by adjusting the number of employees as demand changes, and thus are much less subject to the operating leverage phenomenon.

What are the key elements management can affect in business operations and what is the impact of such decisions on leverage? As we observed earlier, there are three main items in the leverage relationship: *fixed costs, variable costs,* and *price,* all of which are in one way or another related to *volume.* We shall demonstrate the effect of changes in all three by varying the basic conditions in our example.

If management is able to lower the level of *fixed costs* through energetic reduction in overhead elements, the effect can be a significant lowering of the break-even point. As a consequence, the profit boosting effect is moved to a lower level of operations. This is shown in Figure 6–3. Note that a lowering of fixed costs by one eighth has led to a similar reduction in break-even volume, since it will take one eighth fewer units at $500 contribution each to cover the lower fixed costs. Starting from the reduced break-even point of 350 units, 25 percent increments or decrements in volume will lead to profit or loss increases quite similar to the earlier example, as shown in our illustration. The reduction of fixed cost, therefore, is a very direct and effective way to lower the break-even point for an improved profit position.

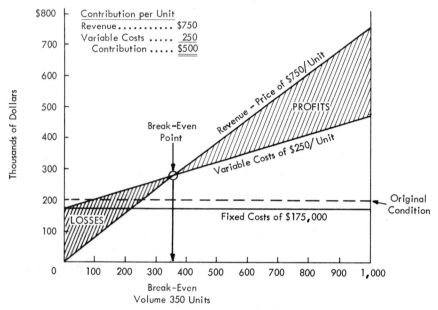

Figure 6– 3
ABC CORPORATION
Simple Operating Break-Even Chart No. 2
Reduced Fixed Costs by $25,000

Profits and Losses as a Function of Volume

Volume	Increase	Profits	Increase
350	—	–0–	—
438	25%	$ 44,000	Infinite
547	25	98,500	125%
684	25	167,000	69
855	25	252,500	51

Volume	Decrease	Losses	Increase
350	—	–0–	—
262	25%	$ 44,000	Infinite
196	25	77,000	75%
147	25	101,500	32
110	25	120,000	18

Any effort expended at reducing *variable costs* (and thereby increasing the unit contribution) can similarly have a salutary effect on profits at current levels as well as on the movement of the break-even point itself. In Figure 6–4 we have shown the resulting change in the slope of the variable cost line, which in effect widens the profit. This is indicated graphically in the shaded area. Loss conditions are similarly reduced. The change in break-even volume resulting from a 10 percent change in variable costs is not as dramatic as we found when fixed costs were lowered earlier by one eighth. The reason for this is that the reduction applies only to a small part of the total cost picture, since variable costs are relatively low in this example. Only at the full capacity of 1,000 units does the profit impact of $25,000 correspond to the amount of reduction in fixed costs in the earlier example. At lower levels of operations, the reduction in unit volume and the low importance of variable costs combine to minimize the effect of this change. Nevertheless, the result is clearly an improvement in the break-even condition, and a profit boost is achieved earlier on the volume scale. Again, 25 percent incremental changes are tabulated to show the specific conditions.

Price changes are perhaps the most complex adjustment to analyze, since heretofore we have concentrated on *cost* effects which are strictly under the control of management. A change in price normally has an effect on the competitive equilibrium and will directly influence the volume a business is able to sell. This it is not enough only to trace the effect of high or low prices on the break-even chart, but an attempt must be made to interpret the likely change in *volume* resulting from the price change itself. In other words, raising the price may more than proportionately affect the volume which can be sold in the marketplace, and the decision may actually lower the total profit achieved. Conversely, lowering the price may more than recoup the lost contribution on all units by boosting the total unit volume which can be sold against competition.

The chart in Figure 6–5 demonstrates the effect of lowering the price by $50 per unit, a 6.7 percent reduction. Note that this action raises the required break-even volume by about 11 percent, to 444 units—which indicates the need to sell 44 additional units just to recoup the loss in contribution on the sale of each unit. For example, if current volume had been 800 units, with a contribution of $400,000 and a profit of $200,000,

Figure 6–4
ABC CORPORATION
Simple Operating Break-Even Chart No. 3
Reduced Variable Costs by $25 per Unit

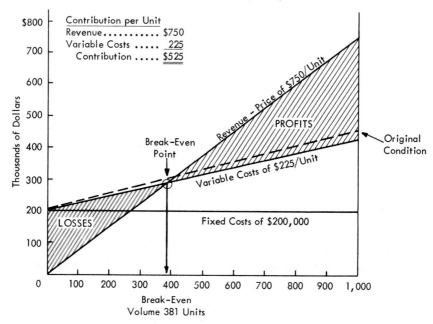

Break-Even
Volume 381 Units

Profits and Losses as a Function of Volume

Volume	Increase	Profits	Increase
381	—	–0–	—
476	25%	$ 49,900*	Infinite
595	25	112,375	125%
744	25	190,600	69
930	25	288,250	51

Volume	Decrease	Losses	Increase
381	—	–0–	—
286	25%	$ 50,150	Infinite
215	25	87,125	75%
161	25	115,475	32
121	25	136,475	18

* First 25 percent change not exactly equal due to rounding.

Figure 6-5
ABC CORPORATION
Simple Operating Break-Even Chart No. 4
Reduced Price by $50 per Unit

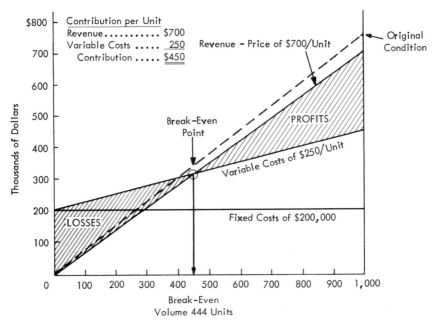

Profits and Losses as a Function of Volume

Volume	Increase	Profits	Increase
444	—	–0–	—
555	25%	$ 49,750*	Infinite
694	25	112,300	125%
867	25	190,150	69
1084	25	287,800	51

Volume	Decrease	Losses	Increase
444	—	–0–	—
333	25%	$ 50,150*	Infinite
249	25	87,950	75%
187	25	115,850	32
140	25	137,000	18

* First 25 percent change not exactly equal due to rounding.

the price drop of $50 would require the sale of enough additional units to recover 800 times $50 or $40,000. This must be done with a lower unit contribution of $450, and the result is 89 units—an increase of 11 percent. Note that this is a more than proportional change in unit volume versus unit price.

Price changes affect the internal operating results, but they may have an even more pronounced and lasting impact on the competitive environment. If a more than proportional volume advantage can be obtained for some time by price reductions, it may be wise to do so. On the other hand, if price reductions can be expected to be met quickly by others in the business, the final effect may simply be a drop in profit for all concerned, since no shift in relative market shares would come about. This is not the place to discuss the many strategic issues involved in pricing policy; the intent is merely to show the effect of this important element on the operating system and to provide a way of analyzing likely conditions.

In the foregoing analysis, cost, volume, and price implications and their impact on profit were analyzed separately. In practice, the many conditions and pressures encountered by a business often affect these variables *simultaneously*. Cost, volume, and price for a single product may all be changing at the same time in subtle and often unmeasurable ways. The analysis is further complicated when several products are involved in a business, as is true of all major corporations. In such cases, changes in the sales mix can introduce many complexities. Moreover, our simplifying assumption about simultaneous production and sales does not necessarily hold true in practice, and this lag effect must be introduced and reflected, if significant. In a manufacturing company, sales and production can be widely out of phase, with inventories absorbing differences. Some of these complications were indicated in our examples in Chapter 3, where of necessity the cash budget and the accounting statements had to be analyzed and contrasted with these elements in mind.

Up to this point we have used very simplified conditions to demonstrate essentially *linear* operating conditions for leverage and break-even analysis. A more realistic framework is sketched out in Figure 6–6. This chart shows the potential changes in both period costs and variable costs which may be encountered over the full range of operations. Furthermore, changed price-revenue possibilities are reflected. While only illustrative, the chart indicates that the simple straight-line relationships used in Figures 6–2 through 6–5 are normally only approximations of the "step functions" and gradual shifts in cost and price behavior often encountered under realistic circumstances. Inflationary distortions occurring over time must also be considered. A few of the possible changes in

Figure 6– 6
GENERALIZED BREAK-EVEN CHART
Allowance for Changing Cost and Revenue Conditions

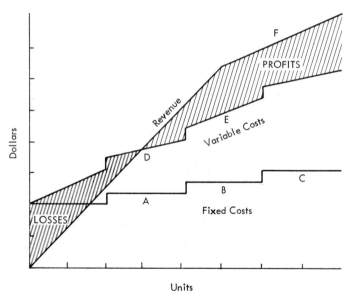

A. A new layer of fixed costs is triggered by growing volume.
B. A new shift is added, with additional requirements for overhead costs.
C. A final small increment of overhead is incurred as some operations require overtime.
D. Efficiencies in operations provide a lesser slope for variable unit costs.
E. The new shift causes inefficiencies and lower output, with more spoilage.
F. The last increments of output must be sold on contract at lower prices.

conditions and sample reasons for these are described below in the chart.

Having dealt with the concept of operating leverage, we now turn to the application of the fixed-variable relationship to the financial structure of a company.

FINANCIAL LEVERAGE

As we stated earlier, a close similarity exists between operating leverage and financial leverage, since in both cases there is an opportunity to profit from the fixed nature of certain costs relative to increments of profit. In financial leverage, as already mentioned in Chapter 5, the advantage arises from the simple notion that funds borrowed at a fixed contractual interest rate can often be employed at an opportunity rate of return higher than the interest paid. Given a company's ability to make investments which provide returns consistently above the going rate of interest, it will be to its advantage to "trade on equity." This means borrowing as much as prudent management will permit and thereby boosting the return on ownership equity by the difference between the rate of return and the interest paid.

Chapter 5 contained a visual display of the effect of financial leverage in the EBIT chart which reflected the earnings per share impact of the choice between different types of capital. In the context of this chapter, we shall employ another form of graphic analysis to display the boosting impact of leverage on return on equity, one of our key measures. We shall also use a formula approach to express the basics of leverage, as it affects both return on equity and minimum investment standards.

In Figure 6–7, the leverage effect on return on equity is graphed for three sample conditions, all under the assumption that funds can be borrowed at 4 percent per year after taxes. If the normal return on capitalization (before interest, after taxes) is 20 percent (A), the introduction of increasing proportions of debt causes a dramatic rise in return on equity, which jumps to infinity as debt approaches 100 percent. Lines B and C

Figure 6–7
RETURN ON EQUITY AS AFFECTED
BY FINANCIAL LEVERAGE
(after-tax interest on debt is 4 percent)

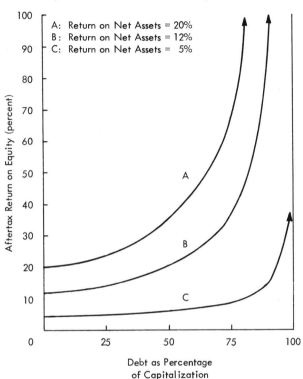

show the leverage effect under more modest earnings conditions. While dampened somewhat, the return on equity still shows sharp increases as the debt proportion rises. As we observed before, one should not forget that leverage works in reversed circumstances also. Such a condition is demonstrated by the widening space between the lines at higher debt levels; should earnings drop, the plunge in return on equity can be massive.

A formal way of expressing these relationships begins with defining the components, as we did in the case of operating leverage. Profit after taxes I now has to be related to equity E

and long-term debt D. We also single out return on equity R, and return on net assets (capitalization) before interest and after taxes r. Finally, the interest rate after taxes i must be noted. First we define the return on equity as

$$R = \frac{I}{E}$$

and the return on capitalization (the sum of equity and debt) as

$$r = \frac{I + Di}{E + D}$$

We now restate I in terms of the components of profit,

$$I = r(E + D) - Di$$

which represents the difference between the return on the total capitalization $(E + D)$ and the aftertax cost of interest on outstanding debt. We then find that our first formula becomes:

$$R = \frac{r(E + D) - Di}{E}$$

which we can restate as

$$R = r + \frac{D}{E}(r - i)$$

This formulation shows that the leverage effect is represented by the positive expression, that is, the proportion of debt to equity, multiplied by the difference between the earnings power of net assets and the aftertax cost of interest. Thus to the extent that debt is introduced into the capital structure, the return on equity is boosted as long as interest cost does not exceed earnings power.

When we apply the formula to one set of conditions which pertained in the graph of Figure 6–7, the results can be calculated as follows. Given $i = 4\%$, and $r = 12\%$, then

for (1) $D = 0$, $E = \$100$ R equals 12.0%
   (2) $D = \$25$, $E = \$75$ R equals 14.7%
   (3) $D = \$50$, $E = \$50$ R equals 20.0%
   (4) $D = \$75$, $E = \$25$ R equals 36.0%

In this illustration, we observe four different sample conditions for debt-equity ratios, ranging from no debt in the first case to a 3:1 debt-equity relationship in the fourth case. Given an aftertax cost of interest of 4 percent and the normal ability to earn 12 percent after taxes on net assets invested, the return on equity in the first case is also 12 percent after taxes, since no debt exists and the total capitalization is represented by equity. As increasing amounts of debt are introduced to the capital structure, however, the return on equity is boosted considerably, since in each case the effectiveness with which investments are made far exceeds the cost of interest paid to the debt holders. This was, of course, demonstrated in the graph of Figure 6–7. The reader is invited to work through the opposite effect, that is, interest charges in excess of the ability to earn a return on investments.

We are also interested in the impact of leverage on the return on capitalization (r), which we obtain by first reworking the formula:

$$R = r + \frac{D}{E}(r - i)$$

into

$$r = \frac{RE + Di}{E + D}$$

Given $i = 4\%$, and $R = 12\%$, we can determine the *minimum* return on capitalization necessary to obtain a return on equity of 12%:

for (1) $D = 0$, $E = \$100$ r equals 12%
(2) $D = \$25$, $E = \$75$ r equals 10%
(3) $D = \$50$, $E = \$50$ r equals 8%
(4) $D = \$75$, $E = \$25$ r equals 6%

This is a useful concept for the investment analysis process. Our approach simply turns the calculation around, by fixing the return on equity standard and letting the opportunity rate of investment vary. The calculation is straightforward. Note that the required amount of earnings on net assets (capitalization) drops sharply as leverage is introduced, until it begins to approach the 4 percent interest cost after taxes. It will never quite reach this figure, however, since normally some small amount of equity must be maintained in the capitalization.

While it is simple to work out the mathematical relationships, the translation of these conditions into the appropriate financial strategies is much more complex. No management is completely free to vary the capital structure of the company at will, and there are realistic constraints on all types of companies to keep some "normalcy" in their financial structures. While no absolute rules exist, the various tests employed by lenders of funds run the gamut of the ratios we discussed in Chapter 2. With enlightened self-interest in mind lenders will impose upper limits on the amount of debt capital to be employed. Manufacturing companies will normally range between 0 and 50 percent debt in the capitalization, while public utilities will vary between 30 and 60 percent. Trading companies with highly liquid assets can reach debt proportions of even greater magnitude.

As stated before, we are interested in the effects of financial leverage to assist us in the broader financial planning for a company. As such, it is only one of several aspects affecting the performance of an operation, and we shall now turn to a more integrated look at financial planning based on the interrelationships discussed earlier.

FINANCIAL GROWTH PLANS AND MODELS

Management can set a variety of possible objectives of a financial nature in planning for its operational and financial future. Foremost among these are growth in earnings per share, growth in total profits, market value appreciation, growth in dividends, growth in ownership equity, and growth in sales volume. None of these can *singly* be used as *the* overall standard, as we observed before. It will be useful, however, for purposes of illustration, to select one of these objectives in order to work through an integrated financial plan. One of the simplest ways in which to demonstrate such integrated modeling is using the objective of growth in ownership equity. Not only is it relatively easy to calculate but it also is one of the key elements through which future earnings growth and stock values are directly or indirectly affected.

The next exhibit, Table 6–1, is an illustration of such a simplified financial growth model showing the several aspects of a corporation's growth, that is, capitalization, profitability, earnings disposition, and financing. With the results we can demonstrate the effect of different financial policies. Three

Table 6–1

FINANCIAL GROWTH MODEL
Three Different Sets of Policies
($000)

	Case I	Case II	Case III
Capitalization:			
Debt-equity ratio	0:1	1:1	1:1
Debt	–0–	$250	$250
Equity	$500	250	250
Net assets	$500	$500	$500
Profitability (after taxes):			
Gross return on net assets* ...	10%	10%	10%
Amount of profit	$ 50	$ 50	$ 50
Interest at 4%	–0–	10	10
Profit after interest	50	40	40
Earnings disposition:			
Dividend payout	0%	0%	50%
Dividends paid	–0–	–0–	$ 20
Reinvestment	$ 50	$ 40	20
Financing:			
Additional debt	–0–	40	20
New investment possible	$ 50	$ 80	$ 40
Results (in percent):			
Net return on net assets†	10	8	8
Return on equity	10	16	16
Growth in equity‡	10	16	8

* Profits *before* interest, *after* taxes related to net assets (capitalization) as a measure of operational return on assets.

† Profits *after* interest and taxes related to net assets, as often shown in financial reports.

‡ The growth in recorded equity based on earnings reinvested after payment of dividends.

cases have been worked out. The first shows an unleveraged company with $500,000 in equity which pays no dividends and reinvests all of its profits in operations similar to its present activities. The second case shows the same company, but in a leveraged condition with a 1:1 debt-equity ratio. In the third case we take the conditions of case II, but assume a dividend payout of 50 percent of earnings. As we discussed in our earlier overview of the business system, we shall assume that the financial strategy chosen will be maintained unchanged in each case.

Let us trace through the data for case I. Given a gross return on net assets after taxes of 10 percent, the amount of profit generated for the year is $50,000, all of which can be reinvested in the company's activities in the form of new investment for expansion, profit improvements, and so on. As we assumed in our business system overview, the reinvestment of annual depreciation is considered necessary to maintain the current facilities in operating condition. These funds therefore do *not* represent investments in *new* profit opportunities. The results of case I are a net return on capitalization of 10 percent, a return on equity of 10 percent, and thus a growth in equity of 10 percent, since all of the profits for the period are assumed to be reinvested in the business. In Table 6-2 we have calculated three additional periods for the operations of this particular business, without changing the assumptions. We can observe quickly that given stable policies and conditions, equity growth will indeed continue at 10 percent per year.

The second case differs only with regard to the use of *debt financing*. Since $250,000 has been borrowed at 4 percent after taxes, $10,000 of aftertax interest must be deducted from profit on net assets, which reduces the amount available for reinvestment to $40,000. If management desires to maintain its policy of a 1:1 debt-equity ratio, an additional $40,000 of debt can be borrowed. This raises the funds available for new investment to $80,000. Compared to case I, the results have changed in several ways. Net return on capitalization has dropped to 8 percent since interest charges were introduced.

Table 6–2
FINANCIAL GROWTH MODEL
Results of Three Different Stable Sets of Policies over Three Periods

	Case I			Case II			Case III		
	Period 1	Period 2	Period 3	Period 1	Period 2	Period 3	Period 1	Period 2	Period 3
Capitalization:									
Debt-equity ratio	0:1	0:1	0:1	1:1	1:1	1:1	1:1	1:1	1:1
Debt	-0-	-0-	-0-	$250	$290	$336.4	$250	$270	$291.6
Equity	$500	$550	$605	250	290	336.4	250	270	291.6
Net assets	$500	$550	$605	$500	$580	$672.8	$500	$540	$583.2
Profitability (after taxes):									
Gross return on net assets*	10%	10%	10%	10%	10%	10%	10%	10%	10%
Amount of profit	$50	$55	$60.5	$50	$58.0	$67.28	$50	$54.0	$58.32
Interest at 4%	-0-	-0-	-0-	10	11.6	13.46	10	10.8	11.66
Profit after interest	50	55	60.5	40	46.4	53.82	40	43.2	46.66
Earnings disposition:									
Dividend payout	0%	0%	0%	0%	0%	0%	50%	50%	50%
Dividends paid	-0-	-0-	-0-	-0-	-0-	-0-	$20	$21.6	$23.33
Reinvestment	$50	$55	$60.5	$40	$46.4	$53.82	20	21.6	23.33
Financing:									
Additional debt	-0-	-0-	-0-	40	46.4	53.82	20	21.6	23.33
New investment possible	$50	$55	$60.5	$80	$92.8	$107.64	$40	$43.2	$46.66
Results (in percent):									
Net return on net assets†	10	10	10	8	8	8	8	8	8
Return on equity	10	10	10	16	16	16	16	16	16
Growth in equity‡	10	10	10	16	16	16	8	8	8
Growth in total profit (after interest)	—	10	10	—	16	16	—	8	8

* Profits *before* interest, after taxes related to net assets (capitalization) as a measure of operational return on assets.
† Profits *after* interest and taxes related to net assets, as often shown in financial reports.
‡ The growth in recorded equity based on earnings reinvested after payment of dividends.

As we expected, however, return on equity has been boosted to 16 percent at the same time as leverage was introduced. Under these conditions, growth in equity can be similarly maintained at a level of 16 percent as long as all of the internally generated funds are reinvested and matching additional borrowings are made for new investments.

In the third case, the introduction of *dividends* is the only change involved. A 50 percent payout reduces the internal funds available for reinvestment to $20,000 and also reduces the available additional debt to $20,000, under a 1:1 debt-equity ratio. Total funds for new investment have thus been reduced to $40,000. The dividend action seriously affects our assumed objective of growth in equity, which now has been cut in half.

This very simple model illustrates the effects of a combination of decisions about investment, operations, earnings disposition, and financing strategy. It permits the analysis of changes in a very easy manner. Clearly the conditions have been oversimplified, but any refinements regarding such items as return on net assets, dividend payout ratios, and increments of additional borrowing, to name but a few, will only be variations on the basic theme expressed here.

If growth in ownership equity were indeed considered to be the chief objective in our illustrative company, it would be useful to express the relationships on the basis of formulas along the lines of our earlier examples.

In case I, when no debt was employed and no dividends were paid, the following conditions held:

$$g = r$$

where g is growth in equity and r is the aftertax rate of return on capitalization. This formula simply expresses the fact that under these basic conditions, return on capitalization is equal to return on equity, and growth in equity is *equal* to return on equity.

In case II, debt is introduced to the capital structure, and the leverage effect is added to the formula as we did before:

$$g = r + \frac{D}{E}(r - i)$$

where D is debt, E is equity, and i the interest rate after taxes. Leverage, as we discussed earlier, is a direct function of the proportion of debt in the total capital structure and the size of the margin between the return on investment and the interest cost of the funds, both after taxes. Since all earnings are reinvested, the rate of growth in equity must be equal to the rate of return on equity—which is a combination of the return on net assets and the boost from leverage.

In case III, the introduction of dividends causes a slowing of the growth in equity, since only the earnings *retained* can be reinvested. We have to adjust each of the two components to reflect this change, and p stands for the proportion of earnings retained as a percentage of total earnings. The resulting formula is shown below:

$$g = rp + \frac{D}{E}(r - i)p$$

We now have the generalized formula for the rate of growth in equity which can be maintained by a business if *stable* conditions and policies hold. If the business, over the long run, is able to invest its funds at the return indicated, if management maintains the debt-equity ratio as indicated, and if interest costs and payout ratios do not change, then the growth in equity obtained will stabilize as expressed in the formula.

As we stated before, growth in equity is only one of several different types of financial objectives. Just to show the applicability of such modeling to other objectives, we have worked out in Table 6–2 the examples from Table 6–1 for three annual periods each. We have added the growth in total earnings as the last line in the results area, to show that under the stable sets of policies, growth in total earnings (profit after taxes) stabilizes at the same rate as growth in equity. In fact, the formula used for growth in equity applies to this objective as well, since profit growth depends on the same variables. As changes in policies are introduced, however, the fluctuations in year-to-year profit changes can be severe, as can be seen in Table 6–3 later. The reader is invited to test the formulation, using these and other examples if desired.

Similar models can be developed for the conditions surrounding earnings per share, dividends per share, debt service, or any other aspect of the financial area of the business. We shall not attempt to go into detail on these, but rather let the examples of growth in equity and growth in earnings stand as a representation of this type of thinking.

Table 6– 3

XYZ CORPORATION

Integrated Financial Plan

Sample Five-Year Projection of Effect of Policy Changes

($000)

	Year 1	Year 2	Year 3	Year 4	Year 5
Capitalization:					
Debt-equity ratio	0.5:1	0.75:1	0.75:1	1:1	1:1
Debt	$ 300	$ 468	$ 489	$ 688	$ 728
Equity	600	624	652	688	728
Net assets	$ 900	$1,092	$1,141	$1,376	$1,456
Profitability (after taxes):					
Return on net assets	8%	7%	8%	8%	9%
Amount of profit	$ 72	$ 76	$ 91	$ 110	$ 131
Interest after taxes	4%	4%	4%	4.5%	4.5%
Amount of interest	$ 12	$ 19	$ 20	$ 31	$ 33
Profit after interest	60	57	71	79	98
Earnings disposition:					
Dividend payout	60%	50%	50%	50%	40%
Dividends paid	$ 36	$ 29	$ 35	$ 39	$ 39
Reinvestment	24	28	36	40	59
Financing and investment:					
New debt, old ratio	12	21	27	40	59
New debt, revised ratio	156	–0–	172	–0–	–0–
New investment	$ 192	$ 49	$ 235	$ 80	$ 118
Results:					
Net return* on net assets ...	6.7%	5.2%	6.2%	5.7%	6.7%
Return on equity	10.0	9.1	10.9	11.5	13.4
Growth in equity	4.0	4.6	5.5	5.8	8.1
Earnings per share					
(100,000 shares)	$0.60	$ 0.57	$ 0.71	$ 0.79	$ 0.98
Dividends per share	0.36	0.29	0.35	0.39	0.39

* Return after taxes and interest.

We can now turn to an illustration of an integrated financial plan over a sample five-year period for XYZ Corporation, which we assume is considering a number of changes in the policies governing its financial behavior. This integrated financial plan is shown in Table 6–3. Changes are introduced over the five-year span in the following areas: debt-equity proportions, return on net assets achieved, interest cost (as debt proportions rise), and dividend payout proportion. While almost any type of assumption can be simulated on a model of this sort, one of the benefits of displaying the key relationships is that any obviously inconsistent conditions will show up in the results. As these appear, the analyst has the possibility of correcting them with more tenable assumptions and calculating the effect of such changes.

XYZ Corporation starts with a debt-equity ratio of 0.5:1 in a total capitalization of $900,000. Current return on net assets after taxes but before interest is 8 percent, which provides a profit of $72,000. Interest after taxes requires $12,000, which leaves a profit after interest of $60,000. Under a dividend payout of 60 percent, cash dividends of $36,000 are required, which leaves $24,000 for reinvestment. Since the debt-equity ratio is to be maintained at 0.5:1, new debt of $12,000 can be incurred, supported by the increased equity.

In expectation of expansion plans, management has decided to raise its debt-equity ratio to 0.75:1 for the second year, which would call for additional borrowing of $156,000 at the end of the first year beyond the increase of $12,000 under the old debt-equity ratio. For simplicity, we have assumed that all changes take place at year-end. The results for the first year show a net return on capitalization of 6.7 percent, a return on equity of 10 percent, and a growth in equity of 4 percent. Earnings per share are $0.60; and dividends, $0.36. The influx of new funds at the beginning of year two raises the capitalization to well over $1 million.

For the second year, the assumption about returns earned is lowered to reflect some inefficiencies as the new funds are invested; the overall return on net assets thus is dropped to 7 percent. After proper allowance for interest, profits available for equity are $57,000. A change in dividend payout to 50 percent calls for only $29,000 in dividends, leaving $28,000 for reinvestment. This is matched with $21,000 of new debt under the existing debt-equity ratio of 0.75:1. These funds are added to the investment base for the third year.

The process is repetitive, as changes in policies are anticipated at the end of each year's operations. For example, we find a new influx of capital into year 4, and as debt-equity proportions are changed to 1:1. Some additional interest cost due to higher rates charged by lenders is assumed, as the capital structure becomes more leveraged and thus more risky. At the same time, however, the effectiveness of employing capital has been left at 8 percent in years 3 and 4, but raised to 9 percent in year 5, allowing some time for the new investments to become effective.

The results at the bottom of the exhibit indicate some fluctuations in net return on capitalization over the years, as either profitability or interest cost is changed. The return on equity, however, after dropping in year 2, rises steadily to a sizable 13.4 percent in year 5. Growth in equity jumps, after some intermediate boosts, to about double the original 4 percent rate in year 5, that is, 8.1 percent. Changes in total profit after interest are quite sizable, as the policy changes from year to year take effect. Similarly, earnings per share fluctuate in their growth, while dividends per share are dampened somewhat.

The results of such a model run raise some realistic questions. For example, it may not be prudent to change the dividend payout ratio in sizable steps as was done. We observe that there was a drop in dividends per share of almost 20 percent in the second year. In the absence of general economic problems, the corporate directors might be very reluctant to do this, since a consistent dividend pattern is generally considered desirable. It would therefore be possible to adjust the dividend payout for the second year back to the original level and to lower the dividend payout only as earnings rise sufficiently to avoid a sharp drop in dividends per share. At the same time, it might be useful to refine the assumptions about return on net assets. We have used an overall percentage, which could be made more realistic by splitting the analysis into return on existing assets and additional assets, and lagging the expected returns on the new assets. Such a practice might be particularly useful if a company were embarking on diversification in its operations, expecting a highly different return from some of these activities. More attention might also be paid to the assumption that depreciation will be reinvested without additional profits. A company contracting some of its on-going operations to redeploy its funds in diversified lines might in fact not be willing to reinvest such amounts in old product lines.

The main purpose of this illustration is to show the usefulness of financial planning in an overall sense. By observing the key result areas of interest to management, the analyst can arrive at a set of assumptions and recommendations which fairly reflect the desires and capabilities of the management involved. Many more refined formats are possible, a process greatly enhanced by the construction of computerized models, as discussed briefly in Chapter 3. Computerized financial models are nothing more than representations of financial and operational conditions like those indicated in the simple approaches used here, but enhanced with a great number of additional details and complications.

SUMMARY

In this chapter we have attempted to integrate some of the key concepts discussed in the earlier parts of the book. Through the use of a simplified systems overview of business and the development of a basic financial planning model, we have demonstrated the need to provide a consistent set of strategies in order to develop creditable plans. In the end, the key test of financial analysis is the viability of the methods and results as predictors of future activity, which was a major point we made in the earlier chapters. Often the optimal approach is the use of quite detailed and sensitive models of all conditions of the business. Yet the outside analyst, and even inside management, will often have to get by with simplified yardsticks and modeling efforts which can sufficiently approximate the solution for broad planning needs. It is for this perspective that the chapter was provided, to represent the capstone to the various techniques of this book.

SELECTED REFERENCES

Break-Even and Leverage Concepts

Anthony, Robert N., and Reece, James S. *Accounting: Text and Cases.* 6th ed. Homewood, Ill.: Richard D. Irwin, 1979.

Horngren, Charles T. *Cost Accounting, a Managerial Emphasis.* 4th ed. Englewood Cliffs, N.J.: Prentice-Hall, 1977.

Moore, Carl, and Jaedicke, Robert K. *Managerial Accounting.* 5th ed. Cincinnati, Ohio: South-Western Publishing, 1980.

Rosen, L., ed. *Topics in Managerial Accounting.* Toronto and New York: McGraw-Hill Ryerson, 1974.

Van Horne, James C. *Financial Management and Policy.* 5th ed. Englewood Cliffs, N.J.: Prentice-Hall, 1980.

Weston, J. Fred, and Brigham, Eugene F. *Essentials of Managerial Finance.* 4th ed. Hinsdale, Ill.: Dryden Press, 1977.

Financial Strategy and Planning

Boston Consulting Group, Inc. *Perspectives on Corporate Strategy.* Boston, 1968.

Childs, John F. *Profit Goals and Capital Management.* Englewood Cliffs, N.J.: Prentice-Hall, 1968.

Donaldson, Gordon. *Strategy of Financial Mobility.* Boston: Division of Research, Graduate School of Business Administration, Harvard University, 1969.

Henderson, Bruce D. *Henderson on Corporate Strategy.* Cambridge, Mass.: Abt Books, 1979.

Porter, Michael E. *Competitive Strategy.* New York: The Free Press, 1980.

Steiner, George A. *Top Management Planning*. New York: Columbia University Graduate School of Business and Macmillan Co., 1969.

Walsh, Francis J. *Planning Corporate Capital Structures*. New York: The Conference Board, 1972.

EXERCISES AND PROBLEMS

1. The ABC Corporation, a manufacturing company, sells a product at a price of $5.50 per unit. The variable costs involved in producing and selling the product are $3.25 per unit. Total fixed costs are $360,000. Calculate the break-even point and draw an appropriate chart.

   a. Calculate and demonstrate the effect of leverage by noting the profit impact of moving in 20 percent volume increases and decreases from the break-even point.

   b. Calculate and graph separately the impact of a 50 cents drop in price, a 25 cents increase in variable cost, and an increase of $40,000 in fixed cost.

   c. Draw a graph and discuss the implications of operating conditions whereby a step increase in fixed costs of $30,000 would occur after 175,000 units, the average price would drop to $5.25 per unit after 190,000 units, and variable costs would drop to an average of $3.00 after 150,000 units. How are the calculations affected?

2. Discuss the implications of financial leverage based on the results of problems 2 and 3 in Chapter 5. What would be the effect if the current interest paid in problem 2 were $3.5 million, current preferred dividends were $2 million per year, and the new preferred had a dividend of 10 percent? Discuss.

3. Develop a five-year financial plan for a company based on the following assumptions:

	Year 1	Year 2	Year 3	Year 4	Year 5
Net assets (000)	$1,500	—	—	—	—
Debt-equity	0.25:1	0.25:1	0.50:1	0.50:1	0.50:1
Return on net assets (after taxes)	8%	9%	10%	10%	10%
Interest rate (after taxes) ...	4.5	4.5	5.0	5.0	5.0
Dividend payout	⅔	⅔	⅔	½	½
Number of shares	200,000	—	—	—	—

    a. Calculate all relevant financial results, such as earnings per share, return on equity, growth in equity, and growth in earnings, and discuss your assumptions and findings.

    b. Demonstrate the sensitivity of earnings per share, return on equity, and growth in equity by varying the conditions of year 5 as follows: debt-equity, 0.75:1; return on net assets, 11 percent; interest rate, 4.5 percent; and dividend payout, ⅔. Discuss your findings.

7   SOURCES OF
       FINANCIAL
       INFORMATION

While the orientation of this book has been the presentation and discussion of financial analysis techniques, we have all along assumed that a great deal of information of a financial and economic nature was readily available to us. The student, analyst, or business executive should be familiar with the various main sources which provide this information, in order to obtain the desired input for the analysis. For this reason, the final chapter in this book is devoted to a brief review of common data sources, and guidelines are given where required for the interpretation of financial data presentations. Familiarity with this type of background will permit more informed decisions about company performance, new financing, temporary borrowing, investments, credit, capital budgeting, and so on.

Again in keeping with the nature of this book, the treatment of the subject cannot be exhaustive. The chapter only introduces the form, extent, and character of financial information which is published daily, weekly, or monthly in current media or is collected and interpreted annually in reference works and investor services of a large variety. The information will be discussed in the following segments:

Current Financial Information
Periodic Financial Information
Background Company and Business Information.

CURRENT FINANCIAL INFORMATION

The most common and convenient way to keep abreast of financial developments is the review of the daily financial pages of metropolitan and regional newspapers. Among these newspapers, the most complete and widely read financial news coverage is found in the pages of *The Wall Street Journal* and *The New York Times*, which contain detailed information on securities and commodity markets; news, feature articles, and statistics on economic and business conditions; individual company news and earning reports; dividend announcements; currency, commodity, and trading data; and a great deal of international business and economic coverage. The major dailies in the United States and Canada also carry key financial and economic data, but the coverage and emphasis vary greatly. Smaller and regional papers will often provide only selected highlights tailored to the area and the readership.

Securities transactions and current financial data represent the bulk of the materials shown in the financial pages. Since the display of this information is not entirely self-explanatory, we shall describe some of the details and give examples of the way in which *The Wall Street Journal* carries data on stock transactions (traded on exchanges and over the counter), bond transactions, and other key financial data. Other newspapers generally present data in a fairly comparable fashion, only in less detail.

Stock Quotations

Exchange Quotations. The transactions of the organized stock exchanges (New York Stock Exchange, American Stock Exchange, and several regional exchanges) appear in total or as excerpts in daily and weekly papers generally in the same format. Figure 7–1, as an example, shows the day's transactions in 10 stocks out of the 1,903 stocks traded on the New York Exchange on Thursday, January 15, 1981, as reported in *The Wall Street Journal* on Friday, January 16. The total share volume for the day was about 45 million, a little above average in a period in which days with well over 50 million shares were quite common and in which volume under 30 million shares came to be considered a "slow day." In fact, the all-time high of 94 million shares traded was reached earlier in January 1981.

The first stock in the listing, Asarco, is recorded as having had, during the past 52 weeks, a high value of $58.50 and a low of $25.50, noting the range in which actual transactions took place in the last 12 months. The quotations are made in dollars and fractions of a point not smaller than one eighth ($0.125). The stock paid a dividend of $1.40 during the period, which reflects the normal annual rate of dividend based on current quarterly payments. The special symbol "a" indicates that extra dividends beyond the normal rate were paid.

The next column shows the dividend yield based on the current market quotations, while the price-earnings ratio based on current reported earnings and current price levels is shown in the adjoining column. Asarco's depressed market value is indicated by the price-earnings ratio of only 4.

The day's transactions in Asarco stock totaled 41,400 shares as indicated in the seventh column, where sales are given in hundreds of shares. The custom of listing sales in hundreds arises from the practice of considering 100 shares a round lot for trading, as contrasted with less than 100 shares, considered an odd lot. Brokerage fee structures allow for somewhat higher commissions for the odd lots.

Figure 7–1

NEW YORK STOCK EXCHANGE STOCK TRANSACTIONS

Thursday, January 15, 1981

Volume: 45,461,140 Shares; 176,400 Warrants

52 Weeks										
High	*Low*	*Stocks*	*Div.*	*Yield*	*PE Ratio*	*Sales in 100s*	*High*	*Low*	*Close*	*Net Change*
58½	25½	Asarco	1.40a	2.6	4	414	39¾	39⅛	39¼	− ¼
9⅜	3⅛	Bas Res	—	—	29	195	8⅜	8	8⅛	+ ⅛
62¾	33½	Crw Zel	2.30	5.0	8	434	46¼	45¼	46¼	−1½
132⅝	48	Dome g	0.60a	—	—	111	84⅛	81½	81½	+1½
11¼	6⅛	Firestn	0.30e	2.8	—	382	10⅞	10⅝	10¾	—
20⅞	13½	Glf Wst	s.75	4.8	4	558	15⅞	15⅝	15⅝	—
20⅛	14¾	Nev. Pw	pf 2.30	14	—	z20	17	17	17	+ ¼
32¾	12⅛	US Home	0.64b	2.1	8	323	30	29½	30	+ ½
10	7⅛	Wn Un	dpf 1.18	14	—	11	8½	8¼	8¼	+ ⅛
40	32	Zapata	wi —	—	—	36	33⅜	32⅝	33⅛	− ⅛

The next four columns indicate the day's price movements of the stock, based on actual transactions during January 15. Successive trades reached a high for the day of $39.75 and a low of $39.13. The net change in the last column indicates the difference between the day's closing price and the close of the previous trading day, in this case a drop of 25 cents.

Unless otherwise indicated, transactions listed in this fashion represent common stocks. If a preferred stock was traded, the symbol "pf" is added right before the amount of dividend shown in column 4. In our example, Nevada Power and Western Union stocks are preferred stocks. The dividend quoted for preferred stock is the annual rate, as was the case with common stock. Thus the Nevada Power stock has a dividend rate of $2.30 while Western Union pays $1.18 per year, with both selling at prices well below par to yield 14 percent, a reflection of the high interest rates of the period.

A number of additional symbols and abbreviations are in common use, all of which are explained briefly in the footnotes of the financial pages. A number of these apply in the cases cited in our brief listing. For example, the "a" next to the Asarco and Dome dividends indicates that the companies had paid extra dividends in addition to the annual rate shown. The "b" after the US Home dividends shows that a stock dividend was paid in addition to the $0.64 annual cash dividend, while the "e" with Firestone indicates the amount of dividends paid or declared in the past 12 months. The "g" with Dome refers to dividend quotations made in Canadian currency. The "d" with Western Union refers to the stock quotation reflecting a 52-week low. Other symbols are used for issues with dividends in arrears ("k"), liquidation dividends ("c"), and so on.

Apart from notations for dividend exceptions, symbols are also used to show such occurrences as new issues ("n"), calls ("cld"), various conditions of rights and warrants, quotations on a when-issued basis—the ("wi") with Zapata is an example of this anticipatory trading—and so on. Two symbols help define the price level and the volume of trading: A stock can be traded ex-dividend ("x"), which can affect the price for the day.

Also, the total sales volume for the day in a stock may be only a few shares ("z" indicates sales in full); in the case of Nevada Power only 20 shares were traded, not 2,000 as we would have assumed without this notation.

The individual listings are supplemented in *The Wall Street Journal* financial pages by various summaries. One of these is the list of the day's most active stocks. On January 15, 1981, the stock with the highest turnover of shares among the 15 stocks listed was Chrysler Corporation (738,000 shares), opening at 5¾ and closing at 6⅛, up ¾. Another summary, the "market diary" for the last six days, showed that January 15, 1981, had a trading volume of 1,903 issues with 789 advances, 691 declines, and 423 unchanged listings. New highs achieved were 28, and new lows were 10. Also shown in a listing are the various closing stock price averages (for example, the Dow Jones Industrial Average, which closed at 969.97), as well as a four-month chart of the Dow Jones averages, by day, showing the range and closing position. All of these summary data and others not mentioned here provide an indication of the mood and direction of the market.

Stock quotations representing the transactions of the American Stock Exchange are generally presented along the same lines, if the newspaper is carrying this information. Transactions from regional exchanges, such as the Pacific Stock Exchange in San Francisco and the Midwest Stock Exchange in Chicago, are often found together with the most important selections from the trading activity on the major Canadian stock exchanges in Toronto and Montreal. Less detail is provided on these quotations: normally, only the number of shares traded, the high and low prices achieved, and the closing prices with changes from the previous close. At times the quotations are limited to volume and closing prices only.

Reference was made earlier to the various stock price averages, which are popular and important clues to the behavior of the stock market in general. Several of these averages are calculated daily and in some cases continuously, with the help of computers. The averages are followed closely by analysts, investors, and financial managers to interpret market movements in view of their plans for recommendations or actions on investing or selling of securities, or for issues of new securities to raise additional funds. Since the various averages, which will be discussed shortly, are averages of a selected and relatively small number of stocks, the upward or downward movement over time is not necessarily a predictor of the likely movement of any particular stock.

As discussed in the earlier chapters of the book, there are many factors underlying the value and market position of a particular security, the most important of which are the current and prospective operating circumstances of the company. The atmosphere of the market and general economic conditions will certainly influence the behavior of a particular stock, but one must caution against the adage that a "rising tide lifts all ships in the harbor," which is a gross oversimplification of the behavior of the stock market. The limitations of the stock indexes are those of averages in general, which can only be broad indicators of a likely trend against which all particulars of a security have to be compared.

The most commonly quoted and publicized stock price averages are the Dow Jones averages of 30 industrial, 20 railroad, and 15 utility stocks, and the composite average of all of these 65 securities. The Dow Jones Industrial Average contains most of the well-known companies in American business, such as General Motors, General Electric, U.S. Steel, DuPont, Procter & Gamble, and so on. Being heavily weighted toward "blue-chip" securities, the Dow Jones average becomes less applicable as one analyzes the securities of lesser known companies, specialized "growth situations," or conglomerate corporations.

A newer indicator is *The New York Times* average of 50 stocks, which includes 25 railroad and 25 industrial stocks. This average is also weighted somewhat in favor of the blue-chip stock variety. A broader index is found in Standard & Poor's averages (composite indexes of 425 industrial stocks, 50 utilities and 25 railroads, and a combination of all these averages into the "Standard 500"). The Standard & Poor's averages more closely approximate the average price level of all stocks listed on the New York Stock Exchange, representing somewhat less than one third of the issues traded there.

As pointed out before, the various stock averages are plotted and charted daily, including the daily ranges and the average price levels; and with the advent of computers the current level of these averages has become available almost instantaneously during the trading period. Continuous adjustments are made for stock splits, stock dividends, and many other changes of the corporate structures of the companies in the index to maintain continuity. Some references are provided at the end of the chapter for those interested in more details about the way the indexes are calculated.

Over-the-Counter Transactions. A huge volume of securities is traded without the medium of the organized exchanges in an "auction market" consisting of hundreds of security dealers and individuals in all parts of the country who are connected by telephone and wire. This over-the-counter market is an amazingly flexible trading arrangement which serves to put in touch with each other prospective buyers and sellers of such securities as government bonds, state and municipal bonds, stocks and bonds of corporations (particularly smaller and newer companies), bank stocks, mutual funds, insurance companies, small issues, and companies whose stocks have relatively infrequent demand or are held very closely. In contrast to the organized exchanges, individual transactions are not recorded and broadcast on the stock ticker. Instead, representative quotations are provided by either the National Association of Securities Dealers, Inc., or by individual dealers who specialize in particular securities, that is, "maintain a market." The important distinction is that the quotations provided by the over-the-counter traders and listed in the financial pages are only indicative of the prices an individual or a dealer would have been willing to pay for a particular security, and at what price an individual or dealer would have been willing to sell during the trading period. The quotations are given in terms of bid and asked prices, the bid price representing the interest of the potential buyer and the asked price representing the position of a potential seller. A dealer specializing in the security and handling both sides of the transactions thus has a "spread" with which to cover his expenses and profit.

In the financial pages we find over-the-counter quotations by geographic regions or by type of company, such as the Eastern market, the National Funds market, and the National market, or listed in categories such as industrials, bank stocks, and insurance stocks. Only a limited number of stocks are shown on a daily basis, while less active issues can be followed on a weekly basis. Again Figure 7–2, from *The Wall Street Journal* of January 16, 1981, provides a sample listing of over-the-counter quotations encountered in the trading day of January 15, 1981.

The format is similar to the one shown for exchange transactions, with the stocks and the annual dividend rate listed first, and the price levels represented by bid and asked quotations. The last column contains the change in the bids, which, as in the case of stock exchange transactions, represents the change from the quoted bid of the earlier trading period. We note that the bid quotations are normally below the asked quotations, as we would expect in an auction market.

Figure 7– 2
OVER-THE-COUNTER MARKET STOCK QUOTATIONS
Thursday, January 15, 1981
Volume, All Issues, 32,687,200

Stocks and Dividends	Div.	Sales in 100s	Bid	Asked	Bid Change
Am Greetg	0.52	205	11⅝	11¾	—
Equitbl Bcp	0.76g	16	14¾	15½	+¼
Gamma B	0.05b	157	13¾	14½	+¾
Pandick P	0.40b	x2	27⅜	27½	+⅛
Olymp Brw	0.90	z64	13¼	13½	—
Sonoma Viny ...	p	20	10	10¼	—
Sonoco P	1.30a	14	35¼	35½	—
Vitramon	0.10e	26	9½	9¾	—

In our sample listing we again encounter a series of symbols which are quite comparable to the symbols of stock exchange listings. For example, the "a" with Sonoco Products refers to an annual dividend rate plus cash extras. The letter "b" with Gamma B and Pandick Petroleum indicates the dividend paid so far in 1981 is not a regular rate. The symbol "e" with Vitramon denotes dividends paid in cash and stock in 1980, while the "x" with Pandick refers to an ex-dividend quotation. The "z" with Olympic Brewing indicates that no representative bid-asked data were available for the trading period. Finally, the "p" with Sonoma Vineyards shows the company has been granted a temporary exception from the requirements of NASDAQ qualification. References are provided at the end of the chapter on the activities of the over-the-counter market for those interested in more detail.

Other Exchange Quotations. Some of the larger newspapers carry limited and selected quotations from major foreign stock exchanges. Trading of internationally recognized securities on the Paris, London, Tokyo, or Frankfurt stock exchanges is reported in the currency of the country involved. At times, the financial pages may contain current stock averages of foreign countries, supplemented by accounts of major activities there.

Mutual funds have gained in importance in recent years and are quoted in a separate space. Price ranges are provided by the National Association of Securities Dealers, and the quotes given normally show the net asset value per share, an offering which includes net asset value and the maximum sales charge, and the change in net asset value from the previous day.

Bond Quotations

The three major types of bonds—corporate bonds, state and municipal debt, and federal government obligations— represent a huge financial market which extends to both the organized exchanges and the over-the counter market. In fact, the overwhelming majority of governmental bonds are traded in the over-the-counter market, while the majority of corporate bond issues are traded on the stock exchanges.

It will be useful to discuss briefly a listing of bond transactions on the New York Stock Exchange to demonstrate the type of reporting of bonds practiced, which is applicable to the bonds traded on the American Stock Exchange and other regional exchanges as well. Figure 7–3 again uses the trading day of January 15, 1981, as reported in *The Wall Street Journal* of January 16, 1981, from which a sample of seven bonds was taken.

Figure 7– 3
NEW YORK STOCK EXCHANGE BOND TRANSACTIONS
Thursday, January 15, 1981
Volume: $18,830,000

Bonds	Current Yield	Volume	High	Low	Close	Net Change
Am T&T 8¾ 2000 . . .	12	140	73⅞	73½	73½	− ½
Bax L. 4¾ s 01	cv	6	113½	112½	113½	—
vj BoM 6s 70f	—	6	117	117	117	+2
Det Ed 12¾ 82	13	4	97½	97½	97½	+ ¼
Kmart 6s 99	cv	135	68	67	67	−1
UPac 8.6s 83	9.4	3	91⅜	91⅜	91⅜	+ ⅞
Xerox 6s 95	cv	15	79	78¼	79	+ ¾

The most important difference to remember vis-à-vis stock quotations is the fact that bond quotations are made in percentages of par value, and are expressed in fractions no smaller than one eighth of a percent. For example, the American Telephone and Telegraph 8¾ percent bonds ranged from a high of $738.75 to a low of $735.00 for each $1,000 of par value during 1981. We note that sales are given in thousands of dollars, since $1,000 is the most common denomination of a single bond. The format of transaction quotations is precisely the same as in the case of stocks, with high, low, close, and net change listed as before. The discount from par reflects the higher interest yields expected during the inflationary climate of early 1981.

The symbols with the individual bonds parallel those discussed earlier. For example, the symbol "vj" with the Boston and Maine Corporation issue indicates its state of bankruptcy and the symbol "f" indicates that the bonds are dealt in "flat," that is, are traded without the payment of current interest due. The symbol "cv" with the Baxter Labs, K-Mart, and Xerox bonds signals convertibility into common. We should observe that the convertible bonds, particularly Baxter Labs, are trading at fairly low yields and high prices relative to the coupon interest rate paid. This is an indication of the boosting effect of convertibility when the value of the shares of common for which they can be traded reaches and exceeds the par value of the bond. Many more symbols are encountered in bond transactions, and all of these are satisfactorily explained at the bottom of the financial pages where they occur.

A slightly different method is used for listing the current quotations for governmental agency bonds and miscellaneous securities which are traded over the counter. Again we have taken a selective listing from *The Wall Street Journal* for the trading day of Thursday, January 15, 1981, and provided in Figure 7–4 are samples of U.S. Treasury Bonds, U.S. Treasury bills, Federal Home Loan Bank bonds, World Bank bonds, and some tax-exempt bonds, which are generally issued by municipalities in special tax districts.

As was the case with over-the-counter transactions for stocks, we find a format of bid and asked quotations, which stand for representative bid and asked prices on the trading day and do not denote specific transactions. An important difference is the custom of quoting prices in percentage of par value and fractions of a percent in 32ds of a point. Thus a quote of 105.14 refers to a price of $105\frac{14}{32}$ percent, or $1,054.38 per $1,000 of par. Added to the picture in the final column is the yield to maturity, calculated on the basis of the bid value. In the inflationary climate of early 1981, we note somewhat lower yields for longer maturities and higher yields for bonds maturing in the short term, which reflects the hope for a moderation of inflation longer term. For example, 6¾

Figure 7–4
GOVERNMENT AGENCY, AND
MISCELLANEOUS SECURITIES QUOTATIONS
Thursday, January 15, 1981
(over the counter)

	Bid	Asked	Bid Change	Yield
U.S. Treasury bonds:				
6¾s, 1987 June n	96.16	96.20	+0.1	14.74
8¾s, 1982 Aug n	93.20	93.10	−0.7	12.95
9¾s, 1983 Sep n	93.20	93.28	−0.1	12.50
11¾s, 2005–10 Feb	96.8	96.16	−1.10	12.19

U.S. Treasury bills:				
Mat				
4–23(81)	15.27*	15.03*		15.86
12–31(81)	12.49*	12.41*		13.82

Federal Home Loan Bank:					
Rate	Mat				
9.55	5–81	97.20	97.24	—	16.06
12.80	7–85	98.80	98.24	—	13.13

World Bank bonds:					
Rate	Mat				
6.50	3–94	60.24	61.24	—	12.49
9.35	12–00	73.16	74.00	—	13.03

Tax-exempt bonds:					
Agency	Coupon	Mat			
Chesapeake B Br&Tun f ...	5¾s	'00	65	68	—
Dallas–FtWorth Airpt.	6¼s	'02	64	68	—
MunicAssist Cp NY	8s	'86	95	99	+½
Penn Turnpike	3.15	'93	89	n.a.	—

* Discount rates.
n.a. = not available.

percent Treasury bonds due in June 1981 would currently yield the prospective purchaser 14.74 percent if he acquired at the bid of 96.16 or $965.00. In the case of the 11¾s, the government has the option to redeem these bonds any time between February 2005 and February 2010. U.S. government securities will be affected by the general outlook for interest rates even more than corporate bonds, since the likelihood of default is extremely remote and the purchaser is normally looking for a safe investment with an assured long-term or short-term yield. Quotations for these issues found in the financial pages will again be clarified by a number of symbols, all of which are explained where listed.

It is worth noting that the Chesapeake Bay Bridge and Tunnel bonds carrying a 5¾ percent coupon rate are currently traded "flat," at depressed bid and asked prices of $650 and $680, respectively. The symbol "f" thus denotes the financial difficulties of that particular agency, which has not been able to meet past interest payments.

As we found in the case of the stock market, bond market quotations are supported by a variety of volume reports, bond averages, summaries of advancing and declining issues, highs and lows for the year, and so on. Again, these provide the investor with a general feel for the daily movements of the bond markets. The most commonly used averages are the Dow Jones Bond Averages (20 bonds: 10 public utilities and 10 industrials). Bond averages are calculated in percentages of par, as were the quotations themselves. On Thursday, January 15, 1981, the New York Stock Exchange bond volume was $18,830,000 for all issues, with the 20-bond average rising slightly to 65.78 (up 0.01), with 736 issues traded of which 258 staged advances, 328 declined, and 143 remained unchanged. New highs for the year were achieved by four issues, and new lows by five issues.

A more recent development in the financial markets is the active trading of options for corporate securities, on the major exchanges including the Chicago Board, the American Exchange, the Pacific Exchange, and the Philadelphia Exchange. Closing prices are generally the New York or American Exchange prices, sales units usually are 100 shares, and securities descriptions include option exercise price. The format reflects the months in which the option is to be exercised, the volume for each exercise period, and the quotation for the last transaction for each period. Similarly, the price movements for Mutual Funds are reported, reflecting net asset values, price offers, and change in net asset value. Clearly, the formats for these more specialized securities must reflect attributes of importance to brokers and clients.

Other Financial Data

Most papers carry, in one form or another, leading business and economic indicators—such as indexes of industrial production, freight car loadings, price indexes, car output, steel production—both in terms of feature stories and at times in tabular form. When supplemented by individual corporate earnings reports, dividend declarations, news about corporate management, analysis and announcement of new financing, and industry analysis, this information can help develop a broad background for the analyst.

Among the more specialized data obtained in the financial pages are transactions in the *commodity markets*. Commodities include a great variety of basic raw materials such as cotton, lumber, copper, rubber; and foods, such as coffee, corn, and wheat. The best-known exchange for commodity trading is the Chicago Board of Trade, while more specialized exchanges include the New York Cotton Exchange or international exchanges such as the London Metal Exchange. Commodity trading takes place both on a "spot" (cash) basis for current delivery and on a "futures" basis, for delivery at some specified later date. This market is far too varied to describe here the many bases on which trades are made and quoted, since each commodity has its own particular trading format, such as cents per pound or dollars per bushel. The pattern of information provided usually involves opening and closing transactions, as well as highs and lows for the trading day and the season. Changes from the previous trading day are often listed as well. A variety of indexes are available, such as the Dow Jones Spot Index, the Dow Jones Futures Index, or the Reuters United Kingdom Index. A company whose operations depend to a large extent on raw materials traded in a spot or futures market can be severely influenced by the fluctuations of these prices. The use of hedging under these circumstances is common practice, and the organized markets for commodity trading allow one to achieve a form of price insurance by buying and selling at the same time with different delivery dates. References are provided at the end of the chapter for more detail on these aspects.

Foreign Exchange

Key prices are quoted in most newspapers by a listing of the major currencies of the world in equivalents of U.S. dollars. Normally, the quotations represent selling prices for bank transfers in the United States for payment abroad, and quotations are given for the current trading day as well as the previous day. Also, prices for foreign bank notes are often quoted in equivalents of U.S. dollars, both on a buying and selling basis.

PERIODIC FINANCIAL INFORMATION

Apart from the financial data contained in the daily newspapers, a wealth of information is provided by the various periodicals published in the fields of finance, economics, and business. Furthermore, there are readily available reference works which contain periodic listings and analyses of financial information oriented toward the investor and financial analyst. The advent of the computer has made possible the rapid collection and analysis of periodic company and economic data, and collective information is now attainable very quickly after the normal closing dates for company, industry, and government financial and statistical reports and series. We shall now discuss briefly the most important sources of periodic financial and business information.

Magazines

Major Weekly Periodicals. For a general business coverage, *Business Week* remains one of the most useful and widely read publications, covering current developments of interest in business and economics, both national and international. It contains analyses of major events as well as reports on individual companies, the stock markets, labor, business education, and so on, and a selective listing of economic indicators as well as a special index of business activity. For a more detailed coverage of stock quotations, security offerings, banking developments, financial, industrial, and commodity trends, the *Commercial and Financial Chronicle* is the most comprehensive source available. The *Wall Street Transcript* contains a great variety of security analyses of individual companies, both on a financial and economic basis and on the technical basis of stock market charts. It further contains major corporate presentations to security analysts about past performance and future plans, and round-table discussions on industry groups by security analsts. *Barron's* covers business trends by individual companies as well as major industries, and provides a great deal of information about corporate securities. The section "The Stock Market at a Glance" is a very useful and detailed picture of the securities markets. *Forbes,* a semimonthly magazine, takes the investor's viewpoint in very detailed and searching analyses of individual companies and their managements. The annual January issue reviewing the performance of major U.S. industries is an excellent documentation of industry trends and provides a ranking of companies by a series of criteria. For an international outlook, the British magazine *The Economist* surveys international and United Kingdom developments in politics, economics, and business, and *World Business* can be considered an international *Business Week.*

Major Monthly Periodicals.   Economic and business trends are covered in considerable detail by the publications of major commercial banks, such as the *National City Bank Monthly Letter* and the *New England Letter* of the First National Bank of Boston. The various Federal Reserve banks issue bulletins and regional bulletins containing regional economic data of interest. *Fortune* magazine comments on national economic trends and sketches profiles of major U.S. and international executives, in addition to detailed research articles on industry, company, or socioeconomic topics. The annual listing and ranking of the "Fortune 500" U.S. companies, and similar listings of banks, and major foreign companies, comprise an excellent reference document. The *Harvard Business Review* is a highly regarded forum for management concepts and tools, including financial insights, presented bimonthly by practitioners and academicians to an extensive worldwide readership of business executives. *Dun's Review* presents trade indexes, failure data, and key financial ratios in addition to articles about industry and commerce. *Nation's Business*, a publication of the United States Chamber of Commerce, presents articles on general business subjects. Statistical information of great depth is provided by the *Federal Reserve Bulletin*, which contains statistical data on business and government finances, both domestic and international, and by the *Survey of Current Business*, which covers business statistics in detail. Detailed stock exchange quotations and data about many unlisted securities, foreign exchange, and money rates are contained in the *Bank and Quotation Record*. The *Journal of Finance*, a quarterly publication, presents articles on finance, investments, economics, money and credit, and international aspects of these topics.

Other Periodicals. Many specialized periodicals are published by trade associations and banking, commercial, and trading groups too numerous to mention individually. Also useful are the great variety of U.S. government surveys and publications, statistical papers by the United Nations and its major agencies, and the various analyses and reviews in journals of the academic community. At the end of this chapter we have provided references to several books on business information sources where the interested reader can obtain detailed guidelines for and descriptions of the type of information available.

Shown below is a brief selection of major periodicals which deal directly with, or relate to, the area of corporate finance. Some of these are specialized and oriented toward a specific community of interest, such as banking, consumer finance, or financial analysts. Others deal with financial conditions in foreign countries or the securities markets within the United States. This listing is given only as a sample to provide some additional guidelines to the reader, and the titles are largely self-explanatory:

Banking
Credit and Financial Management
Journal of Commerce
Corporate Financing
Finance
Financial Analysts Journal
Financial Executive
Financial World
Investment Dealers Digest
National Tax Journal
World Financial Markets

Financial Manuals and Services

The most popular and best-known set of manuals and services is provided by Moody's, with Standard & Poor's a close second. Moody's manuals appear in five volumes: *Industrials; Banks, Insurance, Real Estate and Investment Funds; Public Utilities; Railroads;* and *Government and Municipals.* These annual manuals contain up-to-date key historical data, financial statements, security price ranges, and dividend records of a very large number of companies, including practically all of the publicly held corporations. Helpful summary statistics and industry data are found in the centers of the manuals, the "blue sections." Moody's manuals are updated through semiweekly supplements, with detailed cross-references.

Moody's publishes a *Quarterly Handbook* in which major publicly held corporations are listed, giving one-page summaries of key financial and operating data. Furthermore, weekly stock and bond surveys are published which analyze market and industry conditions. Moody's also provides the semiweekly *Dividend Record*, and a semimonthly *Bond Record* which contains current prices, earnings, and ratings of most important bonds traded in the country.

Standard & Poor's publications include the *Standard Corporation Records*, loose-leaf financial information about a large number of companies, which is updated through daily supplements. A very useful publication is the *Analysts Handbook*, industry surveys which are compilations of key financial data on individual companies and some industries. Other services by Standard & Poor's include weekly forecasts of the security markets, securities statistics, several information services on the bond market, and a monthly earnings and stock rating guide.

Other financial services similar to Moody's and Standard & Poor's are provided by *Fitch's Corporation Manuals*, and by more specialized manuals such as *Walker's Manual* of Pacific Coast securities. An almost overwhelming flow of information, judgments, and analyses of individual companies from an investor's standpoint is provided by the major brokerage houses and their research departments. Furthermore, services available to individuals on a subscription basis provide up-to-date financial analyses of individual companies and their securities. The most important among these services are *The Value Line*, *United Business Service*, *Babson's*, and the new *Investor's Management Sciences*. The Value Line investment survey particularly provides ratings and reports on companies, with selections and opinions for the investor; while Investor's Management Sciences concentrates on providing a great deal of standardized statistical information as the basis on which analytical judgments can be formed. Credit evaluation is made easier regarding small or unlisted companies through the credit information services of Dun & Bradstreet. The advent of computerized data bases has made key company (for those listed on stock exchanges) information available instantly through time-share services.

BACKGROUND COMPANY AND BUSINESS INFORMATION

Annual Reports. The most commonly used reference source about the current affairs of publicly held corporations is the annual report furnished to stockholders. The formats used by individual corporations vary widely: from detailed coverage of facilities, products, and services, and detailed financial and operating statistics, and even discussion of current corporate, industry, and national issues, on the one hand, to a bare minimum disclosure of financial results on the other. Nevertheless, the annual report is generally an important direct source of financial information. Since the disclosure requirements of the Securities and Exchange Commission, the recommendations of the accounting profession, and state laws have become more and more demanding over time, the analyst can usually count on a fairly consistent set of data for analysis in annual reports.

Government Data. More specific details about company operations can often be found in the annual statements which corporations must file with the Securities and Exchange Commission in Washington, D.C., on the so-called Form 10-K, which is available upon request for public inspection. Furthermore, when a corporation issues new securities in significant amounts or alters its capital structure in a major way, the detailed proposal required by the SEC, the *prospectus*, is generally a more complete source of company background data than the normal annual report. It will cover the history of the company, the ownership patterns, directors and top management, financial and operating data, products, facilities, and information regarding the intended use of the new funds.

If a company is closely held, or too small to be listed in the key financial services, information about its financial operations can often be obtained at the corporation records departments of those state governments which require the filing of financial statements from companies doing business in the state. Again, these reports are open to the public for inspection.

Trade Associations. Trade associations are a prime source of information about their respective industries. A great deal of statistical information is made available in annual and even more frequent form, covering products, services, finances, and performance criteria applicable to the industry or trade group. Often the financial and performance data are grouped by types and sizes of firms, to make overall statistics on the industry somewhat more comparable to the affairs of a particular operation. Trade associations include such organizations as the American Iron and Steel Institute, the American Paper Institute, and the National Lumber Manufacturers Association, to name but a few. Sources for listings and addresses of these associations and their publications can be found in the references at the end of the chapter.

Econometric Services. A relatively recent development of interest to the financial analyst is the increasing acceptance and usefulness of the so-called econometric models, which have been built by a variety of academic institutions and economic advisory services. These computerized models of the U.S. economy, and more recently of economies of other countries as well, can provide valuable clues regarding the likely movement of the country's economy within which financial conditions must be viewed. Among the developers of such models whose forecasts are widely quoted and used are the Wharton School at the University of Pennsylvania, Data Resources Inc., and Chase Econometric Associates. Many corporations subscribe to these forecasting services and make use of the projections in their operational and financial planning. Increasingly, corporate and academic economists are testing their own assumptions about economic trends with the help of these models. Another feature of these services is the growing variety of computerized data banks containing a vast array of statistical and financial information.

While the discussion in this chapter merely touches upon the major sources of specific or general information on financial business affairs, the reader is encouraged to make use of these hints as well as the references provided at the end of this chapter. One should not overlook the availability of a great variety of business libraries in corporations, colleges and universities, and cities and counties. The problem facing today's student, analyst, or financial manager is not a lack of data; rather, it is one of selection from among the many sources to find what is truly relevant for the analytical need. This selective chapter has provided a start in this direction for the interested reader.

SELECTED REFERENCES

Background Information

Allen, David E., Jr. *A Reader's Library of Management; Guide and Checklist*. Stanford, Calif.: International Center for the Advancement of Management Education, Graduate School of Business, Stanford University, 1969.

Daniels, Lorna M. *Business Information Sources*. Berkeley, Calif.: The University of California Press, 1976.

Kruzas, Anthony T., and Schmittroth, John, Jr. *Encyclopedia of Information Systems & Services*. 4th ed. Detroit: Gale Research, 1980.

Levine, Sumner N., ed. *Dow Jones–Irwin Business Almanac*. Homewood, Ill.: Dow Jones–Irwin, 1977.

Ruder, William, and Nathan, Raymond. *The Businessman's Guide to Washington*. New York: Collier Books, 1975.

Special Libraries Association. *Handbook of Commercial, Financial and Information Services*. New York, 1976.

———. *Guide to Special Issues & Indexes of Periodicals*. 2d ed. New York, 1976.

Wasserman, Paul, ed. *Encyclopedia of Business Information Sources*. 4th ed. Detroit: Gale Research, 1980.

Financial Markets and Institutions

Institutional Investor Systems. *Corporate Financing Directory*. New York, 1976.

Jacobs, Donald P.; Farwell, Loring C.; and Neave, Edwin H. *Financial Institutions*. 5th ed. Homewood, Ill.: Richard D. Irwin, 1972.

Loll, Leo M., Jr., and Buckley, Julian G. *The Over-the-Counter Security Markets, A Review Guide.* 3d ed. Englewood Cliffs, N.J.: Prentice-Hall, 1973.

Ludtke, James B. *The American Financial System.* Boston: Allyn & Bacon, 1967.

Mader, Chris, and Hagin, Robert. *Dow Jones–Irwin Guide to Common Stocks.* Homewood, Ill.: Dow Jones–Irwin, 1976.

National Association of Securities Dealers. *The NASDAQ/OTC Market Fact Book.* Washington, D.C., 1976.

Pihlblad, Leslie H. *On Options: Fundamentals of Option Investing.* New York: Pershing, 1976.

Robbins, Sidney. *The Securities Markets, Operations and Issues.* New York: The Free Press, 1966.

Zarb, Frank G., and Kerekes, Gabriel T., eds. *The Stock Market Handbook.* Homewood, Ill.: Dow Jones–Irwin, Inc. 1970.

Readings in Finance

Brealey, Richard, and Myers, Stewart. *Principles of Corporate Finance.* New York: McGraw-Hill, 1981.

Childs, John F. *Encyclopedia of Long-Term Financing and Capital Management.* Englewood Cliffs, N.J.: Prentice Hall, 1976.

Fama, Eugene F. *Foundations of Finance.* New York: Basic Books, 1976.

Friedland, Seymour. *The Economics of Corporate Finance.* Englewood Cliffs, N.J.: Prentice-Hall, 1966.

Gordon, Myron J. *The Investment, Financing, and Valuation of the Corporation.* Homewood, Ill.: Richard D. Irwin, 1962.

Hawkins, David F. *Corporate Financial Reporting: Text and Cases.* Rev. ed. Homewood, Ill.: Richard D. Irwin, 1977.

Hirshleifer, Jack. *Investment Interest and Capital.* Englewood Cliffs, N.J.: Prentice-Hall, 1970.

Lerner, Eugene M. *Managerial Finance: A Systems Approach.* New York: Harcourt Brace Jovanovich, 1971.

Levine, Sumner N., ed. *Financial Analyst's Handbook: Portfolio Management.* Homewood, Ill.: Dow Jones–Irwin, 1975.

Myers, Stewart C., ed. *Modern Developments in Financial Management.* Hinsdale, Ill.: Dryden Press. 1976.

Vancil, Richard F., ed. *Financial Executive's Handbook.* Homewood, Ill.: Dow Jones–Irwin, 1970.

Van Horne, James C. *Financial Management and Policy.* 5th ed. Englewood Cliffs, N.J.: Prentice-Hall, 1980.

Viscione, Jerry A. *Financial Analysis—Principles and Procedures.* Boston: Basic Books, 1976.

Walsh, Francis J. *Planning Corporate Capital Structures.* New York: The Conference Board, 1972.

Weston, John F., and Copeland, Thomas E. *Financial Theory and Application.* Chicago, Ill.: Science Research Associates, 1977.

————, and Brigham, Eugene F. *Managerial Finance.* 6th ed. Hinsdale, Ill.: Dryden Press. 1978.

Special Topics

Clasing, Henry K., Jr. The *Dow Jones–Irwin Guide to Put and Call Options.* Rev. ed. Homewood, Ill.: Dow Jones–Irwin, 1978.

Farrell, Maurice L., ed. *The Dow Jones Averages 1885–1970.* New York: Dow Jones, 1972.

Gould, Bruce G. *Dow Jones–Irwin Guide to Commodities Trading.* Homewood, Ill.: Dow Jones–Irwin, 1973.

New York Stock Exchange. *Common Stock Indexes.* Rev. ed. New York, 1972.

Standard & Poor. Method of computation of stock prices indices shown in "Security Price Index Record." Orange, N.J., 1962 edition.

The Wall Street Journal. "Basis of Calculation of Dow Jones Averages." New York, 1960.

INDEX